An Ice Climber's Guide
to Northern New England
Third Edition

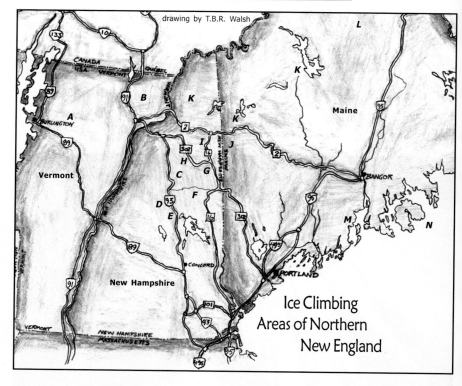

drawing by T.B.R. Walsh

Ice Climbing
Areas of Northern
New England

A.   Smugglers Notch
B.   Lake Willoughby
C.   Franconia Notch
D.   Central New Hampshire Notches
E.   Baker River Valley
F.   Kancamagus Highway
G.   Saco River Valley

H.   Crawford Notch
I.   Presidential Range
J.   Evans Notch
K.   Beyond the Notches
L.   Katahdin
M.   Camden
N.   Acadia

An Ice Climber's Guide
to Northern New England
Third Edition

by
S. Peter Lewis & Rick Wilcox
illustrations by T.B.R. Walsh

TMC
books

Conway, NH

Published by TMC Books, Box 35B Tasker Hill Rd., Conway, NH 03818

ISBN 0-9720307-1-9

Cliff Photographs: David Stone or as credited
Action Photographs: as credited
Maps and Diagrams: T.B.R. Walsh
Layout, Design, Typesetting and Production: S. Peter Lewis, TMC Books
Research: S. Peter Lewis, Rick Wilcox
Editing: S. Peter Lewis, George Hurley
Printed in the United States by J. S. McCarthy, Augusta, ME

Front Cover photo: Conrad Yager climbing Frankenstein's classic hard route Alucard; photo by S. Peter Lewis

DISCLAIMER: Ice climbing is an inherently dangerous activity. You can be hurt or killed. Both subjective (controllable) and objective (uncontrollable) dangers are a part of every climb. This guide is not an instruction manual and purchase or use of it does not guarantee safety or competence. Though great care was taken to ensure that the information in this guide is as accurate as possible, errors will undoubtedly be found, some which could potentially affect safety. A big part of safe climbing involves judgment skills, and that doesn't just mean deciding whether a tool placement is good enough to go on. It may also mean deciding to go left when the guidebook says to go right. Guidebooks cannot take the place of experience. There are many avenues to learn safe climbing technique and quality instruction is recommended before venturing onto the ice. The authors and publisher of this guidebook can in no way be held responsible or liable for any accidents or injuries resulting from ice climbing or winter mountaineering.

PREFACE
to the 3rd edition

On February 1, 1970, Gunks legend Jim McCarthy led a group of four climbers up Pinnacle Gully in Huntington Ravine without cutting a single step. The ice revolution that Yvon Chouinard had started the year before had reached the White Mountains. In their definitive history of Northeast climbing, *Yankee Rock & Ice*, Laura and Guy Waterman talk about that historic group of four and single out one: "a very young Rick Wilcox, who showed his knack for being in the right place at the right time."

Well, Rick has never moved. He's been in the right place for a long time now. In 1976, Rick, with Peter Cole, published *Shades of Blue*, the first ice guide to northern New England. It was a scruffy little yellow book with just a handful of routes and ratings of "easy," "moderate," and "hard." There were no one-piece suits, mono-points, bent shafts, or screws you could spin in by hand. There was one route listed at Lake Willoughby. Many of you reading this guide were not born yet.

A few years later Rick bought International Mountain Equipment (IME) and in 1982 published the first edition of *An Ice Climber's Guide to Northern New England*. It was bigger, and better, and used the New England Ice (NEI) numeric system for rating climbs. There were lots of climbs at Lake Willoughby.

Nine years later Rick and I collaborated on the second edition of that guide. At the time we were in the midst of yet another ice climbing revolution. Crampons, ice tools, screws, and clothing had advanced so far that long sections of really steep ice were now just plain fun (although they still scared me). The old-school desperate climbs like the Black Dike, Repentence, and Last Gentleman, were now being climbed all the time, quickly, and often by folks who had not climbed ice very long.

Since then Rick has gone on to add to his phenomenal list of climbs up huge mountains (including Everest in '91), has made IME a fixture and magnet for New England climbers, and is just about done raising his kids. Last summer I went into Rick's office and said "Isn't it about time we updated that guidebook?" With his typical enthusiasm Rick said "Let's do it," and in five minutes we had the scheme worked out on a scrap of paper. I love doing projects with Rick—it's always the right place and the right time. So I took off, started doing the research, taking pictures, and talking to climbers. In the beginning of 2002 I started a publishing company, TMC Books (Too Many Cats), with a couple of other guys, and now you're holding our second book in your hands.

A lot has happened since 1992 and the ice revolution that Rick and I thought was nearly over has proven to be an opportunistic beast. While there are a limited number of vertical columns in our New England woods, there's a nearly limitless supply of wet cliffs covered with frozen splotches and little drips that today's hotshots love to climb amidst scratches and sparks. So yes, there will likely be a fourth edition to this guide. Rick and I are still in the right place so give us another decade, and when the time is right, we'll hatch another plan on a napkin.

Peter Lewis
September, 2002

ACKNOWLEDGMENTS

This edition of An Ice Climber's Guide to Northern New England was an incredible team effort. It seems boastful for us to list only our two names on the front of this book when so many people helped us so much. Without exception every person we contacted for information, photos, or other help was gracious, enthusiastic and supportive. When this trait was mentioned to one of our major contributors he said he wasn't surprised at all and he felt it demonstrated we truly are a small, tight, supportive community—maybe suffering through all these winters has helped bind us together. We have tried to keep track of everyone who has helped us on this project, but invariably someone will be left out. If you helped us but don't find your name listed here, please forgive us, and consider yourself very thanked. It is with the greatest sense of appreciation that we single out the following folks for very special recognition and thanks.

Frank Hubbell and **Lee Frizzell** for their unwavering confidence and huge support of TMC Books and this, the first big project.

T.B.R. Walsh for his incredible artwork and encouragement during the last hectic months, and Saxon, his sidekick, who provided pleasant diversions.

Jon Sykes for simply smiling and saying "sure" to every request for information or photos about his beloved Franconia, and for letting the cat out of the back on his incredible routes up north. If you want all the beta on Franconia rock and ice routes please buy his book *Secrets of the Notch.*

Pat Viljanen for allowing us to use his excellent book *The Locals Guide to Smuggler's Notch Ice* as the basis for our Smuggler's section. The improvement over the 2nd edition is tremendous; you should buy his book.

Bob Baribeau for all the time spent going over text and photos on Katahdin and western Maine. Without Bob's words and pictures this book would have fallen far short of the mark. He made huge efforts to help us.

Ben Townsend for his gracious permission to use his book *Rock and Ice Climbs in the Camden Hills,* which allowed us to give coastal Maine the attention it deserves. You should buy his book too.

Jim Shimberg for helping us sort out central New Hampshire by editing text and contributing photos—and for those constant encouraging emails and phone calls.

Brad White for his willingness to read just about every word about everything and help us get our lefts and rights straight.

Alden Pellett for taking all the time to help make sure we got Smugglers just right and for his excellent photos; see more at vermontphotographer.com.

Brian Post for his photo work at Smugglers Notch and Katahdin; these areas would have looked pretty pathetic without his excellent slides; see more at wildrays.com

George Hurley for his grand repeat per-

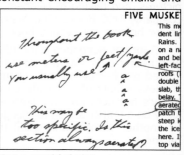

Just a sample of what we were up against when George Hurley sent us in the corrections. Fortunately, we speak fluent Hurley.

formance as our copyeditor. Witthout his help the texct wood have comeout lookng like hiss.

One thing you will notice about this edition is the huge increase in excellent photos. The following folks gave us their best stuff without hesitation or thought for personal gain. We are indebted to them for their generosity and great work.

Bernie Mailhot and **Luca Marinelli** for their outstanding photos of routes at Willoughby and in Franconia. These guys were so generous!

Doug Millen for filling in some very big photo holes (not to mention his general enthusiasm for the whole project); for condition reports go to NEice.com.

Jamie Cunningham for his great shots from Franconia and up north.

Without the efforts of these next climbers lots of new stuff, corrections to old stuff, and photos would have been left out: Kurt Winkler, Paul Cormier, Mark Synnott, Joe Klementovich, Eric Pospesil, Henry Barber, Ron Reynolds, Will Mayo, Jim Ewing, Rob Frost, Kevin Mahoney, Steve Larson, Rich Page, Bob Parrott, Alain Comeau, Eric Seifer, Maury McKinney, Jeff Butterfield, Justin Preisendorfer, Brett Taylor, Joe & Judy Perez, the folks at the Mt. Washington Observatory and the AMC, Peter Cole, Baxter State Park, Ted Hammond, Matt Peer, Doug Huntley, Dave Kelly, Tyler Stableford, Alan Cattabriga, Randy Noble, Paul Ross, Chris Dubé, Steve Matous, Lauren Head, Ed Butler, Mike Arsenault, Steve Weitzler, Richard Doucette, Alexy Shuruyev, Paul Miller, and Matt Elliot.

Without the enthusiastic support of our advertisers and industry friends, this project might not have been feasible. Thanks and best wishes to the folks at:

Grivel	**Climb High**	**Petzl**
IME	**IMCS**	**SOLO**
The Rock Barn	**Trango**	**Ortovox**
Bluewater	**Omega Pacific**	**Rhode Island Rock Gym**
Sterling	**Boston Rock Gym**	

Some behind the scenes work goes on in any project this big and it's easy to forget how much of a contribution some people make. Our thanks go out to Dave Karl, Kristin Gula and Jeff Fongemie for helping us turn our dream into a business and to Jon Wysocki for helping us transform an idea into a book. Special thanks also to the Lewis family; to Karen, who never complained when the work days stretched to 16 hours, to Amanda, who never once asked her mom "who is that man" when the author came home late, and to Jeremiah, who quietly went about the business of preparing for college without bugging his dad.

It would be easy to leave out all the people who helped with the first two editions of this guide. Many of their contributions go back over twenty years and they helped lay the foundation for this latest version. Thanks to: Ed Webster, Bill Supple, Chris Hassig, Bill Kane, Clint Cummins, John Imbrie, Brinton Young, Dennis Drayna, Gustavo Brillembourg, Dave Getchel Jr., Bill Pelkey, Kevin Slater, Todd Swain, Briggs Bunker, Bruce Luetters, Bob Proudman, Doug Teschner, Steve Zajchowski, Rainsford Rouner, Mark Whiton, Dave Walters, Frank Lawrence, John Bouchard, Dave Linden, Michael Hartrich, Mark Richey, Doug Madara, John Bragg, Al Rubin, Sam Streibert, Rich Mulhern, Doug Burnell, Misha Kirk, Chris Hassig, David Stone, Nick Yardley, Marc Chauvin, Jerry Handren, Lee Stevens, John Tremblay, Chris ElIms, Bill Aughton, Bob Timmer, Ben Townsend, Rob Adair, Joe Lentini, Charlie Townsend, Randy Rackcliff, Dennis McKinnon, Paul Boissonneault, Henry Kendall, Ken Henderson, Kevin Codraro, Peter Hovling, and many others.

Finally, thank you to all the climbers in New England who make this such a special place to climb and build friendships.

Contents

PREFACE 5

ACKNOWLEDGMENTS 6

INTRODUCTION 15

WEATHER 17

SAFETY 20

INSTRUCTION 24

EQUIPMENT 26

RATINGS 29

HISTORY 35

SMUGGLERS NOTCH 55

    WEST SIDE *57*

    EAST SIDE *65*

    BEAR NOTCH *70*

BRISTOL CLIFFS 71

LAKE WILLOUGHBY 72

    MT. PISGAH *76*

        THE TABLETS 88

    MT HOR *88*

    CRYSTAL LAKE *90*

    JOBS POND *90*

    MOUNT WHEELER *90*

T.B.R. Walsh

S. Peter Lewis

FRANCONIA NOTCH 93

THE FLUME 95
CANNON 96
EAST SIDE 104
ECHO CRAG 105
PROFILE CLIFF 111
HOUND'S HUMP RIDGE 111
EAGLE CLIFF 114
BIG SLIDE 115
LAFAYETTE LEDGES 115
LONESOME LAKE 116
MT GARFIELD 116
THE NUBBLE 117

CENTRAL NEW HAMPSHIRE NOTCHES 119
OLIVARIAN NOTCH 119
KINSMAN NOTCH 120
WATERVILLE VALLEY 123

THE BAKER RIVER VALLEY 125

NEWFOUND LAKE 126

RUMNEY 128

KANCAMAGUS HIGHWAY 135

BLACK MOUNTAIN 136

MAD RIVER NOTCH 136

MT. HUNTINGTON 138

MT. HEDGEHOG 138

CHAMPNEY FALLS 138

CRACK IN THE WOODS 140

RAINBOW SLABS 140

PAINTED WALLS 140

SUNDOWN LEDGE 142

SACO RIVER VALLEY 145

MOAT RANGE 147

WHITEHORSE LEDGE 148

GUIDE'S WALL 152

CATHEDRAL LEDGE 152

THE NORTH END 162

HUMPHREY'S LEDGE 163

HUMPHREY'S HOLLOW 164

MAIN FACE 164

BLACK PUDDING GULLY 165

BARKING DOG ICICLE AREA 166

CEMETERY CLIFF 167

DUCKS HEAD 167

EAGLE CLIFF 168

IRON MOUNTAIN 169

GIANT STAIRS 170

WHITE'S LEDGE 170

HART LEDGE 171

CARDIAC CRAG 172

MOUNT TREMONT 173

TEXACO SLAB 173

    TEXACO AMPHITHEATER 174

    TEXACO SLAB 175

MOUNT BEMIS 176

ARETHUSA FALLS 177

CRAWFORD NOTCH 179

FRANKENSTEIN CLIFF 180

    SOUTH FACE 180

    THE AMPHITHEATER 184

    THE TRESTLE CUT/PRACTICE SLAB SOUTH 190

    LOST IN THE FOREST AREA 190

    STANDARD ROUTE AREA 192

    THE HANGING GARDENS 196

    LOST HELMET CRAG 198

MOUNT WEBSTER 199

MOUNT WILLEY 202

MOUNT WILLARD 203

    WILLEY BROOK 203

    SOUTH FACE 204

    UPPER EAST FACE 206

    TRESTLE WALL 210

    ELEPHANT HEAD 210

MOUNT AVALON 212

MOUNT TOM 213

PRESIDENTIAL RANGE 215

MT. WASHINGTON 216

    PINKHAM NOTCH 218

    TUCKERMAN RAVINE 219

    HUNTINGTON RAVINE 220

    THE GREAT GULF 226

MADISON GULF 227

KING RAVINE 229

EVANS NOTCH 231

SHELL POND 232
BLUEBERRY MT. 233
THE BASIN 233
EAST ROYCE MOUNTAIN 234

BEYOND THE NOTCHES 239

GOBACK MT. 241
BEAVER BROOK 243
MT. FOREST 243
MT. WINTHROP 244
LARRY FLUME 244
GENTIAN SWAMP 244
REFLECTION CRAG 244
TUMBLEDOWN DICK 245
PINE MOUNTAIN 246
RED ROCK MT. 246
DIXVILLE NOTCH 247
GRAFTON NOTCH 248
MOUNT DIMMOCK 249
SQUAREDOCK MT. 250
BEAR MOUNTAIN 251
KNIGHTS HILL 251
NEEDLE'S EYE 252
BRIMSTONE CLIFF 252
WORTHLEY POND 253
MOUNT KINEO 253

KATAHDIN 257

PAMOLA ICE CLIFFS 263
THE FURRIES 265
SOUTH BASIN HEADWALL 267
NORTH BASIN 276

CAMDEN 280
BARRETT'S COVE CLIFF 281
MAIDEN CLIFF 286
MOUNT MEGUNTICOOK 287
THE MIDDLE CLIFFS.................................... 288
THE CATARACTS 288
THE OCEAN LOOKOUT 290
MOUNT BATTIE 290
ACADIA NATIONAL PARK 291
JORDAN POND 291
OTTER CLIFF 292
THE PRECIPICE 292
INDEX 294

Brian Post

IMCS guide Brad White at the office at Frankenstein

INTRODUCTION

Ice climbing is hot. In the ten years since the second edition of this guidebook the popularity of our drippy sport has grown faster than any of us could have imagined. As rock climbing did in the 1980's, ice climbing has boomed, becoming legitimate, accessible, and well, sane. The lunatic fringe is now the not-so-loony mainstream and frozen hollows in the woods now ring with the cries of folks having fun like never before.

Though there are many reasons, more than any other slice of the climbing pie, the popularity of ice climbing is linked inexorably to advances in technology. Twenty years ago ice climbers wore polypro, pile, wool, and leather, hacked relentlessly with heavy, blunt ice axes and creaky crampons, and twisted clunky screws in by sticking the pick of a tool in and cranking the shaft around in a huge arc. No kidding. You actually had to set yourself up just right so that the almost four-foot diameter swing didn't whack your other tool out or get tangled up in all the stuff hanging off the 1" webbing sling hanging on your shoulder. It took a while to put in a screw, and with big mittens on it was both awkward and cold and...well, you get the point.

Ice climbers today wear light, extremely functional clothing (for goodness sake we can all wear gloves now!), really warm and comfortable boots, we swing our ice tools once (or maybe twice) with ergonomic precision, tic in our mono-points with nary a kick, and spin screws in by hand anywhere while chatting with our belayer. There is very little foot stomping and arm swinging to stay warm, picks rarely break, the movement is fast—ice climbing has become safer and a lot more fun.

Northern New England is one of the best places to ice climb in the world. Our climate produces vast quantities of groundwater which leaks out each winter, flowing down our hillsides and cliffs forming frozen fun-parks all over the place. From late November to mid April, somewhere in Vermont, New Hampshire, or Maine, there is always something really cool frozen and waiting for us. The driving is easy, most of the approaches are reasonable, and the weather is fairly predictable.

Now don't get us wrong. Winter climbing in northern New England is fickle and it can bite. Conditions vary dramatically from year to year (2001 was incredible; 2002 was disappointing) and every season comes with its perils and dangers. The process by which waterfall ice forms is so variable that no rule of thumb applies. Each winter presents a unique set of climatic variables. The amount and type of precipitation, wind velocity, temperature, freeze/thaw cycles, elevation, and the direction toward which the climb faces are all factors which affect the condition of a climb during any given winter. It takes a significant amount of mountaineering experience, research, intuition, and a healthy dose of common sense to be able to read the conditions of an ice climb or a snow slope and climb safely. There are no short cuts to gaining this knowledge; you must still put in your time in the mountains with an experienced partner.

Water ice forms in New England each year regardless of snowfall and by mid winter most areas are in good shape. Some routes, like those at Lake Willoughby, and the big routes on Cathedral and Cannon take sustained winter weather to form up well, and late January through early March is the most popular time to climb the big routes. When routes like The Black Dike, Repentence, or the Last Gentleman do come in, you had best be quick to take advantage of the situation because as little as a few days of unseasonably mild temperatures can destroy months of ice build-up.

The expression "patience is a virtue" seems appropriate to characterize the local attitude toward some of the extreme ice routes found in New England. While the majority of routes are generally in shape for the duration of the season, there are a select group of climbs which form fleetingly, once each year or once a decade! The Myth of Sisyphus is one prime example. It will tantalizingly form for a few hours each season, an inviting drip-line easily seen from North Conway, yet sometimes just a few minutes of sunshine are all it takes to bring it all crashing to the ground. In twenty-six years it still has had less than a dozen ascents. For these routes, all we can say is keep your tools sharp, wait, watch, and strike while the iron is, well, cold.

This book is substantially bigger—and we think much better—than the 1992 edition. There are many more routes and even some new areas. We have cleared up some confusing things from the last guide, reorganized the material, updated the safety and logistical data, given you new maps and photos, and provided icons for easy reference. Our goal is simple. We want you to know how to get to the climbing areas and the climbs, what to expect "on route," and then how to get down efficiently. We have worked hard to ensure that our information is accurate and comprehensive. And while we have made every attempt to document the climbing in our region, we are not attempting to record every leaky drain in northern New England. Given the vast frozen resources of the region, it would be an impossible task anyway. There will always be flows, tucked in here and there, that offer that wonderful combination of great climbing and adventure. We want to help you find great climbing but we do not want to squelch the pioneering spirit that has characterized this region forever. Be adventurous. Go to new areas. Find great climbs that aren't in this book (at any one time, prolific New Hampshire climber Jon Sykes has a dozen crags he's "working" that the rest of us have never heard of). See what's around the next corner. And when you come back from discovering new things in the wilderness, please let us know what you've found. Please send corrections or new route information to the addresses below. To insure that your routes will be included, please provide all pertinent data: area, name of climb, relationship to existing routes, grade, approach and descent directions, route description, names of first ascent party and date, availability of photos, your address and phone number, etc. We appreciate your cooperation and look forward to hearing from you.

Peter Lewis
TMC Books
Box 35B Tasker Hill Rd.
Conway, NH 03818
TMCbooks.com

Rick Wilcox
International Mountain Equipment
Box 494, Main St.
North Conway, NH 03860
ime-usa.com

WEATHER

Although we have made great strides improving our equipment and clothing (one piece suits create a nearly climate controlled micro-environment), we have never managed to control our weather. Recent advancements have made predicting the weather more accurate—we can now access moving satellite images at the click of a mouse and download forecasts based on our zip code—but heading out on a winter day in New England is still a bit of a crap shoot. The climate in northern New England is notoriously variable and old Yankee wisdom says if you don't like the weather just wait a few minutes. In no other activity is that saying more relevant than winter climbing, where sudden changes in temperature, wind, or visibility can turn a pleasant day's climbing into a nightmare struggle for survival. In far too many instances tragedy in New England's mountains can be linked to weather.

Wind-borne clouds roll over Boott Spur on Mt. Washington
S. Peter Lewis

New England weather conditions are complicated by a number of geographic factors including: elevation, aspect (north facing, south facing, etc.) proximity to mountain ranges, etc. These determine what can be very site-specific weather conditions. Though ice climbing locales in New England are often geographically close, drastic differences can be seen between areas just a few minute's drive apart. For instance, it isn't unusual at all for the weather to be sunny, calm and 25⁰, in North Conway, a perfect day for ice climbing on Cathedral Ledge, while just twelve miles away in Crawford Notch it's overcast, windy and ten degrees cooler. And move just eight miles farther north and climb up 3,500 feet to Huntington Ravine on Mt. Washington and it can easily be near zero, with gale force winds and no visibility.

New England's winter weather is not to be underestimated. Each year there are climbers who get into trouble because the weather turns bad and they are not prepared. Mt. Washington is a major attraction for winter mountaineers in northern New England, yet almost every season lives are lost there, many the result of unexpected bad weather.

As an aid to understanding the complexities of northern New England winter weather, and planning for a day's climbing, the following chart gives data for three stations that monitor conditions from the relatively mild valley areas such as North Conway, to the more harsh notch conditions found in Pinkham Notch, to the severe weather common on summit areas like Mt. Washington. Throughout the book, in the introduction to each major area, a designation will be given (valley, notch or summit) depending on how that area's site-specific conditions line up with the standards on the chart. This in no way guarantees that a valley area will always be 20 degrees warmer than a "summit" area. Temperature inversions can reverse this situation, but in typical weather patterns, the relative differences between the valleys, notches and summits are fairly consistent.

Of special interest to climbers planning to venture to the higher elevations of New England, particularly Mt. Washington in the White Mountains and Katahdin in northern Maine, is the role that extreme temperatures and wind velocity can play on any given day.

The summit observatory on Mt. Washington has recorded minimum temperatures from -20° in November and April to between -38° and -47° in December through March. Along with severe low temperatures add an average daily wind velocity of 42 mph during winter months and almost any prolonged outdoor activity becomes extremely dangerous. And though Katahdin does not have a weather station on its summit, conditions there are certainly similar.

Poking their summits into the winter jet stream, these areas have weather more akin to the arctic regions of Labrador and should be treated with extra caution. There are plenty of other places to climb on a bad day.

CONDITION REPORTS

When you're looking for places to climb, or wonder what's in and what's not, or are curious about avalanche conditions, check out the following two websites:

NEice.com
NEclimbs.com

Valley, Notch, & Summit Weather	Average High Temp. (°F)	Average Low Temp. (°F)	Average Snowfall (in.)
NOVEMBER			
N. Conway	45.8	26.9	4.4
Pinkham Notch	**41.5**	**24**	**19.5**
Mt. Washington	*27.3*	*13.9*	*40.4*
DECEMBER			
N. Conway	34.3	14.6	19.4
Pinkham Notch	**30.5**	**11.5**	**30.6**
Mt. Washington	*17.1*	*0.6*	*42.6*
JANUARY			
N. Conway	29.3	6.9	22.2
Pinkham Notch	**25.4**	**4.6**	**29.5**
Mt. Washington	*12.3*	*-4.6*	*40.1*
FEBRUARY			
N. Conway	33.5	9.2	16.4
Pinkham Notch	**27.7**	**6.9**	**31.3**
Mt. Washington	*13.1*	*-3.2*	*40.7*
MARCH			
N. Conway	41.9	20.1	15.4
Pinkham Notch	**35.9**	**15.9**	**25.2**
Mt. Washington	*20.1*	*5.4*	*42.5*
APRIL			
N. Conway	53.8	31.3	5.5
Pinkham Notch	**47.1**	**27.7**	**16.3**
Mt. Washington	*28.7*	*16.1*	*30.9*

Note: Each recording station used a different set of years to compute their data and thus this chart should be used for general comparison only.

The highest point east of the Rockies and north of the Carolinas, Mount Washington, is most famous for its 231 mph blast—the highest ever recorded on the surface of the earth—on April 12, 1934. Always barren and with just a handful of weather and radio station staff on duty in the winter, the summit (a state park) becomes a veritable zoo in the summer crowded with folks "from away."

S. Peter Lewis

SAFETY

Climbing is really dangerous. Even those with the best equipment, skill, and judgment, can be injured or killed. And with ice climbers the dangers are even more apparent. Consider for a moment all the implements an ice climber carries on a climb. Ice tools, crampons, and ice screws are all sharp and potentially dangerous. Even a short fall on ice can result in serious injuries. A caught crampon can snap an ankle; an ice tool can inflict a nasty puncture wound. In rock climbing, the saying once was that the leader must not fall; on ice this concept is still important!

Ice climbing areas tend to be more isolated than most summer rock areas, so a rescue, should it be necessary, is not a matter of minutes away. In winter, many hours could pass between an accident and the arrival of the first rescuers. While winter temperatures hover at or below zero, this elapsed time becomes very critical indeed. Since an injured climber's body temperature will drop rapidly unless immediate insulation can be provided, an extra down jacket and pack with a built-in foam pad can literally become a lifesaver.

The Mountain Rescue Service (MRS) of New Hampshire was formed in 1972 to assist the local and state rescue organizations during technical rock and ice rescues in New Hampshire's mountains. Prior to 1972, the Fish and Game Department, legally responsible for all rescue efforts in the state, would contact climbers from as far away as Massachusetts to come to the aid of other mountaineers. Fortunately, there were only a few technical rescues during those years.

At the present time, the MRS works in conjunction with a large number of other organizations including the Appalachian Mountain Club, the U.S. Forest Service, the State Police, Androscoggin Valley Search and Rescue, and North Conway Rescue. A core of about twenty-five climbers make up the first response team, with many more in reserve if needed. The team is on call twenty-four hours a day year round, and is composed of highly qualified and dedicated local climbers and guides. With thirty years of rescue experience, the team has become a cohesive and exemplary organization. In its role of assisting climbers in trouble, the MRS deserves the respect and continued support of all climbers, visitors, and residents. Other rescue organizations exist throughout northern New England and experienced climbers are often available, but be forewarned: rescue is not guaranteed. In places like Mt. Washington, Smugglers Notch in Vermont, and certainly on Katahdin way up in the woods in Maine, rescue may be many, many hours away. Don't count on your cell phone. Don't count on MRS or other rescue organizations, don't count on other climbers. Do everything you can do to prepare yourself technically for self-rescue, keep your eye on your team and the weather, and be ready to bail. Conservative climbers live longer.

By their very nature, technical rescues are extremely hazardous, especially in winter. Some climbing accidents are the consequence of objective, and hence, uncontrollable dangers: rockfall, avalanche, etc. While other accidents, perhaps the majority, are the result of inexperience or poor decision-making—"pilot error" if you will. And not all rescues end happily.

In January, 1982, Albert Dow, a seasoned member of the MRS and a professional climbing instructor for the EMS Climbing School, lost his life while on a rescue mission on Mt. Washington. During this period of extremely bad weather and high avalanche danger, all the team members were aware of the risks, yet persevered in searching for two ice climbers who had not returned from a trip into Huntington Ravine. After spending several days and nights out in below -20⁰F weather, the stranded climbers were found on the opposite side of the mountain and subsequently rescued by helicopter. They went on to recover, but suffered life-changing and lifelong injuries.

Many climbers recognize the risks to which the rescue members are exposed. Rescuers are volunteers in the purest sense. The decision to go, or not to go on a rescue, is based as much on personal safety as on the tremendous desire to help a fellow climber in trouble. If the risk is too great, the choice to stay home is understandable.

MRS members in arctic conditions during Mount Washington's best known and most tragic rescue in 1982.
David Stone

Before heading out into the mountains, each individual climber must try to accurately gauge his own preparedness, skill and judgment. The possibility of an accident must be realistically determined, and the necessary equipment and skills for self-rescue should be in place long before the climb begins. After such self-evaluation, use this guide to assist you in locating a climb suited to your abilities.

In addition to climbing as safely as possible, you should strive to climb as responsibly and respectfully as possible. As more and more of us climb, the potential for damaging our environment and the likelihood of access issues increases. Although winter climbers are less likely to adversely affect their environment because of the snow cover, we should still strive to meet the standards of the Leave No Trace program, a national nonprofit organization advocating minimal environmental impact by folks like us.

- Plan ahead and prepare.
- Camp and travel on durable surfaces (snow, while not durable, is fine).
- Pack it in, pack it out.
- Properly dispose of what you cannot pack out.
- Leave nature as you found it.
- Minimize use and impact from fires.

AND WHILE ICE CLIMBING, FOLLOW THESE PRINCIPLES AS WELL:
- Do not chip or drill holds in rock (some ice climbs are rock climbs in the summer).

- Use removable protection whenever possible. Bolts and pitons permanently change the rock.

- Take extra care not to damage the rock when mixed climbing on summer rock routes, at sport crags, or sensitive areas (The Flume in Franconia)

- Do not use motorized drills in wilderness areas. Placing bolts is a privilege; follow the rules (and local tradition).

- Consider the overall environmental impacts of developing a new area or route. Traffic, trails, and disturbance to wildlife may follow.

- Leave anchors that blend in. If you place bolts on a new route, or leave a fixed anchor at a belay, or leave slings, make them as invisible as possible.

- Do not rappel directly from trees. Use dull-colored slings and rappel rings instead; trees can die if they are rappelled from repeatedly.

- Clean up after yourself. Spend a few minutes cleaning up before you leave—even if it's not your trash.

- Keep the noise down, especially in urban areas. Be sensitive to the solitude enjoyed by residents and other users.

- Park where you should and keep a low profile along the road.

- Ask permission—private land is often open to climbers; help keep it that way by checking with land owners if you have any doubt about access privileges. Follow regulations, respect closures (for example, for nesting raptors), get involved in solving access problems, consider joining the Access Fund (303-545-6772, accessfund.org), a climber advocacy group that works to keep climbing areas open.

- Lastly, be nice. Our climbing areas can get crowded and if everyone is respectful there can be plenty of fun climbing for all. Be kind to land owners, climbers, and other users of the resource. Don't control popular toprope sites for hours at a time. Be extra careful about falling ice if there are other parties on your route. Consider climbing elsewhere if there is already someone on your planned route. Don't pass other parties without permission. Share information with other climbers about weather forecasts and route conditions—and don't be a sandbagger. Before sharing a rope at a popular spot, ensure that the system is set up properly. If you see a dangerous situation developing, step in and politely offer advice and assistance. And if something bad happens be prepared to drop your plans and help.

S. Peter Lewis

INSTRUCTION

Many ice climbers start out as rock climbers, and these days that start is usually in a climbing gym. The transition from gym climbing to outdoor rock climbing is complex and fraught with dangers—and the transition from gym climbing to ice climbing is even more challenging. If ice climbing intrigues you but your experience level is not such that you feel you can climb safely on your own, consider hiring a guide or going to a climbing school.

Traditionally, climbers have learned their trade from fellow climbers. Organizations such as the Appalachian Mountain Club (AMC) and the Harvard Mountaineering Club have sponsored trips into the White Mountains of northern New England since the 1920's, and many of today's great climbers got their start from such outings.

Today's aspiring ice climber can benefit from the recent growth and maturity of the profession of mountain guiding. The American Mountain Guides Association (AMGA) administers the only internationally recognized instruction and certification program in the United States. Their guide certification programs represent the worldwide standard and many instructors and guides in our region have become certified. If you are looking for quality instruction in our region, consider visiting the AMGA website, AMGA.com, or giving them a call at 303-271-0984.

Here is a list of many of the organizations, climbing schools, and guides that operate in northern New England.

International Mountain Climbing School, Inc.
Box 1666
North Conway, NH 03860
603-356-7064
ime-usa.com
AMGA accredited; AMGA certified guides on staff

Eastern Mountain Sports Climbing School, Inc.
Box 514
North Conway, NH 03860
603-356-5433
EMSclimb.com
AMGA accredited; AMGA certified guides on staff

Mountain Guides Alliance, Inc.
Box 266
North Conway, NH 03860
603-356-5310
mountainguidesalliance.com
AMGA certified guides on staff

New England Mountain Guides
Alain Comeau
Box 883
North Conway, NH 03860
207-935-2008
newenglandguides.com
AMGA certified

Chauvin Guides International
Box 2151
North Conway, NH 03860
603-356-8919
chauvinguides.com
IFMGA certified
AMGA certified

Rhinoceros Mountain Guides
Jim Shimberg
Arlyn Farms
Tenney Mountain Highway
Plymouth, NH 03264
603-536-2717
rhinomtn@worldpath.net

Longtime area guide Nick Yardley smiling on the pillar on Pegasus.
S. Peter Lewis

Mark Synnott
Box 705
Jackson, NH 03846
603-383-6976
marksynnott.com

Outrigue
Danielle Gelinas
RR 1 Box 354
North Conway, NH 03860
603-383-9430
outrigue.com
AMGA certified

Bartlett Backcountry Adventures
Steve Nichipor
Box 93
Bartlett, NH 03812
603-374-0866
bartlettadventures.com
AMGA certified

Acadia Mountain Guides
Jon Tierney
198 Main St.
Bar Harbor, ME 04609
888-232-9559
acadiamountainguides.com
AMGA accredited; AMGA certified

Green Mountain Guides Climbing School
Tom Kontos
PO Box 421
Jeffersonville, VT 05464
802-644-8131
AMGA certified guides on staff

Appalachian Mountain Club
5 Joy St.
Boston, MA 02108
603-523-0636
outdoors.org

Yvon Chouinard once described ice climbing as a slippery game. It is a sport where physical and mental preparedness are paramount, where only the best quality equipment should be used at all times, and even the slightest slip or break in concentration can lead to injury or worse. We hope you enjoy New England's mountains safely.

EQUIPMENT

Oh how things have changed. If any climbing activity is gear intensive, it's ice climbing and winter mountaineering. Unlike the shorts and T-shirt clad rock jock with a pair of sticky shoes and a chalk bag who frequents the neighborhood boulder after work, ice climbing demands the use of gear. And there's lots of it and it's expensive. The equipment and clothing innovations of the last couple of decades have made it possible for this once fringe sport to attract masses of outdoor enthusiasts who want to use ice and snow as their playground. In the old days, suffering was mandatory. Today, suffering is optional.

For climbing ice and snow, equipment generally plays a greater part in determining the speed, security, and at times, the severity of the ascent, than it does in rock climbing. The ice climber is a tool user extraordinaire; here's what works well in northern New England:

HARDWARE

BOOTS

Because of our cold temperatures, most Northeast climbers choose the warmest double boots they can find. While the specialized, light, single boots made for the latest mixed climbing may work great in Colorado, and even here on some days, there are many occasions when such footwear would put you at real risk for frostbite. Big, beefy, plastic double boots are the norm here. Gaitors or supergaitors (those with a rubber rand that wrap around your boot) are a really good idea: they protect your expensive Gore-Tex® pants and help keep your feet warm and dry.

ICE TOOLS

Three kinds work well on our routes: long, straight-shafted ice axes with straight picks for climbing on nontechnical terrain above timberline and for straightforward snow climbs (e.g. Right Gully in Tuckerman Ravine in mid-season); moderately long, straight-shafted, reverse-curved ice axes with an adze on the other end for steep snow and moderate ice climbs (Willey's Slide); and short, bent-shafted, reverse-curved ice hammers for steep ice and mixed climbing. The decision on what kind of tool to use is usually based on the characteristics of the climb and its grade. And don't think that erring on the side of higher tech is always the best option. Carrying a pair of Black Diamond Cobras on Willey's Slide is going to be miserable (and embarrassing when the guys with the straight tools walk right past you.) A spare tool for every two climbers is also a good idea, especially on the longer routes where a broken pick or dropped tool could turn an outing into an epic.

CRAMPONS

Again, there are three basic choices: flexible crampons for tramping above timberline and easy snow and ice climbs; rigid, dual-point crampons for steep ice; and rigid crampons with mono-points for steep ice and mixed climbing. Although the choice is less critical here than with ice tools, it can still be very important to pick the right crampon for the right job. Climbing The Last Gentleman at Lake Willoughby in flexible crampons could be dangerous; climbing Mount Washington's Central Gully wearing the latest mono-points is overkill.

HARNESSES

Because none of our climbs require a night out, wear whatever is most comfortable. You won't need light, alpine-style harnesses that can drop when you need to relieve yourself (unless your timing and biorhythms are just way off.)

HELMET

Yes, wear one.

ROPES

Most climbers are carrying 60-meter dry ropes. Shorter ropes will work (it's ice climbing—you can belay almost anywhere), but ropes not dry treated will turn into cables. A spare rope will be necessary if you plan to rappel. (Note: Many winter routes here do not have fixed anchors. Use trees, bollards, and V-threads as anchors.)

The history of ice climbing (and its equipment) in three volumes.
S. Peter Lewis

Ice Protection

Most climbers carry 8 to 12 screws for climbs here, most in the 17cm to 22cm range. A couple of stubbies are often helpful and some folks carry the real long ones to sink at belays. Because our ice is often really hard and brittle bring the newest, sharpest screws you can get. Pound-in protection, while occasionally useful, is not standard—the pound-in tubular screws are hard to remove (and take more effort to put in anyway), and the pound-in, pick-style protection devices are not particularly secure.

ROCK PROTECTION

Rock gear is only occasionally needed and will usually be mentioned in the written description. Unless otherwise noted for a particular climb, a few wired nuts, Tricams, and cams to 2" are usually sufficient. Pitons are rarely needed.

SUPPORT HARDWARE

For most climbs a half dozen quickdraws, a dozen free biners, a pair of cordelettes, 6 to 8 slings, and a belay/rappel device is all you'll need. In addition, the wise climber will bring a first aid kit, headlamp, compass, map, food, water (don't drink out of the streams), heat packs, and a small repair kit including a spare pick and wrenches. Use your head. Don't overload yourself so much that you can't climb efficiently, and don't skimp and risk your neck.

CLOTHING

It's cold here. Climbers should be prepared to spend the day out in the wind and shade, often at temperatures around zero. Although it is often much warmer than that, it can also be much colder and a cold climber is a miserable climber. A layer of thin synthetic underwear followed by a mid-weight insulating layer and topped with Gore-Tex® will usually keep you warm if you're active and well fed and hydrated. For colder days add a fleece jacket or down vest and consider a down jacket for those belays below zero. Layering is the key so wear a selection of clothing that can be mixed and matched for the conditions. And remember, cotton kills, so stick to synthetics. Mittens are best on really cold days; the new gloves work well in all but the worst conditions and are much easier to climb with. Bring a pair of liner gloves and at least one extra pair of warm gloves or mittens for each climber. A fleece hat is usually fine although everyone should carry full-coverage headwear like a balaclava. A neoprene face mask and goggles should be in every climber's pack if they're headed for Mt. Washington or Katahdin. Most folks wear a thin liner sock followed by a thicker insulating sock. Some swear by vapor-barrier socks; others swear at them. Here's a tip to keep your feet warmer—wear your big socks with the fuzzy/bumpy side out (smooth side in lessens friction and helps prevent blisters, less compression keeps you warmer, better moisture transfer keeps you drier). For outerwear, Gore-Tex® or some other waterproof-breathable material is the way to go. Tops and bottoms work fine but many people find the one-piece suits more comfortable, less bulky, and warmer.

WINTER CAMPING GEAR

If you plan overnight trips in the winter in Northern New England you should be prepared for very cold temperatures and potentially high winds. High quality, four-season mountain tents, sleeping bags rated to -20° (down or synthetic), and stoves capable of burning at arctic temperatures are the norm. Be conservative, err on the side of quality and warmth, and you're less likely to become a statistic.

A decade from now the equipment for winter climbing will be even better than it is today. But no matter how high-tech things get, the most important piece of gear you have is between your ears. Plan ahead, make good decisions, and make sure you come home.

RATINGS

Rating ice climbs has always been a slippery affair. Unlike rock climbs, which, save for the occasional flake disappearing, remain virtually unchanged from season to season, the difficulty of a given ice route is entirely dependent on its condition. And that is affected by a number of factors: thick or thin, mush or bulletproof, hacked up or smooth, and the list goes on. Thus, by definition, ice ratings are subjective, and the grades given are best viewed as generalizations. It is unlikely that you will ever see ice grades broken down into a, b,c,d as in rating rock. Pluses and minuses are about as exact as the ice will allow, and that only on routes that come in consistently each year.

As a rule, the technical grades given in this guide are representative of the climb in its typical mid-season condition, and on a day with average weather conditions. Below zero temperatures, high winds or heavy snowfall can add a full grade or more to a given route, while a sunny day with the thermometer in the 40's can make a hard climb feel easy. A good example of how variable ratings can be is Welcome to the Machine at Frankenstein. This late 1970's grade 5 developed a fearsome reputation over the years as one of the area's hardest and most ephemeral grade 5's. Many years went by without a single ascent. Then along came the winter of 00/01 and for some odd reason the route came in fat. It grew thicker than anyone had ever seen it and by mid February was as pegged out as Standard Route. It was done several times in a day; it was guided; it was soloed. People came into town strutting and bragging that they had done "The Machine." Well, the reality was that it was just a chunky grade 4 that year. So consider the grades to be representative of the typical difficulty of a climb in a typical year and be prepared if it's different on the day you're standing under it. And on climbs with only one ascent, the rating is very subjective and subsequent ascents may alter it, so beware.

Other factors that should be taken into account that are not included in the overall grade are approaches and descents. Adding a three mile thrash through pucker brush to a three pitch grade 3 route increases the commitment dramatically. For example, while Elephant Head Gully in Crawford Notch, and Point in the Madison Gulf are both given the overall grade of 3+, the fact is that the approach to Elephant Head Gully takes thirty seconds while getting to the Madison Gulf entails a six mile hike through deep snow that has been described by veteran bushwhacker Todd Swain as "the most horrendous I've ever experienced. Five times worse than Huntington's." It is wise therefore to take the entire trip from car to car, and not just the technical rating, into consideration when planning a day's climbing.

Up until the late 1970's technical grades for ice climbs could best be described as vague. In Peter Cole and Rick Wilcox's first ice guide to the area, *Shades of Blue*, published in 1976, climbs were simply graded "easy,' "moderate" and "hard." By the late 70's with many more climbers active there was a real need for an accurate rating system to compare the levels of difficulty and commitment of the increasing number of climbs in the region. Rick adapted the Scottish ice grading system, a simple numerical scale from 1 to 4, and called it the New England Ice Scale or NEI for short. (Climbers had casually been using such a system for years, but it had never been nailed down.) A fifth grade was soon added and, with the additions of pluses and minuses, the relative accuracy and simplicity of the scale helped it endure. During the early 1980's ice climbing continued to grow in popularity. The first edition of *An Ice Climber's Guide to Northern New England*, which appeared in 1982, was the first place that the NEI system was published. It was quickly accepted by the climbing community.

In the following years, the simplicity of the system and its reliability as a purely technical grading system was demonstrated by the adoption of similar systems across the U.S. and Canada. In areas such as the Canadian Rockies, (where the length and difficulty of the climbs can be much greater than in New England), grade 6 was added for such 1980's test pieces as Polar Circus, and grade 7 came a few years later with the ascents of such horror shows as Terminator and Reality Bath, the latter put up by New England local Randy Rackliff with Marc Twight. At the time of the second edition in 1992, the area consensus was that grade 5+ was tops for New England. (Kurt Winkler's ascent of La Pomme d'Or in Quebec in the mid 1980's was the first ice climb in this part of North America to be rated a grade 6.)

By the late 1990's and into the early part of this decade, pure ice climbs were being done in northern New England that were just plain harder than grade 5+. So, as typically stubborn New Englanders, we have grudgingly added the 6th grade. Only a handful of routes in this guide carry that grade but, like all things in climbing, that will surely change.

These days the numeric grade for pure ice climbs is quite consistent worldwide. A grade 5 in France is much like a grade 5 in Vermont, Colorado, and British Columbia—at least that's the theory. Obviously length and commitment can differ radically from one area to another; fortunately there are other recognized standards to describe these factors. As grades became more consistent in the early 1990's, the NEI designation was dropped and is now just a bit of New England climbing trivia.

Grade 2: laid back, stand and rest anywhere—George Hurley on Cinema Gully.
David Stone

RATING SYSTEMS

The following systems describe virtually every aspect of a particular climb.

ICE TECHNICAL RATING

Classic climbs are listed for each grade to illustrate the transition in difficulty from one grade to another. Bear in mind that this grade is for the pure technical difficulty of the ice climbing but does not take into account length' there are one pitch grade 4's and five pitch grade 4's. All grades are technical and require the use of ropes, belays and ice climbing equipment.

Grade 1

Low angle water ice less than 50^0 or long, moderate snow climbs requiring a basic level of technical expertise for safety: Willey's Slide (Crawford Notch), Central Gully (Huntington Ravine).

Grade 3: steep bulges and rests—Charlie Townsend guiding on Chia.
S. Peter Lewis

Grade 2

Low angle water ice routes with short bulges up to 60^0: Cinema Gully (Mt. Willard), Yale Gully (Huntington Ravine).

Grade 3

Steeper water ice of 50^0 to 60^0 with short 70^0 to 90^0 bulges: Pinnacle Gully (Huntington Ravine), Standard Route (Frankenstein Cliff).

Grade 4

Short, vertical columns interspersed with rests on 50^0 to 60^0 ice. Fairly sustained climbing. Dracula (Frankenstein Cliff), Twenty Below Zero Gully (Lake Willoughby), Waterfall Gully (Katahdin).

Grade 4: steep, rest, then steep again—Hobbit Couloir.
Joe Klementovich

Grade 5

Generally multi-pitch ice climbs with sustained difficulties and/or strenuous vertical columns with little rest possible: Repentence (Cathedral Ledge), The Last Gentleman (Lake Willoughby). Routes graded with the 5+ rating are climbs with a heightened degree of seriousness, long vertical sections, and extremely sustained difficulties—the classic hard ice climbs in New England: Remission (Cathedral Ledge), The Promenade (Lake Willoughby), Omega (Cannon Cliff), Mainline (Mt. Kineo).

Grade 6

The longest sections of vertical ice in the region (or short and viciously steep), often interspersed with overhangs and free-hanging daggers; the new age of pure ice: Call of the Wild (Lake Willoughby, VT), Valhalla (Goback Mt., NH), Cold Cold World (Eagle Cliff, NH).

Grade 5: straight up, few rests—Mark Synnott on the classic Dropline.
Rob Frost

THE COMMITMENT GRADE

In addition to the pure technical grade the international system for commitment is used throughout the guide and is designated by a Roman numeral just before the technical grade. This grade represents the amount of time a competent party can expect to spend on a given climb under normal conditions. Again, particularly foul weather, or a route in bad conditions, can affect this grade as well. And, as mentioned before, approaches and descents should also be figured into the equation. The following breakdown will help you determine your choice of routes. In

Even here in New England some routes like this ridge on Katahdin are committing undertakings.
Bob Baribeau

this guide, if a route does not have a commitment grade it is assumed to be grade 1.

I   Up to several hours.

II   About half a day.

III   A full day, up to seven or eight hours.

IV   A substantial undertaking; a very long day, possibly including a bivouac.

V   A big wall climb of 1-2 days; could be done in a one day by a fit team.

VI   Multi-day big wall climbs over two days.

VII   Big wall ascents in remote alpine situations.

AID RATING

On some routes, aid climbing moves or pitches will be found and the traditional A1 to A5 ratings will be used.

A0   pulling on a piece of protection or doing a rappel on a free climb.

A1   easy aid climbing with solid pieces all the way.

A2   less secure, often steep or awkward, most placements will hold a fall.

A3   advanced aid, some specialized gear needed, up to several marginal pieces in a row.

A4   body-weight placements and long sections without solid protection; true expert terrain.

A5   body-weight placements for a really long way; extremely long and dangerous falls are possible.

Jared Ogden trying to keep his points only on ice on the mixed terrain of the Hanging Gardens at Frankenstein Cliff.
Mark Synnott

MIXED RATING

The "M" system attempts to give the climber a sense of how hard the moves are by comparing them with rock climbing moves. There are not a lot of mixed climbs yet in our region but the tide surge is definitely coming our way. This is a subjective and relatively new system but here are the basic numbers.

M1 feels like 5.5

M2 feels like 5.6

M3 feels like 5.7

M4 feels like 5.8

M5 feels like 5.9

M6 feels like 5.10

M7 feels like 5.11

M8 feels like 5.12

M9 and above feels ridiculous

Out of a sense of tradition we have chosen to leave the old rock climbing free ratings (e.g. 5.6) on many of the older routes—only occasionally have we converted the rock grade to an "M" rating. Most of the newer routes have been reported with "M" grades (and so New England gets dragged into the future with the rest of the climbing world). In some instances climbers have simply rated their climbs as "mixed" and we will leave it to you to sort that out—there should still be a little mystery in our sport shouldn't there?

PROTECTION RATINGS

We use the standard protection rating system.

no designation—protection is good throughout.

R protection is hard to get or only fair quality and you should expect to run it out.

X protection poor to nonexistent and if you fall you may die.

FIRST ASCENT INFORMATION

Throughout this guide first ascent information will be as follows: no designation—first ascent; FRA—first recorded ascent; FWA—first winter ascent (for rock routes).

PUTTING IT ALL TOGETHER

So there you have it—all of our crazy numbers. After each route's name we will organize the ratings as follows: grade (commitment), followed by the relevant ratings based on the character of the route and proportionately how much of each type of climbing there is. So, if the "M" grade comes first, that's the predominant type of climbing; if the aid rating comes first, then the climb has more aid climbing than anything else. If there are alternate grades based on the style of the ascent the alternative will be included in parenthesis. The written description will also help you determine the characteristics of the route, and therefore what gear to bring. For example, if you did the first winter ascent of a five pitch route that is primarily an ice climb but has one pitch of aid (which can be freed) and a short section of moderate mixed climbing that isn't well protected, the rating would look like this:

MY GREAT ROUTE III 4 A2 (5.10) M3 R

This is the greatest climb in the world and you should all run out and do it.
FWA Me, Myself and I, February 15, 2001

Please bear in mind that the written descriptions vary in terms of length and quality depending on the detail supplied by the first ascent party. One person may climb a horrendous new route on a huge cliff and tell us that it goes right of some other route and was scary while someone else will give us a nearly move by move description of their one-pitch wonder. In every instance we tried to get as much information as we could.

In addition to the traditional rating systems, this edition introduces a series of icons to help you see the characteristics of a route or climbing area at a glance. We have tried to be spare with our icons however, so you won't find them next to every climb. If a climb does not have any particularly distinguishing characteristics, but is rather just a typical route for its grade that comes in reasonably and is protected with normal gear then it won't have any icons. Nebulous routes that don't get much travel won't typically get icons either; their vague status will likely be mentioned in their description. However, routes that are notoriously thin, crowded, strenuous, need rock gear, or for some other reason stand out, are likely to get an icon or two. For instance, Pegasus and Hobbit Couloir at Frankenstein are both rated grade 4 but Hobbit has an infamous vertical crux so is likely to get the "steep" icon. In some instances an entire area (e.g. Champney Falls) may get icons because all the routes there share common characteristics and putting icons all over the place would just clutter things up. Please note that the lack of icons, especially warning icons such as those for Avalanche Hazard, Falling Ice, or Poor Protection, does not mean that these conditions will not be found on a particular route—this is ice climbing after all and any route is susceptible to any number of hazards. Use these icons to get a sense of what to expect—but use good judgment. We hope you find these helpful.

ICON KEY

 Typically Arrives Early

 Sunny Spot

 Steep!

 Typically Stays Late

 Often High, Cold, and Windy

 Mixed

 Typically Fat and Dependable

 Backcountry Route (far from help)

 Rock Gear Needed

 Typically Thin

 Roadside Area/Route

 Poor Protection

 Rare Visitor

 Falling Ice Hazard

 Good Toproping

 Often Crowded

 Avalanche Hazard

HISTORY

Technical ice climbing in New England has been recorded as far back as 1894. On December 26th of that year, Dr. R.C. Larrabee, Herschel C. Parker, and a Mr. Andrew attempted to climb the headwall of Tuckerman Ravine. Unfortunately, their efforts were foiled by the large amount of ice they encountered. Not to be deterred so easily, Parker returned alone on February 27th, 1895, and completed the first recorded ascent of the Tuckerman Ravine headwall. On his successful ascent he carried an ice axe, a useful piece of equipment he'd neglected to bring the first time.

As early as 1915 Howard Jackson and Frank S. Mason had been working on boot and crampon designs to use in the White Mountains. They had rejected Swiss crampons because they felt they were too heavy and wouldn't work properly on soft-soled boots. And some early New England climbers felt that the crampons would conduct too much heat away from the foot, increasing the danger of frostbite. Jackson and Mason's solution was a boot with a thick leather welt which held the metal spikes in place and protected the climber's feet from the extreme cold characteristic of New England winters. Their design, while adequate for winter hikers, failed to satisfy the needs of technical climbers. European equipment, although not as warm as the Jackson-Mason design, simply performed better on water ice.

During the early years of New England ice climbing, just about all recorded activity centered in Huntington Ravine on Mount Washington's east flank. Not until the 1950's did the focus begin to shift to other areas of New England. One extraordinary exception was the 1923 ascent of Katahdin's Chimney route by a party of seven (including three women) led by Willard Helburn. Considering the terrain, the weather, and the modern logistical challenges of climbing on Katahdin in 2002 this 1923 ascent is astounding.

The 1923 party on the first ascent of Katahdin's Chimney route.
Arthur Comey

The first technical winter ascent in Huntington Ravine was made on February 23, 1927, when A.J. Holden and N.L Goodrich climbed Central Gully, the easiest of the six main gullies in the ravine. The second ascent of Central Gully was done a year later on February 12, 1928. J.C. Hurd, Noel E. Odell, B. Bronson, O.W. Linscotte, K.D. McCutchen, N.W. Spadavecchia, R.S. Sperry, L.S. Southwich, and Daniel Underhill left the Glen House at 7:30 a.m. on snowshoes. After a quick trip up to the ravine, they donned crampons for the ascent of The Fan. At the base of Central Gully, the party roped up for the ascent, and with Hurd and Underhill in the lead, reached the Alpine Garden by 1:30 p.m. No protection was used on the climb, but steps were cut up a difficult icy slab, the crux of the route.

On March 16, 1928, Noel Odell, J.C. Hurd, Lincoln O'Brien, and Robert L.M. Underhill returned to Huntington Ravine with a new objective, the wide prominent gully now known as Odell's Gully. The climb proved substantially harder than Central Gully. Although the three climbers were roped together and belayed, not one ice screw was used for protection. The June, 1929, issue of *Appalachia* contained an interesting note, predicting that for the future of ice climbing on Mount Washington, "apparently nothing remained to be done."

Hardly had the print dried when Samuel A. Scoville and Julian H. Whittlesey made the first ascent of Pinnacle Gully, certainly one of the most famous ice climbs in New England. Earlier attempts by the leading climbers of the day, O'Brien, Underhill and others had been unsuccessful, their attempts usually cut short by darkness. Scoville and Whittlesey were far from being the best climbers; in fact they were rank novices. But they did possess the one quality that has so often been evident in climbing history—in today's parlance they were willing to "go for it." Reflecting on the climb years later, Whittlesey admitted cheerfully to historians Guy and Laura Waterman that not only was it the hardest climb he had ever done, but that Pinnacle Gully was "the only one"

Pinnacle Gully first ascentionist Jullian Whittlesey in 1992
courtesy Julian Whittlesey

he had ever done. Their remarkably fast one day ascent of the gully, the hardest of the Huntington Ravine gullies, was a landmark climb. During the next five years, the proficiency and skill of these first climbers were proven time and time again; it wasn't until the fifth ascent of the route by W.V. Graham and Matthew and James C. Maxtwell in March, 1948, that Pinnacle Gully was repeated in a single day! Another interesting bit of history concerning Pinnacle Gully occurred on the second ascent on March 30, 1934, by Alan Wilcox and William M. House. They completed the climb with ten-point crampons and again didn't use a single ice screw for protection. Ice climbers of this era, obviously men of uncommon mettle, usually carried steel carabiners in their pockets for occasional use at belays.

In late March, 1941, an attempt was made by a party consisting of William P. House, Kenneth A. Henderson, Maynard Malcolm Miller, and Andrew J. Kaufman to climb the left-hand of the two northern gullies in Huntington Ravine. The attempt, however, was cut short by a storm, approaching darkness, and difficult conditions. Thus, the gully which had handed them defeat was appropriately named Damnation Gully. The following winter, Maynard Miller and William Latady climbed North Gully, just east of Damnation. Then on January 31, 1943, William Putnam and Andrew J. Kaufman returned to complete the first successful ascent of Damnation Gully—the last gully in Huntington Ravine to feel the swing of the climber's ice axe. (Note: Robert Underhill and Lincoln O'Brien had climbed all but the crux bulge in Damnation (then called Nelson Crag Gully) in 1929.)

Until the 1950's all ice climbs in New England were credited to members of either the Harvard Mountaineering Club or the Appalachian Mountain Club. As a result, lessons in ice climbing were to be had only from these two climbing organizations. However, the pace of winter climbing activity was remarkably uneven. During the 1920's and 30's, the AMC had regularly scheduled trips to Mount Washington, yet between 1933 and 1954, not a single visit was scheduled. The twenty-one year hiatus ended in March, 1954, when twenty-five people participated in an AMC ice climbing trip to the White Mountains. A healthy interest was subsequently rekindled in the sport and the AMC has sponsored such trips ever since.

Although the precise date of the first ascent of Willey's Slide in Crawford Notch is not known, it is known that climbing trips to the area commenced as early as 1954. Finally, after over 60 years of technical climbing in the gullies of Mount Washington, climbers began to turn to the multitude of other ice-laced crags and gullies in the White Mountains to enliven their sport and seek new directions. One of the next major winter ascents accomplished in the region occurred on February 7, 1954, when David Bernays and Andrew Griscom, members of the Harvard Mountaineering Club, made the first winter ascent of Standard Route on Whitehorse Ledge. Their seven hour climb involved several tricky sections, including a pendulum over the infamous "brown spot" and some direct aid in the final overlaps. Surprisingly, it was another ten years before Cathedral Ledge, just a few hundred yards north of Whitehorse, was climbed in winter.

Cutting steps up Odells Gully in 1962. Seven years later cutting steps would go the way of the dodo on neighboring Pinnacle Gully.
Henry Kendall

On January 19, 1964, Hugo Stadtmuller and Henry W. Kendall climbed the Standard Route up Cathedral in difficult verglas conditions. Their ascent of the notorious "cave wall" ushered in a new level of difficulty in mixed climbing (M2 in modern terms). In that same year, in April, tragedy struck the New England ice climbing community for the first time. John Griffen and Hugo Stadtmuller, both experienced climbers, failed to return to the Harvard Cabin after a day's ice climbing in Huntington Ravine. John Porter, who was staying at the cabin, reported to Ranger Richard Goodwin that his friends were overdue. The next morning, a joint Forest Service and AMC rescue team hurried into the Ravine where they found evidence of a massive avalanche which originated in Central Gully. The climbers, whose bodies were uncovered at the base of The Fan, were apparently at the junction of Central and Pinnacle Gullies when the slide occurred.

A year later, another fatal ice climbing accident occurred in Huntington Ravine on March 14, 1965. Daniel Doody, a member of the successful 1963 American Everest Expedition, and Craig Merrihue fell from near the top of Pinnacle Gully. A corkscrew-type ice screw found clipped to the climbing rope was assumed to be the belay piton. When the leader fell, the belay failed and both climbers fell 800 feet down the gully to the rocks of The Fan below.

As these accidents point out, ice climbing up until the late 1960's was a dangerous and slippery game. Prior to 1968, the standard technique for ice climbing was to chop a ladder of steps up the slope. Ten-point hinged crampons, long-shafted straight-pick ice axes, and a handful of crude ice screws were the climber's standard gear. The introduction of nylon rope in 1947 had increased greatly the margin of safety, but ice climbing was still a dangerously precarious sport. Standards of difficulty were not rising during these years. But in the late 1960's, an American hardware manufacturer set out to revolutionize the sport.

Yvon Chouinard travelled to Europe, climbing in Chamonix, France, the center of European climbing. There, climbers were using rigid 12-point crampons and short ice axes and hammers with steeply drooped picks. Without cutting steps, and with an economy of energy, climbers frontpointed quickly up steep faces of nevé ice. Two hand tools, an alpine hammer in one hand and short axe in the other, afforded them much greater stability and security. After a particularly successful alpine season in 1968, Chouinard returned to the U.S. with some grand plans. In his Ventura, California, machine shop, he produced the first American-designed, rigid, 12-point crampons, alpine hammers, and ice axes. Made in Europe to his specifications, Chouinard's new ice gear hit the New England ice climbing scene in the winter of 1969. Equipped with drooped tools and rigid crampons, climbers could now ascend even the steepest ice without having to resort to the laborious techniques of step cutting. Almost overnight, new ice climbing areas in New England, once thought to contain ice much too steep to climb, became approachable. Armed with these latest technological weapons, New England ice climbers began to scour the cliffs with renewed intensity, pushing the limits higher than ever before.

In the winter of 1969-70, Jim McCarthy headed north to try out his new ice equipment on Mount Washington. On February 1, 1970, he along with Bill Putnam, Rick Wilcox, Rob Wallace, and Carl Brandon made the first ascent of Pinnacle Gully without cutting a single step. Their historic, five-hour ascent, proved once and for all that steep water ice could be climbed swiftly, surely, and safely with all the new gear and by only standing on frontpoints

Frankenstein's classic route Chia climbed thousands of times in the last three decades. George Hurley making the umpteenth ascent in the 1990's.
S. Peter Lewis

The new technology that Chouinard developed not only made the standard routes easier and safer, but opened up a whole new world of possibilities. Areas that had always been passed over because they were obviously too difficult, could now be explored with confidence.

During the same season as Pinnacle Gully's first step-less ascent, Sam Streibert and Al Rubin discovered the amazing ice climbing potential at Frankenstein Cliff in Crawford Notch. The classic frozen waterfall, Standard Route, was climbed first, then Chia and Pegasus the next year. Word soon spread of this fantastic ice climbing area, with its short approach, variety of routes, and relative lack of objective dangers.

John Bouchard on the second ascent of the Black Dike in 1973. His 1971 solo first ascent is considered by many to be the most impressive first ascent in New England ice climbing history.
Rick Wilcox

It was during this time as well that Vermont's Smugglers Notch began to see high caliber activity, initially spearheaded by Dave Cass and Phil Koch.

In an article in the 1971 issue of the Sierra Club mountaineering journal *Ascent*, Yvon Chouinard singled out The Black Dike on Cannon Cliff in Franconia Notch as one of the last unclimbed "plums" on the East Coast. Excitement mounted as climbers wondered who would accept Chouinard's challenge of "a black, filthy, horrendous icicle 600 feet high. Unclimbed." It didn't take long. Much to everyone's surprise, the first ascent was made by a young ice climber, John Bouchard, on December 18,1971. His ascent was an epic in every sense of the word. On the first pitch his rope jammed, so he dropped it. Then the pick on his axe broke, and he dropped a mitten. Just as darkness was about to overtake him, Bouchard clawed his way to the woods, completing what even today is considered one of the most impressive individual accomplishments in New England climbing. To remove any doubt regarding his first ascent, Bouchard returned the following winter with Henry Barber, John Bragg, and Rick Wilcox to climb The Dike a second time. The Black Dike, the first ice climb in the region to be graded 5, was undeniably a major ascent in the history of New England ice climbing.

Soon afterwards, new ice routes of all grades of difficulty were recorded throughout the area. At the same time, ice climbing possibilities were investigated at Mt. Katahdin in northern Maine, a mountain whose remoteness and severe winter weather attracts only serious mountaineers. John Porter, Jeff Wood, Larry Hodin, and Dave Isles ascended a major new line, the Gallery Route, the first winter route up the South Basin Headwall's West Face, during the 1972-73 season. Following this came the first ascent of the Waterfall Route by Bob Proudman and Mark Lawrence, one of a number of their first ascents in the South Basin area. Also on Katahdin, Dave Cilley and Henry Barber ascended a long, narrow ribbon of ice, the Cilley-Barber Route, almost directly to the summit of Baxter Peak, a route that has become an all-time New England classic.

Back on Frankenstein Cliff, activity also began to increase. John Bragg and Rick Wilcox ascended Smear, Bragg and A.J. LaFleur climbed Dracula, and Al Rubin and Oriel Sola-Costa did Waterfall. On Humphrey's Ledge, Rick Wilcox, Peter Cole, and A.J. LaFleur made it up Black Pudding Gully for the first time.

The culmination of the 1972-73 season was undoubtedly John Bragg and Rick Wilcox' first winter ascent of Repentence on Cathedral Ledge, an ice climb now ranked among the finest in all of North America. A modern ice climber's test piece, Repentence was the second ice climb in New England to be granted a rating of 5. As testimony to its difficulty and significance, an ascent of Repentence today is still considered a major accomplishment and for many aspiring climbers it remains a route to be dreamed of.

Each winter to follow brought new ice climbers to the forefront and the discovery of new areas in which to climb. In northern Vermont, a new area took on appeal and challenge. The flanks of Mt. Pisgah above Lake Willoughby promised routes steeper and colder than most others. Mike Hartrich, Al Rubin, and Henry Barber were the first to accept the challenge, ascending the appropriately named Twenty Below Zero Gully. Also in Vermont, Smugglers Notch provided John Bouchard and Steve Zajchowski, then students at the University of Vermont, with as many new routes as they could systematically climb.

John Bragg on the first ascent of Repentence on Cathedral Ledge, perhaps the most famous route in New Hampshire. And no, it has never come in this fat again.
Rick Wilcox

The big climb at Frankenstein in 1973-74 was the first ascent of the Bragg-Pheasant, a series of thinly-iced runnels on the Main Cliff. John Bouchard, Steve Zajchowski, and Roger Martin added yet another NEI 5 to Cannon Cliff in December, 1975, by climbing the ice ribbon of Fafnir, just to the right of The Black Dike. The crux was a section of difficult mixed climbing at the top of the flow.

A new and more aggressive group of climbers arrived during this season, and many of the last big unclimbed lines fell to their determined efforts. At Cathedral Ledge, Rainsford Rouner, his brother Tim, and Peter Cole made the long sought-after winter ascent of Remission, the sister ice route to Repentence. Although the first ascent team used etriers and direct aid on the column, it was soon climbed free. Graded 5+, Remission remains a serious and rarely climbed route.

February, 1976, was one of those rare months in the history of any ice climbing area when the combination of exceptionally good conditions and a talented core group of climbers mix to produce a string of superior climbs. On Frankenstein Cliff, Rainsford Rouner, Peter Cole, and Rick Wilcox climbed the impressive icicle, Dropline (grade 5) and on Humphrey's Ledge, Mark Richey and Rainsford Rouner managed a quick ascent of The Senator (grade 5), an ephemeral ice route which has never returned.

Michael Hartrich on the first ascent of Twenty Below Zero Gully at Lake Willoughby; the beginning of the frenzy.
Henry Barber

Several of the routes climbed during this month were in the same, rare condition. Michael Hartrich and Mark Whiton made the first winter ascent of Thin Air on Cathedral Ledge climbing ice all the way; over on the South Buttress of Whitehorse Ledge, the Rouner brothers ascended the Myth of Sisyphus, a beautiful line which has also seldom formed again. On Cannon Cliff, the ice was also in unusually good "nick," and John Bouchard and Rainsford Rouner were quick to take advantage of this opportunity. Their superb climb, Omega (grade 5+), is considered to be one of the hardest ice routes on Cannon and ranks also among the finest in the region. As in the case of all of the previously mentioned routes, Omega is rarely in good condition and has been repeated infrequently.

Marc Chauvin attempting an early repeat of North Conway's most ephemeral route, the Myth of Sisyphus, in 1981.
S. Peter Lewis

An increased interest in a long neglected ice climbing area and a new trend in winter climbing both occurred in the winter of 1976-77. Noteworthy winter ascents were made of the difficult aid climbs on Cathedral Ledge, including Bryan Becker and Alain Comeau's ascent of Mordor Wall (IV 5.7 A4 as a rock climb). They sieged the climb over a period of three days, wisely preferring to bivouac in town! Earlier, with Eric Engberg, they had warmed up with a winter ascent of Mines of Moria. Comeau and Tony Trocchi also climbed Cathedral Direct, finishing up the ice-choked upper chimney. Later, Doug Madara and Trocchi did Diedre, finding difficult mixed and aid climbing on the route.

Over on the icy flanks of Mt. Pisgah above Lake Willoughby in Vermont, the golden age was just beginning. The Rouner brothers, Rainsford and Tim, in impeccable style, climbed the centerpiece of that area, The Last Gentleman (NEI 5) in December, 1976. The Rouners returned the next month with Peter Cole to do battle with The Promenade (grade 5+), a terrifyingly steep ice flow immediately to the right of the former route. Members of the Harvard Mountaineering Club were also active at Lake Willoughby doing numerous arm-destroying climbs. The principle climbers involved in the action were Clint Cummins, John Imbrie, Brinton Young, Dennis Drayna, and Gustavo Brillembourg. Some of their best efforts are classic routes of the Lake; among them are Plug and Chug, Mindbender, and Crazy Diamond.

A variety of other unique and noteworthy new ice routes were climbed in that same winter of 1976-77 as activity grew in scope to encompass nearly all ice climbing areas in New England. Bill Kane and Doug Madara completed the first winter ascent of The Girdle Traverse of Whitehorse Ledge. Matt Peer, Danny Costa,

Steve Larson on the incredibly steep Mindbender in the late 1970's
Paul Boissonneault

No, this isn't the Canadian Rockies. Jim Shimberg heading up, and up, and up, on the Kineo classic, Maine Line

Joe Terravecchia

Doug Strickholm, and Alec Behr were the main explorers of the Madison Gulf of Mt. Adams. In the winter of 1977-78, Jim Dunn, the master of hard, free rock climbs in the Mt. Washington Valley, garnered a few short, steep ice routes, particularly, Great Madness (then called by the bland name of Gully #3) at Mt. Willard, Angel Cake on Frankenstein, and Way in the Wilderness off the Kancamagus Highway (all grade 5). The latter route, a steep ribbon east of Rainbow Slabs on the Painted Walls, was climbed with Peter Cole and Michael Hartrich.

Also that year saw Cummins and Imbrie make the long trek to northern Maine where, on the face of Mt. Kineo, overlooking Moosehead Lake, they climbed Maine Line, a tremendously steep route that was as hard as it was spectacular. Maine Line unfortunately suffered from the "out of sight, out of mind" syndrome and few took the six hour drive to follow in their footsteps. Subsequent investigation has revealed that Maine Line was actually climbed first a couple of years before by a pair of climbers more interested in adventure than fame—bravo.

As the 1970's drew to a close, the flurry of activity that had made this perhaps the most important decade in the history of the sport, waned. With almost all of the major lines now established, the question was "what next?", but the answer was not obvious. With climbs rated at 5+, and no clearly harder lines to be found, the advance of pure technical difficulty came to a virtual standstill. It would be almost 20 years before a spark struck and climbers once again broke new ground.

The Watermans have defined the period of the late 1970's and 1980's as "primarily one of consolidation...and perfection of style." With some of the psychological barriers of the unknown broken by the ascent of the hardest routes, and with the ongoing evolution of equipment, the high standards established by a handful of climbers in the 70's now became reachable for the masses.

With the fearsome reputation of routes such as The Black Dike and Repentence somewhat mellowed, ascents became commonplace, and a nice Saturday at Cannon could see several parties queued up for the Dike, where just a few years before, only the hardmen dared tread.

Frankenstein and Huntington became more like playgrounds than ever and by the mid 1980's it wasn't uncommon to see nearly every popular route occupied on a nice winter day.

As the popularity of ice climbing increased, any icy drip in New England became fair game. "The modern age of ice climbing had permeated every piece of frozen verticality in the Northeast," reported the Watermans.

The answer to "where next" really boiled down to "how next," and though the early 1980's saw many routes of tremendous difficulty put up such as Reign of Terror by Matt Peer and Tom Dickey at Lake Willoughby, and the incredibly steep Geographic Factor, by Brian Bodeur, Tim Gotwols and Chris Hassig at Rattlesnake Mountain in the Baker River Valley, these routes tended to be shorter and, though unquestionably hard, were not breakthroughs in the sense that climbs like The Black Dike or Repentence had been. While those pushing the limits in the late 1970's developed techniques for overcoming relentless verticality such as hanging from wrist loops, hanging from their tools to place protection and in some instances (such as the first ascent of Remission), even employing etriers, the 1980's would see a reversal of this trend with climbers finding the challenge in completing the hardest routes in the purest style.

Unlike the nearly naked rock climbers of today with their slippers, chalk bag and rack of quick draws, ice climbers by necessity are "tool users" who depend to a much greater degree on their equipment to engineer their way up a climb. Thus the definition of "good style" in ice climbing has always been somewhat vague. Everyone agrees that not using etriers is more pure than using them, and that placing protection without hanging from the tools is more pure than hanging. In a sport festooned with gear, the philosophy that the less you use, the better, gradually began to take hold.

A leading practitioner of this trend toward purer style was longtime North Conway guide Kurt Winkler, whose list of ascents in the best of style was rivaled by few and inspiring to many. With Ed Webster in 1982 he made the first complete ascent of the mystical Rouner route The Myth of Sisyphus on Whitehorse Ledge, a delicate hollow runnel that narrowed and steepened to vertical 400 feet off the deck. But it was his ascent with Alec Behr and Joe Lentini of Eagle's Gift in Glen, N.H., that was representative of the opportunities for development in the mid 1980's. Though only two short pitches long, the climb was horrendously thin and poorly protected. After sixty feet of verglas, the second pitch followed a fractured, detached runnel only a couple of feet wide, and demanded a delicate, controlled style radically different from the full-on bashing of the hardest thick flows..

Kurt Winkler gently tapping on the fragile Eagle's Gift on the first ascent.
Joe Lentini

Two other climbers, Todd Swain and John Tremblay, though radically different in their approach to ice climbing, also figured prominently during the middle years of the decade.

With all the major areas developed, Swain focused on the obscure, systematically searching out and climbing every bit of ice he could find. During the winter of 1982-83 he was out almost every day, his appetite for first ascents sometimes giving him several new routes before dark.

Though few of Swain's climbs were at the top of the difficulty scale, the sheer volume of new routes that he ferreted out of the New England woods has earned him a permanent spot in the region's history.

Tremblay's reputation for devouring ice was legendary as well, although he focused almost exclusively at the highest difficulty. And though his list of first ascents isn't long, the seriousness of some of these routes has diminished little over time. In December of 1986 Tremblay climbed nearly every hard route in New Hampshire (and many elsewhere), many in marginal condition. Later in the

The ubiquitous Todd Swain on yet another chunk of new ice.
Brad White

season he decided to really test the limits. Thriving on insecurity he put up perhaps his best known route, Overload, with Dave Rose. This route, on Duck's Head, took over where Eagle's Gift had left off. One hundred feet of vertical verglass with imaginary protection, Overload barely had enough ice to still be called an ice climb. And with the level of commitment extremely high, the need for total control was essential.

Mr. Tremblay at the office.
Joe Lentini

Not to be left out of the picture, Lake Willoughby saw perhaps the most activity, at the highest standard. The huge wall stretching north from The Last Gentleman had always been home to a number of thin runnels that rarely if ever reached the ground. In the early years there had been so many thick flows to climb that no one paid much attention to the skimpy routes. But by the mid 1980's the urge to climb new terrain brought some of New England's best talent to the base of these ephemeral routes. First to fall was the all-ice Who's Who in Outer Space, a spectacular thin line to the immediate left of The Last Gentleman, by Mark Richey and partner in 1984. 1986 saw the addition of two serious and committing mixed routes, Aurora by Ted Hammond and Chris Rowins, and Starman by Brad White and Rowins, go up side-by-side in the same month.

Equally extreme and committing was the practice by a few of linking many hard routes together in a day, often solo. With the latest equipment, the security of climbing vertical ice had been greatly enhanced, and with tremendous energy and confidence, some climbers could get up an almost unfathomable stretch of ice in a day. While ten years before it had been quite an accomplishment to solo all the major gullies in Huntington Ravine in a day, people like Randy Rackliff, John Bouchard, Steve Larson, Andy Tuthill and others took the notion a few steps further. The ultimate in this sort of 'link-up' may have been Larson and Tuthill's one day ascent of The Black Dike, Standard Route at Frankenstein, Repentence, and Pinnacle Gully—the latter by headlamp.

No great leap in difficulty or commitment was seen in the late 1980's and early 1990's. The steepest ice, Lake Willoughby, and the thinnest ice, several Tremblay routes, were now known to be climbable. The fearsome reputation of routes like The Black Dike had mellowed, becoming a pleasant day's outing. Even the somber air of seriousness that had characterized Huntington Ravine a generation before had been replaced with a much more casual confidence, though for the unprepared, unfortunate, or inexperienced few, the ravine continued to be a place of tragedy.

For those with a flair for exploration, this period provided the opportunity to take well-honed skills and climb extreme routes way out in the woods. The sparsely populated hills in western Maine were host to a number of quality routes by climbers like Bob Parrot, Rob Adair and Paul Boissonneault. In the Baker River Valley, Jim Shimberg, Ted Hammond and others found very steep, often thin ice-cragging in abundance. Katahdin continued to attract those seeking a committing alpine environment, with a small, dedicated group of climbers leading the exploration. Among the most active were Kevin Slater, Landon Fake, Bob Baribeau, Kurt Winkler, Ben Townsend, and Kevin Codraro.

Bob Baribeau has been to Katahdin dozens of times and has climbed every recorded route—a tremendous feat.
courtesy Bob Baribeau

This period was a time of maturing for New England ice climbing. Most, but certainly not all, of the major routes had now been climbed. And while ice climbing had been viewed as eccentric, it was now established as just one more way to squeeze adventure out of life. There were now many more climbers, and with more modern equipment and techniques they began climbing better and faster than ever before. Ten years before, an ascent of Repentence may have been the culmination of a climber's career; now it was not unusual for a climber new to the sport to tick off Repentence early in his career.

Standing on the shoulders of those who paved the way, ice climbers in the 1990's headed out into the mountains with the assurance that almost any ice can be climbed, equipped with the tools to give them the confidence to try. Thus prepared, Willoughby routes like Dave Wright and George Hurley's masterpiece China Shop and Ted Hammond and Dave Karl's Bullwinkle, with its incredibly long pillar, pointed the way for the next generation.

At the end of the history section in the 1992 edition of this guide, we drew the following conclusion: "The future of New England ice climbing is anyone's guess. Will there be harder routes? Certainly. Better climbers? Of course. Somewhere there are youngsters that have yet to wear crampons, but who have the ability, determination and vision that will one day make the hardmen of today shake in their boots." So here we are, ten years later; how did we do? Well, we got it right—sort of. There certainly are better climbers and harder routes around, but oddly, it's not just the youngsters who are creating the newest boot-shaking routes. Sure, there are hot young climbers around doing amazing things, but a review of the last decade's activities shows that the "hardmen" are still around. In fact, they're kicking pretty well these days.

In the first few seasons after the second edition of this guide, things coasted along slowly. Bullwinkle was still the hardest chunk of ice around and people seemed satisfied repeating the old (and new) standard routes. The great improvement in hardware and clothing was making climbing a safer, more comfortable, and easier sport. The huge difference that the new gear made was summed up well by one colorful local guide who was heard to say "I love ice climbing. Everything is 5.8!" Not trying to patronize the sport, he was just excited about the fact that bashing up steep ice just didn't seem as desperate as it did a decade earlier. And he was right. The old hard-core routes like The Black Dike,

Jon Sykes has been a leader in exploring our frozen resources since the early 1990's, here he cuts new ground at Echo in Franconia Notch.
Jamie Cunningham

Repentence, The Last Gentleman, and the like were seeing nearly constant ascents when in condition and it was no big deal for a new climber to tick one of these climbs early in their first season.

The year the second edition came out, 1992, was a quiet one, with little in the way of dramatic new lines. Over on Squaredock Mountain in western Maine, home to the backcountry classic Big Science, Bob Baribeau out in the woods alone climbed Sanctum of Privilege (II 5 5.8). A dramatic line on a big cliff far from the crowds, Baribeau described the route as "pretty tough sleddin'." As you will see later on, being alone in the woods on a big route isn't unusual for Baribeau.

In 1993 Jon Sykes, with an insatiable appetite for new routes, started developing Echo Cliff on the east side of Franconia Notch. A short, rambling wall that has become home to many fine one pitch rock climbs, Echo also had abundant possibilities for ice. Typically in the company of Mike Lee, Jamie Cunningham, Chris Marks, Gareth Slatterly, Art Mooney, Bill Keiler, Chuck Woodman, Kris Kratt and others, Sykes has scoured Echo and the other crags on the Lafayette side of the notch ever since, unearthing dozens of little pure ice and mixed gems.

In February of 1993, Baribeau with his frequent partner P. Marten, set out to best Baribeau's old friend Geoff Heath's marathon on Katahdin and succeeded in climbing the Cilley-Barber Route and Waterfall in just over nine hours—an amazing accomplishment.

Perhaps the biggest winter route of the year was Kurt Winkler and Chris McElheny's ascent of Cannon's huge wall route One Drop of Water. A true grade 5 with hard, scary, free and aid climbing throughout (5.9R A3), this was one of the last of the big routes on Cannon to see a winter ascent. In horrendous weather, over four days, Winkler and McElheny climbed, fixed, rappelled, and climbed again. Hoping for a bivy on the wall, the weather was just too nasty and the climbers made the trip up the ropes each way. See more in the history of this huge route with its description.

The year 1994 was highlighted by a long new route on Katahdin, a monster link-up in the Presidentials, and some short nasties lower down. In northern Maine Baribeau and longtime northcountry climber Landon Fake climbed Tower Ridge, a variation to the Waterfall that breaks out left and climbs a big buttress (first climbed by an AMC party in 1928) directly to the Knife Edge. Winkler with Doug Huntley, in preparation for bigger routes on other continents linked Pinnacle Gully in Huntington Ravine, Wait Until Dark Gully in the Great Gulf, and a new grade 4 route in the Madison Gulf over four days. Climbing with all their gear, above timberline most of the time, and ascending and descending thousands of feet in often nasty weather makes this one of the all-time great Presidential marathons. Down in the valleys longtime local climbers (the "youngsters" still hadn't shown up yet) and one notable visitor started scratching up some new mixed stuff. At Champney Falls, during the annual icefest, visiting superstar Alex

Lowe climbed Champin at the Bit, a scary M8+ located on the wall opposite the traditional ice climbs. It was as if Lowe was saying "turn around folks, the future is over here." Over in Rumney, Jim Shimberg and Joel O'Connel had also seen the future and straightened out the line of Artificial Intelligence to give a new M5 start. And, not to be outdone, over on Cathedral, veterans Steve Larson and Henry Barber clawed their way up Off the Hook, a terribly thin grade 5 on the Barber Wall. In the years to follow, many would take up the challenge of scratchy routes such as these and see the old stomping grounds with new eyes.

In 1995 Baribeau again found himself out in the middle of nowhere with icicles in front of him. At Evans Notch, alone, he climbed French Canadian Reality and Love Diet, two grade 5 pillars up high on East Royce Mountain. But his big route of the year was up in his backyard at Grafton Notch. After years of looking and effort he finally managed to bag The Sty on the Eyebrow cliff above the Appalachian Trail. Two pitches of thin climbing culminating in a 90 foot pillar characterize this ephemeral route. Over on Cannon John Bouchard and Mark Richey, two of the regions best known alpinists had been using the cliff as an outdoor gym for years. In preparation for their big routes in the Himalayas, the pair went to Cannon and simply climbed rock and ice as fast as they could. Their multi-thousand foot days on Cannon became legendary with their finest effort arguably the first winter ascent of the Magical Mystery Tour—the left to right girdle traverse of the cliff. This route, with over 6,000 feet of technical climbing and rated IV M5 5 A0 is about as much climbing as you can squeeze into a New England winter day. And after 5,500 feet of constant movement, Bouchard and Richey finished by climbing the Black Dike—for most people that's a good day's climb in itself.

Wildman Jim Shimberg breaking through the ice ceiling on the first free ascent of Call of the Wild (6) at Willoughby.
Tyler Stableford

Perhaps the biggest news of the year was the first ascent of an ice climb at Lake Willoughby that finally blew the lid off the pure ice rating scale. For over a decade the hardest routes in this part of the country got the rating of 5+. Like the 5.9's of the 1950's before anyone would admit to the 5.10 grade, the 5+ routes in New England got jammed up against the ice ceiling and got harder and harder (many thought Hammond and Karl's Bullwinkle deserved to be graded harder than 5+). In March of '95 Dan Lee and Mike Moran climbed a nearly independent line just left of the Willoughby classic 5+, Mindbender. The pair found long stretches of overhanging ice and two roofs and when they looked over at Mindbender, they realized that 5+ just wasn't going to work. After hanging to rest on the second pitch the pair climbed to the top of Call of the Wild, the first grade 6 in the area. Three days later Jim Shimberg returned and bagged the coveted free ascent of the route, blowing the lid off the scale.

The following two years were relatively quiet. Kurt Winkler and Richard Gunning found The Howling at Frankenstein. This 4+X route demonstrated that even venerable old Frankenstein wasn't climbed out, at least if you were willing to climb ice so thin that you protected (?) it with "Spectres, tied off screws and small trees." In February of 1996 a remarkable ascent occurred. Long eyed by many locals, the thin streak that dribbled down the vertical wall beneath Cathedral's classic Remission, finally got close enough to the ground to get a pick in it. Dan Lee got on the route early and succeeded but returned to tell Kurt Winkler that he had seen tic-marks in it all the way up. The mystery was solved when it was discovered that Bob Baribeau, alone (as usual) had taken a look a day or so before, started up, got committed, and soloed the pitch. And if that wasn't impressive enough, not wanting to continue up the route, he quietly replaced his tools and crampons below him in the tic-marks and downclimbed the pitch. As word got out that the pitch was "in" a host of folks got in line including Jeff Fongemie, Jeff Lowe, Alex Lowe, Steve Larson, and Kurt Winkler with Charles White. To add to the confusion, Jim Shimberg had done the route during this time and was told by John Bouchard (who certainly should know) that it was the first ascent. When Shimberg and company climbed the pitch they saw no evidence of previous ascents. The thin and tenuous nature of the route makes it extremely unlikely that it "healed" enough between ascents to look virgin to Shimberg, so it is the opinion of the editor that Shim got the first ascent. But regardless of who did what when and how, this pitch, graded 5+ (how traditional) is one of the hardest, rarest visitors to the cliff and who knows when it will come in again. (When it does we hope someone takes better notes.)

In 1997 Jim Shimberg, Ted Hammond and Dave Rioux hiked into Mad River Notch off the Kancamagus Highway and climbed the severe Aye Karumba at M5 4+, a sister route to the classic route in the notch, On the Drool of the Beast. Back on Cathedral longtime Colorado climber Duncan Ferguson and Henry Barber finished an old Tom Callaghan mixed route near the North end. Just Laughing, 4+ M6 linked a series of grooves, overhangs and smears to give the cliff one of its hardest, albeit short, new lines. But the big news of the year, also on Cathedral, was George Hurley and Mike Kahn's ascent of Black Crack. Graded a stiff 5.10 in the summer, this notorious offwidth crack made for terribly insecure climbing and required nearly every technique in the book. And at 5 M7 5.10R it was, and remains one of the hardest mixed climbs in the region. (Editor's Note: Here we are, five years after our own prediction that a bunch of "youngsters" would come in and blow our doors off, and look who does Black Crack. Hurley was 62 at the time of the first ascent and Kahn was certainly old enough to know better.)

As the 1990's waned the action started to pick up (and some of the young guys finally showed up). In 1998, Rob Frost climbed One Pickle Shy in the Flume in Franconia Notch. Though short, this fierce M7+ R sure got Frost's attention. Several times he found himself partway up with no points of contact and had to start over. Near the top of Crawford Notch, Mount Willard received much of the attention in 1998. Tom Burt, Kevin Mahoney, Paul Cormier, and Ben Gilmore teamed up to climb the first recorded ascent

Mark Synnott heading up into the M zone on the Lowe Down at Texaco.
courtesy Mark Synnott

of a twisting pencil of a drip they called The Corkscrew. The obvious pillar had been distracting local climbers for years as they drove down the notch. Three additional hard routes were climbed on Willard this season. Out of Touch, by Mike and Chris Dubé, climbed a difficult smear up the right wall of The Cleft. Henry Barber and visiting Australian climber Jay Reilly climbed the first pitch of a new mixed route on The Trestle Wall near the head of the notch. Shortly afterward Paul Cormier and Greg Cloutier climbed the difficult second pitch to complete The Snot Rocket (5 M5). Over on the big slab of the South Face of Willard, Cormier and Jim Shimberg climbed a new full-length line that followed (approximately) the summer lines of Across the Universe on the lower slabs and then continued up the upper wall. Parallel Universe, graded III 5 M5 R/X is the longest hard route on the cliff and one of the most serious in the Notch.

Further south at the Texaco Amphitheater, Arthur Haines fixed protection and then climbed a new mixed route. The route was repeated by several locals and visitors including a more direct ascent (without clipping the bolts), by Rob Frost. Although the bolting was controversial (some might say Haines was ahead of his time), The Lowe Down, 6 M5, became instantly popular.

Elsewhere in the Saco River Valley newer locals like Mark Synnott, Kevin Mahoney, Eric Seifer, Rob Frost, and others found incredible mixed climbing on little crags.

Not to be left out, the boys over in Smugglers Notch put up a number of new routes during the late 1990's. During 1998 and 1999 a number of new ice and mixed routes went in that demonstrated just how much potential the notch has for stout routes. The pure ice dagger of Prenuptial Agreement (5+) by Carl Tobin got things going and then in quick succession a number of hard mixed routes went in. In 1998 Alden Pellett and Dave Furman put up Scream Queen (M5 4+), Dominatrix (M6 4+), and, with western visitor Mark Wilford on the sharp end,   climbed Freeze Dried (M6/7), and the pair added French Tickler (M6 4) in 1999. Also in 1998 Bob Timmer and Bert Severin climbed the outrageous arete of The Beginning of the End at grade 5 M7+. Timmer also climbed a variation to the right at a similar grade. Other activists of the time included Pat Viljanen (author of the excellent locals guide to the area), and longtime Smugglers regulars Alex Sargent, Bill Pelkey and Tom Kontos. In the late 1990's Timmer and Sargent began

Alden Pellett on the scratchy first ascent of Dominatrix; the sign of the times in Smugglers.
Dave Furman

climbing at a new area a few miles north of the notch called Bear Notch. Here they found a steep, short cliff bristling with ice. Among the plums picked was Bear Right, a 5+ that is as steep as anything in the area. Perhaps more than the popular crags in New Hampshire, the geology of the Smugglers region seems destined to produce some of the best new mixed routes and the recent activity noted here is likely just the beginning.

With two dramatic exceptions 1999 continued the trend of the short, mixed, and hard. Kevin Mahoney climbed Submission (5), a thinly iced water groove left of the first pitch of Repentence. Over in Rumney, Jim Shimberg and Jon Brown found the free-hanging Dagger (4+) just left of Fangmanship. In the coastal Maine town of Camden, Tim Martel and Justin Preisendorfer found hard mixed climbing up icicles and over a roof to create Neverdrip (M5 3+). Back on Mount Willard in Crawford Notch, Keven Mahoney and Ben Gilmore put up two quality pitches to the right of Lower Hitchcock Gully: Zip Pig and Peace of Mind, both rated M5 4. Down in Kinsman Notch, known for decades as a great short practice area (and presumably climbed out), Robert Adams and Eric Pospesil climbed a stout pillar and then did a mixed finish out left (in 2002 Brad White and Jamal Lee-Elkin would drytool out a finger crack in a 15-foot roof, "hooking on packed dirt," to give the route, Hanging by a Moment, an M6 finish).

Two spectacular mixed lines rounded out the short routes of the season. Over at Frankenstein's Hanging Gardens, to the right of Tremblay's classic Without Reason (another one of those 80's style 5+ routes), Jared Ogden, followed by Mark Synnott and Randy Rackcliff, flashed Something About You Makes Me Wild. This severe M8 connects hanging curtains up and over a roof on an over-hanging wall. At Eagle Cliff in the village of Glen, Ogden, Synnott, and Rackcliff teamed up to climb one of the hardest mixed pitches in the state. Cold Cold World, a dramatic M8+ to the right of the old-style classic Eagle's Gift, climbs icicles over a really big roof.

On the longer side of things, at Cannon, Tom Nonis and John Courtney freed the hard mixed aid and free winter route Lila. This full-length route right of Fafnir is a long, serious undertaking graded IV 4 M6. Also noteworthy from years past are hard finishes to this route by Kurt Winkler and Harold Hunt as well as John Bouchard and Joe Josephson. And finally, at Lake Willoughby, Jim Shimberg and Jon Brown climbed a terrifyingly thin line up a strip of ice left of Float Like a Butterfly. The White Strip, II 5 M6 X was one of those lines that Shimberg and Brown were happy to scratch up just once. Not knowing of Shimberg and Brown's ascent, Canadian climber Bernie Mailhot climbed the route several days later and added protection bolts and a belay anchor to the lower part of the route. Discussing the route later all parties decided that the bolts were a good thing. "We talked, no big deal, now it will get done more often," Shimberg said.

Also during the late 1990's the mixed revolution made it's way to Acadia where Jeff Butterfield, Chris Kane, and others found that just after a big, cold, Nor'easter, the nearly vertical face of the Precipice on Champlain Mountain be-came plastered with ice. For a few fleeting hours they found conditions akin to the high mountains and revelled in mixed delight. So ephemeral are the lines and fickle the conditions that the routes go unnamed and ungraded.

The three seasons since Y2K have seen an increase in activity, difficulty, and exploration in Northern New England. Far from climbed out, the region has proven to be ripe with new frozen (or at least partly frozen) winter routes.

On the short, scratchy side, the early millennium season gave Chris Marks, Art Mooney, Jon Sykes, and Peter Ducette the hardest mixed route at Echo in Franconia Notch. Lip Service, 4 M7, climbed successfully after attempts over several seasons, climbs skinny ice to an icicle over a big roof on the formation called The Shield. In Pinkham Notch, Tim Martel and Justin Preisendorfer found the hardest route in the notch, Pass the Quiche (M7), above Lost Pond. Preisendorfer with Andrew Davenport climbed a new M5 route down east in Camden which they called Stairmaster. Over at Sundown off the Kancamagus highway in New Hampshire, Mark Synnott and Eric Seifer scratched their way up what Synnott has called "the best mixed route I've ever done in the Mount Washington Valley." The Mongol (M7) starts with an overhanging groove, originally dry-tooled (back before there was a name for it) by Bob Parrott and Bill Holland in 1986, that leads to a roof, hanging icicles and more difficulties above.

At Frankenstein, the obscure route Wrath of the Valkyrie received several first ascents (!) and became an instant classic. On the first ascent only the bottom of the route was climbed. On the second ascent in 1981 John Drew, Todd Swain and Brad White sorted out the blank granite above the ice by tossing a cluster of pitons into a fork in a tree at the top. Drew then gingerly climbed

"The best route I've ever done in the Mount Washignton Valley. Mark Synnott on the Mongol.
courtesy Mark Synnott

the rope. The first, first free ascent came by way of Jim Ewing and Evan Sanborn in December 2000. Ewing found very hard mixed moves above a bolt so bad he almost didn't clip it. After that Steve Larson and Doug Madara and then Brad White all climbed the route free—each thinking they were first. After all was said and done everyone involved cared more that the 4+ M5 route was really good than who clawed up it first.

Two big routes were climbed on Cannon in 2000. Aboriginal Rhythmic Implement by Tom Nonis and Tom Callaghan wiggled its way up shattered rock to the right of the mega-classic Omega and came in at III 3+ 5.9 (sounds tame don't it? don't bet on it.) Just right of Omega Kevin Mahoney climbed Prozac at 6R M6, a desparate independent line up very steep and sketchy ground. Now if you thought Omega was hard...

Up Katahdin way, Bob Baribeau (after over 30 trips to the mountain over the years) and Landon Fake hung it all out on Ambejejus Boom House Buttress (III M4 3), a long mixed route up a buttress in the remote North Basin.

Way up on the shores of Moosehead Lake in Maine, Bob Baribeau rope-soloed, with some aid, a new, incredibly steep line a hundred feet right of the all-time northeast classic, Maine Line on Mount Kineo. Two seasons later Jim Ewing and Will Mayo would free Baribeau's fine Les Enfant Blue de Kineo at a hard core 5+/6- M5.

Jim Ewing hanging it all out on the first free ascent of Les Enfants Blue de Kineo.
Will Mayo

In 2001 the Canadian contingent came back to Lake Willoughby and found fine new stuff. After Alden Pellet and Will Mayo loosened up a new route left of Aurora by taking a huge whipper, Jean Francois Morin, Bernie Mailhot, and Mathieu Peloquin flashed the route coming away with a new 400 foot line rated M6+ 5+. Originally the Canadians were going to call the route Three Musketeers but since they benefitted from some of the gear left by Pellet and Mayo, they offered to change the name to Five Musketeers in the name of good sportsmanship. Down the cliff and to the right of the 1980's testpiece The Promenade, Benoit Marion and Mailhot pieced together two routes, the most impressive being Power Test, a three pitch M7+ 5+ that is surely one of the hardest climbs on Mount Pisgah. The final pitch climbs a desperate mixed traverse past bolts placed on the lead by Marion in failing light. Also on Mount Pisgah, Jon Sykes and John Mallory climbed Super Nova (IV 4+ M4 A2) to the left of Aurora over three days in temperatures never higher than 5⁰.

At the other end of the region, on Mount Kineo, Jon Sykes and John Mallory found an independent line just left of an older route around the corner to the right of Maine Line. White Line Fever, with its thin start and beefy upper pillars turned out to be one of the longest grade 5 routes in the northeast at 650 feet.

Talk about your plums, there aren't too many routes left like Five Musketeers.
Bernie Mailhot

Down in the banana belt of Rumney long-time locals found two new hard routes. Ted Hammond and Alan Cattabrigga climbed Reasons to be Cheerful and the pair, with George Lutz, found Twit. Both routes are rated (watch out), 5+.

If 2001 is remembered for anything it will be for the discovery of Valhalla by Jon Sykes, Eric Pospesil, Nick Farley and Shad Lawton. The combination of pure chance and the drive to explore led the group on a long and difficult bushwack into Goback Mountain, a remote 3,485 foot peak in Northern New Hampshire. After hours in deep snow they turned a corner and found the stuff of dreams. While the right wall of the big cliff was dripping with several obvious hard lines, it was the left wall that left everyone speechless. The wall was dead vertical, blank, about 150 feet high, and ended with a roof. And lo and behold two pencil straight drips spilled out from under the roof. After an oath was sworn by all, two trips to the mountain, and the first ascents of most of the other lines,

Reasons to be Cheerful indeed; great ice and warm sport routes for the afternoon. Ted Hammond on the first ascent.
Tim Gotwals

Sykes finally got on the right-hand drip. Valhalla turned out to be 110 feet of grade 6 ice with no room for error (and no way to get lost). Returning a few days later Sykes brought along Will Mayo who confirmed the grade and added the difficult M6 finish. Valhalla is one of the most stunning lines ever done in northern New England and is destined to become a super-classic.

This past season, the winter of 2001/2002, continued the trend of recent years: hard new mixed routes and great finds on the established crags. On good old Whitehorse Ledge Steve Larson and Henry Barber found exquisite climbing on the first winter ascent of Sleeping Beauty (5 M5/6). Steep drytooling up a corner followed by smears of ice and torquing in cracks with good rock pro will surely make the pitch popular. At Sundown, Eric Seifer and Kevin Mahoney found Pimpsicle, another barely-there M6 route similar to the nearby Mongol. At Frankenstein Seifer, Carrie Shea and Seth Green eeked out a new pitch right of Widow's Walk. Widow's Run climbs a series of three disconnected ice tiers that drip off overhangs and checks in at a harsh M7.

On Cannon, directly above the belay on the first pitch of northern New England's best know hard route, the Black Dike, Philippe Pibarot, Bernard Mailhot, Charles Laliberté and Jean Martel looked at the wall and saw something new. Their Dark Crystal (5 M4) takes a hard independent line to the right of the Dike up through a bizarre chimney.

In 1992 we predicted that new climbers would climb new routes and that the future would lie in "redefining the possible." We were right, and we were wrong. Certainly there is a crop of new climbers that have helped push the standards. But we underestimated the drive and talent of the old guard. Many of the great routes of the last ten years were done by the same folks that set the standards in the decade prior to 1992. But we certainly got it right about a new definition for what's possible. (In all fairness, it wasn't much of a stretch. All historians have always been safe in assuming that generations to come would redefine the standards.) So where do we go from here? What will happen between now and 2012? Well, our guess is that the old guys will continue to crank and the "youngsters" will push the limits ever upwards. (Pretty safe guesses huh?) Perhaps the best way to point toward our future is to look at some of the routes of the last few seasons and draw conclusions:

There will always be great new stuff right under our noses (Dark Crystal, The White Strip).

Mixed climbing is really cool, "hooking on packed dirt" is here to stay, and it opens everything up again (Hanging by a Moment, Cold Cold World, The Mongul, The Beginning of the End).

The next Valhalla lies just around the corner.

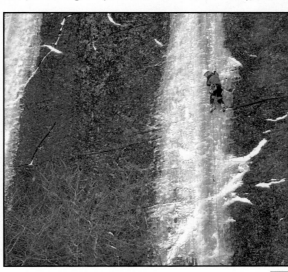

Folks, it just doesn't get better than this in New England. Jon Sykes ascending Valhalla on the first ascent.
Jamie Cunningham

BlueWater Ropes

Photo by Scott Cramer
Alpine Adventure Images

Elephant's Head, the most recognizable feature at Smugglers, is flanked by classic routes.
T.B.R. Walsh

SMUGGLERS NOTCH

Nestled in the heart of the Green Mountains, Smugglers Notch is one of the two major centers of ice climbing activity in Vermont. Similar to Frankenstein Cliff in New Hampshire, although somewhat more remote and certainly more alpine, this scenic notch is lined on either side by climbs from one to four pitches in length encompassing all grades of difficulty.

Although the approaches to the routes themselves are usually fairly short and straightforward, everyone who climbs at Smugglers must hike, ski or snow-shoe in for a half an hour or so from the end of the plowed road to reach the first ice. Route 108, which runs through Smugglers Notch between Stowe and Jeffersonville, is not maintained in the winter, leaving about a three mile gap. From either direction you will find a large parking lot at the end of the plowed road. The top of the notch is about 1.5 miles from either side and the approach adds spice to the day (sometimes it is possible to hitch a ride on a snowmobile). Most of the descent routes are the typical New England variety; wade, stumble, or glissade down through the woods on either side of your climb. Often rappelling will be the easiest choice and will be noted in the text. There are no camping restrictions in the area and several excellent campsites will be found at the top of the notch, especially in boulder caves in the vicinity of the obvious stone hut (an information center in the summer; closed in the winter).

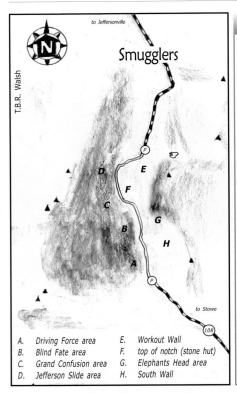

T.B.R. Walsh

Smugglers

to Jeffersonville

to Stowe

108

A. Driving Force area
B. Blind Fate area
C. Grand Confusion area
D. Jefferson Slide area
E. Workout Wall
F. top of notch (stone hut)
G. Elephants Head area
H. South Wall

AREA HIGHLIGHTS

Location:	Rt. 108 between Stowe and Jeffersonville, 30 minutes northeast of Burlington, VT
Routes:	Grades 1 to 6, wide variety from toprope to desperate
Access:	park at either end of notch, hike or ski about a mile
Descent:	walk off (can be a bushwhack) or rappel
Weather:	"Notch," see page 18; can be cold and windy; December through March
Equipment:	standard ice rack+ rock gear
Superlatives:	Very secluded, good camping, easy access to many mid-range routes: *Elephant's Head Gully, Blind Fate, Dave's Snotcicle,* plus hard ice and mixed routes
Amenities:	Both Stowe and Jeffersonville have everything; Stowe is bigger
Attention:	Rt. 108 is not plowed, heavy snowfall can make approaches difficult and increase avalanche danger

To reach the Stowe end of Smugglers take exit 10 off Rt. 89 in Waterbury, follow Rt. 100 north to Stowe and then take Rt. 108 into the notch. To reach the Jeffersonville end of the notch from the Burlington area take Rt. 15 east through the town of Cambridge to a right turn onto Rt. 108 in Jeffersonville.

Smugglers Notch has been tramped by ice climbers for decades and the history of many of the routes is a bit fuzzy. With such a muddled history, despite our best efforts, you won't find details on every frozen dribble here. The early forays of John Bouchard and Steve Zajchowski in the 1970's and visits by Adirondack and N. Conway climbers as well as a swelling cadre of locals in the 80's and 90's including Pat Viljanen, Alex Sargent, Bert Severin, Bob Timmer, Tom Kontos, Bill Pelkey, Alden Pellett, and others have filled in many of the lines, but this is a complex area and there is so much stuff! Smugglers is a fantastic winter playground and its growing popularity in recent years is no surprise. The mixed climbing rage that has taken ice climbing by storm has reached Smugglers too and in the coming era this area is likely to see a resurgence of activity by those who love dry tooling and scratching up outrageous lines (they'll likely leave the rest of us scratching our heads).

Smugglers is at a relatively high elevation (at least by Eastern standards) so be prepared for cold and windy conditions. The area also gets inundated with snow so be wary of the snow slopes after a storm—avalanches are quite common here. Smugglers is a unique natural area with fascinating geology and flora including many rare plant species; please climb responsibly here. Routes in the notch will be described loosely from south to north on the Mansfield side (west), then back from north to south on the Elephant's Head (east) side.

A final note. The authors are greatly indebted to the local climbers at Smugglers for helping us gather and organize this information. Without the enthusiastic help this section would have been pretty pathetic. Special thanks to Pat Viljanen (author of the excellent and comprehensive *Locals Guide to Smugglers' Notch Ice*), Alden Pellett, and others for their help and encouragement.

SMUGGLERS NOTCH: WEST SIDE

DRIVING FORCE 2-3+

This and the following two routes are well below the main climbing areas. Approaching from Stowe, and just after a straightaway, the road bends; Driving Force will be found low and not far from the road. Leave the road near the end of the guard rail just north of a bridge, cross a small stream, head over a ridge just south of a small hill, cross another stream and head on up to the route. There are several potential lines here, the easiest climbs the middle of this one pitch route. The left side is harder and the right side is harder still. This is a good choice if recent snowfall has made approaching routes further up the notch difficult.

unknown

TERROR-TORY 2-3

November

April

Farther uphill is this short route. It is to the left of the more readily apparent Blue Ice Bulge, at the southern end of the notch on the Mansfield side. There is no obvious snow gully leading up to this 150 ft. flow, so bushwhack approximately 300 yards through the woods from the road to the base. Climb easy snow and ice to a steeper flow at the top. Climb it directly or bypass it on the left and traverse back right. Walk off to the right.

FRA: Jeff Lea, Jay Amico, George Seiveright & Roger Hirt, January 12, 1980.

Several short flows have been climbed between Terror-Tory and the next route.

BLUE ICE BULGE II 3-4

November

April

Below the high-point in the notch on the Mansfield side of the road is an area with a high concentration of quality routes. Approach up one of several long snow gullies (beware of avalanche danger). Blue Ice Bulge climbs the prominent gully on the left bordered on its left by a buttress. An easy pitch leads to steeper ice above with several variations possible.

Chet Callahan & Dave Cass, winter 1969-70

The next area is an obvious amphitheater with several lines and a long snow-slope approach. For these routes descend down to the right through the woods and then rappel with one rope down the buttress just left of Cass's Gully.

PICK AND CHOSS M4

This is the left-most climb in the amphitheater and offers a thin, challenging line up a buttress. It may be easiest to approach the route by starting up as for Blue Ice Bulge and then continuing right. Climb blocky rock to a short pillar then continue up a thinly iced slab to trees.

FRA Alden Pellett, solo, winter 1995-96

NORTON-GIBNEY II 4

To the right of Pick and Choss but still left of the center of the amphitheater this climb works up icy slabs over bulges to a belay below the obvious steep column. Climb the steep pillar, and continue past several more bulges until the angle lies back.

Dave Norton & Frank Gibney, Winter 1974-75.

CALIFORNIA DREAMING II 4

Right of Norton-Gibney a 35' drip sometimes touches down. Approach by climbing the lower section of Blind Fate and then break left to the obvious icicles dripping down about 40 feet left.

Dale Bard, Bubba Parker & Dave Gustasson, January 1977

BLIND FATE III 4

This classic notch route is the next flow to the right. Two pitches and two columns characterize this sustained line. The latter steep section is some thirty feet high. Rappel twice or descend to the right and then rappel once.

John Bouchard & Rick Wilcox, Winter 1974-75.

BLIND FAITH II 3

Begin at the base of Blind Fate but stay right in an icy corner and then finish up bulges.

Bob Olsen, Chuck Bond & Alan Long, Winter 1971-72.

BLIND FATE AREA

A. Blue Ice Bulge
B. Pick and Choss
C. Norton-Gibney
D. California Dreaming
E. Blind Fate
F. Blind Faith

CASS'S GULLY 1-2

To the right of Blind Faith is a large tree-covered buttress. The gully on its right-hand side is Cass's Gully. It is easily seen from the road at the top of the notch. The gully is typically full of snow, but there could be a little ice mixed in. Pass by a large chockstone at the top of the gully to where the angle eases, then descend via rappel down the tree-covered buttress to the left.

Dave Cass, Winter 1968-69

HIDDEN GULLY II 3/4-

The route is only visible to the west several hundred yards south of the top of the notch. The approach gully starts at a pullout on the west side of the road just a hundred feet or so below the top of the notch. The initial portion is quite narrow. Climb easily past a few ice bulges to the first snowfield. Continue to the next larger snowfield and then either descend Easy Gully on the right, or do a third pitch up any of the three more difficult finishes. From left to right they become progressively easier. If you climb one of the harder finishes, the descent is a tough bushwhack off to the right toward the Bear Pond Trail which eventually leads you back toward Easy Gully. This can be a long and difficult descent so plan ahead.

Dave Cass and Phil Koch climbed up to the second snowfield and presumably descended Easy Gully. John Bouchard soloed the hardest finish in the winter of 1973-74

Several ice and mixed routes have been done on the buttress right of Hidden Gully but little is known about them. One route, referred to as The Slot, climbs a mixed corner about 100 feet right of Hidden Gully.

EASY GULLY 1-2

This is the largest slide/gully at the top of the notch. Around a buttress to the right of the former route climb a snow-filled gully that leads up and then left toward the second snowfield on Hidden Gully. It is steepest at the top. Most climbers use Easy Gully as a means of descent from the middle of Hidden Gully,

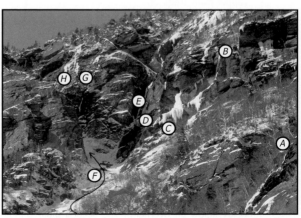

EASY GULLY AREA

A. Grand Confusion
B. Poster Child
C. Grand Contusion
D. Three Sheets
E. Grand Illusion
F. Easy Gully
G. Scream Queen
H. Dominatrix

Brian Post (wildrays.com)

or as an easy snow climb. The easiest approach is to follow a snow gully from behind the stone hut and then move up and left before reaching Grand Confusion. An alternate approach starts just north of the high-point on the road, passes a huge boulder, and then follows a slide path. Avalanches are not uncommon in this area so take care.

unknown

GRAND CONFUSION 3+

Named because it was commonly mistaken for Grand Illusion, it lies to the north of that route. Approach this one or two pitch climb from behind the stone hut. Head in just left of large boulders for a hundred yards then trend left to a long snow gully (can be good skiing). Climb over short bulges to a snow gully with a couple of possible lines at the top. To descend either rappel from trees on the right or make a long hike down left to Easy Gully.

unknown

Bob Timmer finds awesome climbing at the start of Grand Confusion. You can rappel from trees on either side of the fop of the gully.
Alden Pellett

POSTER CHILD 4/4+ M4

This route is on the right just above where Easy Gully turns left. Start from a large ledge and climb ice next to a right-facing corner. In lean conditions the route has a mixed start (rock gear needed) up a finger crack past a piton leading to the ice on the right. Rappel from trees.

unknown

GRAND CONTUSION 3+

Several variations are possible on this flow up a buttress right of the Easy Gully. Climb directly up the buttress (not well protected), come in easily from the right, or climb much harder terrain further right up an overhanging crack (M6) to a ledge below the obvious overhang. All variations lead to a piton belay below an overhang. The second pitch climbs the ice curtain on the left to easier ground and then a final hard pillar. A harder variation on the second pitch, moving up and right to gain a hanging drip, has not yet been successfully completed. Rappel the route twice with one rope.

FRA Bert Severin & Pat Viljanen

THREE SHEETS II 4

This two or three pitch route climbs a steep, left-facing slab between Grand Contusion and Grand Illusion on the right wall of Easy Gully. A thin start (rock gear) leads to steeper ice trending right and then wider flows above with several variations possible. Hike off right to the Bear Pond Trail and then down Easy Gully or rappel from trees on the right.

unknown

THE GRAND ILLUSION 4+

This classic route can be done in either one or two pitches depending on where you start. The climb ascends the dark slot directly up from where Easy Gully turns left. Climb an easy gully to typically thin climbing in a corner (pitons on the left and additional rock gear helpful in lean conditions) and then steeper ice above. Walk off right to the Bear Pond Trail.

John Bouchard & Steve Zajchowski, February 1975

SCREAM QUEEN M5 4+

Up Easy Gully a short distance left of the obvious slot of Grand Illusion is good rock with cracks and a right-facing corner with a thin crack. Climb up this and dry-tool the crack, or climb thin ice in the corner, to gain a ramp which is followed to a belay below a roof (pin). Dry-tool to the right under the roof to its end and then step down to a spectacular stance. Climb the roof (good gear) then tiptoe back left to a thin ice smear and climb a short, skinny pillar to more thin ice, a corner and the trees. When in condition, this is one of the best mixed routes in the notch.

Alden Pellett & Dave Furman, winter 1998

FRENCH TICKLER M6 A0 4

This route is in between Scream Queen and Dominatrix on the wall left of Grand Illusion. Start near the base of Dominatrix and head up and right making mixed moves to reach a roof (bolt). On the first ascent there was a free-hanging pillar that promptly fell off when it was weighted (such nerve) and the leader made one aid move off a bad pin to clear the roof. Overhanging ice then leads thinly to a corner and a flat belay stance. Pitch two climbs 15 feet up a flake below overhanging rock and then moves left and down and then left again on an airy traverse into a hanging corner. Climb the corner up and out left to gain the top part of Dominatrix.

Dave Furman & Alden Pellett, December 1999

Stout indeed. Alden Pellett on serious terrain on the first ascent of Dominatrix.
Dave Furman

DOMINATRIX II M6 4+

Conditions on this stout route are variable and rock gear is essential. Start uphill about 100 feet from Grand Illusion on the right side of Easy Gully. Climb a ramp to an overhanging crack on the right, step right above the crack, then back left and up thin ice to a belay. An alternate start avoids the crack by moving up and left above the ramp. Pitch two climbs thin ice for 100 feet to the top.This is a serious route; the direct line has only had two ascents.

Alden Pellett & Dave Furman in 1998; the P.1 variation was climbed by Tom Yandon

BLACK SUNSHINE 3+/4

Near the top of Easy Gully climb either of two short flows on the right. Descend Easy Gully.

FRA Bert Severin & Bob Timmer

The next bunch of routes are found near the large Quartz Crack Face that is obvious above the stone hut parking area. Approach up the snow gully as for Grand Confusion and then move up and right.

A'S ANGUISH (A K A GOLDEN ICE CHIMNEY) 4/4+

This is the farthest route on the left beginning just left of Rubble Gully. Climb an easy pitch then up to a cave (several variations) then out right. Rappel. There is an alternate start that goes at M4/5.

Alex Sargent, Tom Kontos & Bill Pelkey

RUBBLE GULLY 3 mixed

Climb up easy ice just right of the previous route to bulges and a narrower steep section and then climb easily to a large ledge. Several mixed variations are possible from the ledge including staying in the gully, climbing the corner to the right above a spruce tree, or stepping off a block on the right and then climbing an overhang to moves left to a corner and an old belay.

Bob Timmer climbed the lower pitch; the mixed variations were climbed by the group of Tom Kontos, Bill Pelkey & Pat Viljanen

TRI-SCAM 3+ mixed

Just right of Rubble Gully climb a right-slanting corner (mixed) to a ledge, move left to steeper, thin ice, then snow in the low-angle corner to spacious belay on the left. The final section climbs a narrow ice runnel to a cave and fixed belay. Rappel twice with one rope.

Bob Timmer

QUARTZ CRACK II 5.8R

A winter ascent of this summer rock route is a serious undertaking with cold and sometimes loose rock and sections of thin ice. Bring rock gear to 4". Start at a tree ledge right of Tri-Scam, climb a right-facing corner then step left to a ledge and belay. Tackle the namesake crack above and step left at its top. Pitch three traverses right to a corner under a huge roof and the awkward moves out right and up to the top. Head up and right to the Bedouin Trail which heads toward Jefferson Slide and then down.

unknown

THE SNOTCICLE II 4+/5-

This dramatic route is seen as a yellow drip down the wall to the right of Quartz Crack. The route is often thin and rock gear is needed. After the typically thin and mixed start a piton belay will be found on the right on a right-

QUARTZ CRACK AREA

A. *A's Anguish*
B. *Rubble Gully*
C. *Tri-Scam*
D. *Quartz Crack*
E. *The Snotcicle*
F. *Pub Crawl*

Brian Post

 slanting ramp (possible rappel). Steeper ice leads up to another belay under a roof and a rappel from a V-thread (there is no fixed anchor). Rappel twice with one rope or once with two ropes.

FRA Bob Timmer

The next set of climbs are located along the buttresses north of the Quartz Crack Face. This is an easy place to get in a short pitch at the end of the day.

PUB CRAWL M4

This route climbs the big right-facing corner to the right of Quartz Crack Face and is best climbed just after a storm (bring rock gear). Climb the corner to a ledge. Continue up the corner or the wide crack 25 feet to the right and then head back left. Continue up the corner to trees (mixed) or climb snow and turf 30 feet to the right. Two single-rope rappels will get you down.

Bill Pelkey & Pat Viljanen

THE BUSHWAY ROUTE M4+

This route climbs the mixed corner system between Pub Crawl and Positively 4th Street for two pitches with a couple of variations possible along the way.

Pat Viljanen & Chris Bushway

POSITIVELY 4TH STREET 3+

About 300 feet north of The Snotcicle is a small amphitheater. This short route climbs an obvious line on the left up a ramp to a pillar and then left to trees.

Pat Viljanen & Steve Lulek

RAINY DAY WOMEN 3-/3+ M4+

Climb the wide flow on the right side of the amphitheater with many variations possible—including a hard mixed toprope climb on the right—to easier ice above.

Bill Pelkey, Tom Kontos & Pat Viljanen

HALFWAY GULLY 3

A hundred feet or so right of Rainy Day Women is this short gully. It is best approached by heading up from behind the outhouse and then going up and left 100 feet before reaching Ent Gully.

FRA Pat Viljanen, Bert Severin & Steve Lulek

ENT GULLY II 2

Approach the route from the Bedouin Trail from behind the outhouse. The climb, a two-pitch low-angled, right-trending gully with large rock walls on both sides, is not visible from the road. Many parties only do the first pitch. It is a fantastic early season mixed route with several possible finishes. There are fixed pins in the roof in the upper slot. Later in the season the route typically fills with snow. Rappel the route.

Todd Swain, Chris Taylor, Don MacDougal & Ned Getchell, Winter 1980

THE BEGINNING OF THE END 5 M7+

This is one of the notches hardest lines climbing the arete left of Ent Gully. Start up Ent Gully and after about 40 feet look for a crack on the left. Dry tool left to reach the ice (some fixed gear including two bolts near the arete) and then continue on difficult mixed ground to the top.

Bob Timmer & Bert Severin, February, 1998 (with some rock gear pre-placed)

THE END OF THE BEGINNING 5 M6+

Start to the right of the previous route, climb up a small left-facing corner to a tree under a roof, traverse left (pins) toward the arete to gain hanging ice.

Bob Timmer, winter 1997-98

LOW RENT M1

This short rock route climbs the low-angle wall on the right side of Ent Gully past a piton and bolts. Sometimes there is ice offering a mixed ascent.

Pat Viljanen & Tom Kontos

HIGHER RENT 3- R

Just uphill from Low Rent climb thin ice to a rock finish. Poorly protected.

unknown

NATURAL LIGHT 3- mixed

About 100 feet right of Ent Gully is a narrow gully between rock walls. Climb a short rock bulge to a cave and then tunnel up through one of two very tight slots to reach a big ledge. Rappel either the route itself or Ent Gully.

Alex Sargent, Bert Severin & Pat Viljanen

NATTY ICE M5+

This cool mixed route climbs the cave/corner/chimney 50 feet right of Natural Light. Traverse left near the top and descend as for that route.

Alex Sargent, Pat Viljanen & Bert Severin

JEFFERSON SLIDE 2-4

This is the huge slide/gully best seen while hiking in from the Jeffersonville side of the notch. The slide is about 200 feet wide and 1.5 pitches tall with many lines possible from grade 2 to 4. It comes in early and stays late. Approach from first bend in road north of the parking lot. Descend left in trees after two pitches. There is also a short M5 mixed route 50 feet to the left of the bottom of the slide.

unknown

NORTH GULLIES 2+/3+

Right of Jefferson Slide lie three moderate flows each less than a pitch high.

unknown

The following three routes are located in an area called Notch North and are in the vicinity of the obvious rock buttress a couple of hundred feet up and right of the top of Jefferson Slide. They can be approached by climbing the slide itself or by thrashing through the woods to the side.

HAPPY BIRTHDAY 3+ M4

This short route climbs a series of short tiers in the groove on the right side of the buttress. Bring rock gear.

Bert Severin

THE RUSTINATOR 3+ M5

This route climbs discontinuous ice near the center of the buttress. Start up a short pillar in a corner, move right and follow a corner with a crack to a roof, then step left over an arete to bulges and the trees.

Pat Viljanen & Alex Sargent

THE GOLDEN SHOWER 3+

About 300 feet up and left of the previous route is this short ice climb. An excellent mixed variation (M4⁺) climbs a corner just left.

Bert Severin

SMUGGLERS NOTCH: EAST SIDE

Routes will now be described north to south on the east (Spruce Peak) side of the notch.

WORKOUT WALL 2+/4+

This is the first area you will come to on the east side of the notch when approaching from Jeffersonville and is about a mile from the parking lot. There are lots of short climbs here including good mixed routes and it's a great area for toproping. A little bit of everything will be found here from a low-angled flow to the right, columns and mixed routes on the right side of the main area, longer pillars in the middle and hard mixed climbs on the left.

unknown

LOUIE'S LEAP (bouldering)

This small area offers good ice bouldering and is found several hundred feet in the woods on the opposite side of the road from the outhouse.

unknown

Even something called the "Workout Wall" looks pretty impressiive at Smugglers Notch.

Luca Marinelli

STERLING CLIFFS AREA 3-/4-

Several one pitch climbs will be found in this area although the approach is a long one. Hike up the Sterling Pond Trail to a snow gully which will bring you to the ice (you can see the climbs from near the stone hut high up on the east side).

unknown

H&D GULLY 2+/3

This gully is named after the Hunter and His Dog rock formation which can be seen from just south of the high-point on the road. Between the stone hut and the high point climb a snow slope to reach the gully. A short ice pitch leads to easier ice and snow above.

unknown

THE PLAYGROUND 3-4

Found on the Elephant's Head side of the notch just south of the so-called "top of the Notch," the Playground is a very popular practice area, even though most of the routes are fairly difficult. A steep open slope below the ice flows is the best approach. Most of the flows are about 50 feet high. The routes are easily top-roped.

unknown

The following routes are all found in the vicinity of the Elephant's Head, the prominent rectangular nose of rock on the east side of the notch. A deep gully is found on its left side and a blocky buttress to its right. Some of the notch's finest routes are found here.

INTELLIGENCE BYPASS 3

This route takes an independent line for two pitches just to the left of the following route. Rappel with two ropes or bushwhack north and rappel with one rope.

unknown

ORIGIN OF INTELLIGENCE IN CHILDREN III 4-5

North of Elephant's Head is a wide wall with several flows. This route climbs the wide flow on the left side of the face. Climb up the center of the flow finishing up and right on a steep pillar. Descend as for the previous route.

Steve Zajchowski & John Bouchard, Winter 1974-75

UNNAMED 4+/5

Just right of the former route is a buttress. Occasionally a

Origin of Intelligence in Children.
Brian Post

ELEPHANT'S HEAD AREA

A | B C D | E

Brian Post

A.	Origin of Intelligence...	B.	Watership Down	E.	Ragnarock
		C.	Elephant's Head Gully		(variation
		D.	Elephant's Head South Face		starts)

free-standing pillar drips off the prow of the buttress onto the lower slabs. Protection on the lower portion of the route is poor. The route has rarely been repeated.

unknown

WATERSHIP DOWN II 3+/4+

This is the large flow to the left of Elephant's Head Gully and there are a number of possible lines. From a ledge at mid-height you can make a 100' rappel down and to the right into Elephant's Head Gully or continue up the upper pillar (it doesn't always form). A popular variation start is down and to the left.

Steve Zajchowski & John Bouchard, winter 1974-75

ELEPHANT'S HEAD GULLY II 3

This is the obvious gully that climbs the left side of this notch landmark. The route is quite easy except for one section of roughly ten feet on the second pitch. The first pitch climbs low-angled ice for a long pitch to a fixed belay on the right. Pitch two trends up and left to the top. Rappel the route with two ropes. This route comes in early and stays late.

Chet Callahan, Bob Olsen & Chuck Bond, winter 1969-70

ICE SCREAM MIXED (HARD)

Instead of moving left on pitch two of the former route, continue up the corner on mixed ground to thin ice smears.

Bob Timmer, toprope

ELEPHANT'S HEAD, THE SOUTH FACE II 4 M4

This often sketchy route climbs the corner formed by the right side of the

Elephant's Head Buttress. Bring rock gear in addition to your ice rack. Start at the bottom of the buttress at a rock overhang, or on thin ice down and to the right (harder). Follow the corner to a chimney and then head out right to easier climbing and the top. Descend by rappelling Elephant's Head.

John Bouchard, Winter 1973-74

FREEZE DRIED II M6/7

Start as for the South Face but head out right after the first pitch to a finger crack in a corner and a thin ice finish. Bring rock gear.

Mark Wilford, Alden Pellett & Dave Furman, winter 1998

RAGNAROCK II 4+

Ragnarock, one of the Notch's great routes, with both starts obvious.
Luca Marinelli

One of the Notch's early difficult routes and still a classic. This route climbs the huge right-facing corner to the right of the South Face. Angle up and left on ice bulges to the base of the corner and a bolted belay. (there is an alternate start straight up on the right.) The next pitch climbs (often thinly) up moderate ice to another fixed belay. The last pitch climbs out right on bulges to a final upper pillar. The pillar rarely forms completely but the nature of the terrain allows for a fun mixed ascent. Rappel Elephant's Head Gully or from trees at the top.

John Bouchard & Steve Zajchowski, Winter 1974-75; in past editions of this guide the Creighton-Korman Route, was described left of Ragnarock; it was the same route.

TALL TALES 4/5 M5 R

Extending up and right from the base of Ragnarock is a snow ramp and below this is a blocky wall that occasionally ices up. This route climbs thin ice on the right side of the wall about 100-150 feet right of Ragnarock and left of a snow gully. Even with rock gear the climb is typically poorly protected.

unknown

SARGENT-SEVERIN 3+/4+

Just south of the rock buttress to the right of Ragnarock is a prominent flow with several variations. Approach as for Blue Room and then bushwhack up and left. Start at a small saddle bordered by snow gullies. The left variation climbs a steep flow for a couple of pitches to easier ice while on the right is a ramp with several steep pillars on its left side. Two ropes are helpful to rappel.

FRA Alex Sargent & Bert Severin

Several thin flows occasionally form on the buttress up and right of Ragnarock and are approached up a right-diagonalling snow ramp. About 200 yards south of Ragnarock is the next area, the South Wall, which is home to a number of excellent routes. To get to the South Wall Area follow a trail from the Big Spring parking area and follow it up and left to reach Blue Room. For routes

SOUTH WALL AREA

Brian Post

A.	Sargent-Severin	D.	Doug's Route
B.	Blue Room	E.	Prenuptial Agreement
C.	Dave's Snotcicle		

right of Blue Room head up and right about two thirds of the way up the trail. This is a sunny area which can provide relief on bitter cold days.

BLUE ROOM II 3+/4-

This is the left-hand of a cluster of routes in the South Wall area and one of the most reliable climbs in the area. Three steep sections, the middle the longest, characterize this climb. Rappel on the left from a tree.

unknown

DAVE'S SNOTCICLE II 3-4

This is the biggest flow on the sunny south wall and features a huge roof and then a left-trending ramp. Climb steeply up to a belay near the roof (the steep start can be avoided by coming in from the right), then climb up and left on pitch two. Two ropes are required for the rappel (60m helpful).

unknown

Smuggler's fat Blue Room on the South Wall.
Alden Pellett

DOUG'S ROUTE II 4

Just right of Dave's Snotcicle climb one pitch up to a cave. A second pitch climbs the steep pillar above to easier ice and the top.

Bubba Parker, Geoff Radford & Dale Bard, February 1977

PRENUPTIAL AGREEMENT 5+

Climb the awesome free-hanging pillar dripping off an overhanging wall just right of the former route. Rock gear is helpful in thin conditions. This is the hardest ice pillar in the notch.

Carl Tobin, winter 1996-97

Two moderate flows (2⁺ & 3⁺) lie around to the right of the former route. They offer quick access to routes in the next area, the Upper South Wall. The upper wall can also be approached up a snow gully that starts near the road about 300 feet right of the regular South Wall approach. Near the top of the gully you will see the moderate flows mentioned above coming in from your left. When above them head left and then up to these additional short routes.

LEFT SKI TRACK 2+/3-

This is the moderate flow on the far left of the upper wall.

unknown

RIGHT SKI TRACK 3-

Climb short bulges right of the previous route.

unknown

SINK 'EM AND WEEP 4

Less than 100 feet right of the ski tracks and near the center of the wall climb up a typically thin start and then up and right finishing in a corner.

unknown

LEFT BASTARD 3+

On the upper right side of the Upper South Wall lie a trio of short routes that drip down a steep wall. This is the left-hand route beginning under a rock roof. Rock gear may be helpful.

unknown

MIDDLE BASTARD 4-

The middle pillar leads to easier ice.

unknown

RIGHT BASTARD 4

The hardest and longest of the trio.

unknown

SMUGGLERS NOTCH: BEAR NOTCH

In recent years the tremendous ice and mixed climbing potential of this area just north of Smugglers has begun to be tapped. From Jeffersonville head north on Rt. 108 then turn onto Rt. 109 and follow it about 8 miles to the town of Waterville. Just past the Waterville Market (after a bridge) turn left onto Lapland Rd. and follow it for about 2.5 miles until you see ice up and left. The main cliff is above a sharp turn in the road just past a short steep section. There is no parking area so park responsibly by getting off the road as far as possible. The area was first explored by Bob Timmer, Alex Sargent and Bert Severin and what follows is just a sampling of what can be found here. Hike across (or around) a pond and up a slope for about twenty minutes to reach an amphitheater dripping with ice. The easiest descent for all routes is via rappel.

GRIN AND BEAR IT 3+ M4

Start in a corner/chimney about 100' left of Bear Right on a ledge near a dead tree. You can avoid the top pillar by heading left.

Bert Severin

BEAR RIGHT 5/5+

To the right of the previous route is an obvious series of pillars, said to be harder than nearby Smugglers Prenuptial Agreement. On the first ascent the top pillar was even harder as the bottom of the top pillar had been shot off (!) and mixed climbing was needed to regain the ice.

Bob Timmer & Alex Sargent

Bear Left 4

After the first pitch of Bear Right, head left on a ramp to the trees (mixed).

Bob Timmer, Bert Severin & Alex Sargent

CUB SCOUT 3+

This is the right-hand climb in the amphitheater about 50 feet right of Bear Right up an obvious flow trending left near the top.

Bob Timmer, Bert Severin & Alex Sargent

THREE BEARS 4

This route is located on the right wall of Bear Notch above a (currently) blue cabin. Climb pillars to a ledge then move left to more steep ice and the top.

Bert Severin, Marty Novia & Jim Rooney

BRISTOL CLIFFS

BRISTOL CLIFF FLOWS 2-4

This small area about 45 minutes southeast of Burlington has been a popular practice area for years. Take Route 116 south from Burlington to the traffic light in Bristol, turn left, drive about 2.5 miles and the ice will be obvious on the left. There are a number of routes here up to three short pitches and ranging across the grades. Descend by walking off left, rappelling the ice, or rappelling off the back side into a snow gully that leads back to the base. There are other short flows in the area that may be of interest. Parking may be tricky.

LAKE WILLOUGHBY

Longtime New England climber Bob Baribeau relates how visiting climber Joe Josephson once said to him that Lake Willoughby "might be the greatest ice climbing cliff in the world." Now many people have praised "The Lake" over the years, including Henry Barber, Michael Hartrich, and Al Rubin, the first guys to stand slack-jawed under Twenty Below Zero Gully back in 1974. But back then everything was inspiring. But when it's the new millenium and the comment comes from a guy like Josephson, whose backyard ice playground spans the globe, you should sit up and take notice. In terms of the sheer volume of vertical ice, there's just no place in the eastern United States like Lake Willoughby. The cliffs of Mount Pisgah rise up for hundreds of feet from the fiord-like valley that cradles one of the deepest lakes in Vermont. In most years the nearly mile-long cliff is simply plastered with ice columns up to 500 feet high. In total there is certainly

Pillars. That's what Lake Willoughby is all about. Tom Mazola on the classic Mindbender in lean conditions.
Doug Millen

over a mile of steep ice here—more than enough to keep even the hardest of hard climbers happy for a long time. For us New England climbers it is a point of pride that such a gem sits right here in the rolling hills of our backyard—the nearest ice that rivals this is found either way up in Quebec or way out in the Rockies. Easy approaches and descents, a sunny aspect, and reliable steep ice has made Lake Willoughby tremendously popular in recent years.

Climbs here are substantial undertakings. While the cliff is roadside, the easiest route is a two pitch grade 3, and most of the routes are much longer and much harder. Nestled in the comparatively remote Northeast Kingdom of Vermont, Lake Willoughby is also a long way from a town of any size and climbers need to be self-sufficient and know their limitations. Organized rescue is at least two hours away so don't get in over your head and know how to get out of trouble yourself if something happens.

Lake Willoughby is located about two hours northwest of N. Conway and an hour north of Franconia North in NH (five hours from Boston). The nearest large town is St. Johnsbury, VT, about 20 miles to the south. The fastest approach is via Interstate 91 which follows the New Hampshire and Vermont border from top to bottom. From the South, take exit 23 off Rt. 91 and take Route 5 north

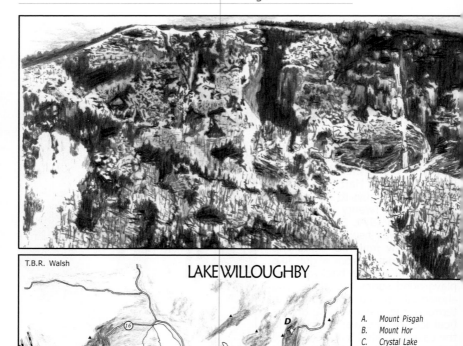

T.B.R. Walsh

LAKE WILLOUGHBY

A. Mount Pisgah
B. Mount Hor
C. Crystal Lake
D. Jobs Pond
E. Mount Wheeler

AREA HIGHLIGHTS

Location: Rt. 5A about 15 miles north of Lyndonville, VT

Routes: Grades 3 to 6, most routes are 4 or harder and two pitches or more; many climbs

Access: park below routes, 30 to 60 minute approaches

Descent: hike down around south end of cliff or rappel

Weather: "Notch" (weather section); sunny but can be windy and cold; January through early March

Equipment: large standard ice rack, double ropes make rappelling easy

Superlatives: a lot of vertical ice, Last Gentleman, Promenade, Called on Account of Rains, Mindbender, Bullwinkle, Power Test, White Strip, Five Musketeers, Call of the Wild, and even a bunch of moderate (4+) routes like Twenty Below Zero Gully

Amenities: Lyndonville is small with hotels and restaurants; St. Johnsbury is a small city

T.B.R. Walsh

MOUNT PISGAH OVERVIEW

see detailed photos at the end of the chapter

through the village of Lyndonville (last place to get gas or inhale a pile of pancakes). Several miles north take a right onto Rt. 5A in W. Burke and continue for another seven miles or so to Lake Willoughby. Parking at Lake Willoughby is a bit hit or miss. The parking lot at the lodge south of the Tablets may or may not be available to climbers based on the decisions of local landowners—don't count on it. You can park at pulloffs below the Last Gentleman and again farther north below Mindbender. There is additional parking at the south end of the lake in an unplowed parking area across from the campground and another (plowed) farther south near the "Cheney House." Be prepared to walk some distance to your route (30 minutes—or more in tough conditions).

The land around Lake Willoughby is managed by the Vermont State Department of Natural Resources (DNR) and the managers have been working with climbers for several years to keep the area open. The relationship between the DNR and climbers has been a good one so far. Please climb respectfully and responsibly here to help ensure that ice climbing will continue to be allowed without restriction.

While the climbs do receive afternoon sun, the wind chill factor can be extreme at Lake Willoughby so dress accordingly. The approaches to the climbs take up to thirty minutes and are straightforward in good conditions; simply walk straight up to your route from below. Bear in mind however, that the approach slopes can vary from hard ice that requires the use of crampons, to deep snow that could avalanche. Don't hesitate to rope up on the approach if conditions warrant it. A hiking trail follows the cliff's edge from the south end up to the top of The Last Gentleman, after which it turns uphill to the summit of Mount Pisgah. For all routes south of Renormalization you will usually find a climber's packed trail that skirts the edge of the cliff connecting with the main trail above The Last Gentleman. To reach the parking lot, leave the trail near the bottom and descend a short gully on the right, either downclimbing or sometimes rappelling if conditions are dangerous. If climbing on the trio of routes at the north end of the cliff, one long rappel with two ropes from the top of Renormalization will get you to the base, and another short rappel from a tree will get you down.

Deep snow or poor weather can make Willoughby's relatively easy descents treacherous so be on the lookout for rappel anchors (V-threads will work well) as you climb and don't hesitate to bail out if things don't go according to plan. Routes will now be described north to south.

WILLOUGHBY: MT. PISGAH

This is the main wall at Lake Willoughby forming the east side of the dramatic, fiord-like notch. A mile and a half long and in places over 600 feet high, this is the most spectacular ice climbing area in the entire Northeast. The easiest climb here is a 3+ (and there is just one), most are significantly harder, and they average about three pitches long. The cliff catches afternoon sun so the climbs take a little longer to form early in the season and they fall down early. A trail runs near the top from the south end to about the middle of the cliff. Climbs on the north end are best descended by rappel.

PLUG AND CHUG II 5

The farthest left ice flow on the west face of Mount Pisgah, and the left-hand of a group of four major ice climbs. A two-pitch ice route, not as serious as its neighbors, Call of the Wild or Mindbender, but strenuous enough. Don't run out of energy on the crux pillar. Descend left or rappel.

Clint Cummins, Brinton Young & John Imbrie, February 20, 1977

CALL OF THE WILD II 6

This is one of the hardest pitches of pure ice in New England. Left of Mindbender a thin line sometimes drips down from top to bottom. On the occasion of the first free ascent the crux was climbing up through and then out of a huge cave formed by a freestanding pillar on the second pitch. Start 20' left of Mindbender and climb 80' of vertical mushrooms and then another 20' of hollow grade 5+ ice and belay. Pitch two climbs a vertical, mushroomed pillar up and over a 4 foot roof to 35 feet of 95°-100° ice to another 4' roof.

Plug and Chug is one of Willoughby's, um, "moderate" climbs. Brian McGillicuddy having a moderately good time.
Luca Marinelli

The route was first climbed by Dan Lee and Mark Moran with one long hang for a rest on the second pitch on March 3, 1996; Jim Shimberg made the historic

There it is folks: grade 6. Long the bastion of the top-heavy 5⁺, New England finally caught up with the rest of the world in March 1996 when Dan Lee and Mark Moran climbed the first ascent of this line of pillars left of Mindbender. Jim Shimberg making the first free ascent of Call of the Wild a few days later.
Tyler Stableford

first free ascent of this route several days later.

MINDBENDER II 5+

The central ice flow, steep and unrelenting. A two-pitch route which has a notoriously sustained vertical pillar on the first pitch and additional hardships higher up. Descend left or rappel as described above.

Clint Cummins & John Imbrie, February 13, 1977

RENORMALIZATION 4

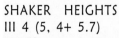

The right-hand flow of the quartet and the most reasonable route of the four. Its close proximity to the road, shorter length, and less severe technical difficulties make it a popular route.

John Imbrie & Nancy Kerrebrock, February 20, 1977

SHAKER HEIGHTS
III 4 (5, 4+ 5.7)

Luca Marinelli starting a full pitch of typical Willoughby straight-up ice on Mindbender.
courtesy Luca Marinelli

Situated immediately left of the northern end of the main rock face of Mount Pisgah, this route offers an alternative to the typically arm-destroying routes found at Lake Willoughby. A highly recommended route with generally moderate bulges and three or four pitches of climbing. The route can be done all the way to the top of the cliff but this does involve harder climbing. The left finish is up steep ice (4+) and then some 5.7 mixed climbing while the right-hand finish climbs a grade 5 ice column over an overhang. From the top of the cliff, descend by hiking up and then right linking with the trail from the top of The Last Gentleman. If you choose not to do either direct finish, then rappel the route from trees.

Ken Andrasko & Chris Field, Winter 1974-75; direct finishes: unknown

SHAKY HEIGHTS III 3+ mixed

Fifty feet left of the last pitch climb a mixed start to fatter ice above for a full pitch.

Jon Sykes, Mike Lee & John Mallory, February 15, 1999

LEDGE APPROACH III 4

Beginning Just to the right of Shaker Heights gain a fairly obvious ledge system which leads right to the upper ice on Called on Account of Rains. This is also a good approach to The Gantlet. Two or three ice pitches lead to the top. Rappel with double ropes to the left end of a ledge system, then again to the ground.

John Imbrie & Clint Cummins, February 19, 1977

CALLED ON ACCOUNT OF RAINS IV 5+ M4 R

A very impressive mixed route, the left-hand of a group of ice flows that rarely, if ever, reaches the ground. Very dicey mixed rock and ice climbing gains the base of the ice flow, which is followed to the top in another three pitches. You should carry rock gear including pins. There is a two-pitch pillar (5+) on the left at the top (see variation).

Clint Cummins & John Imbrie, December 28, 1977

THE GANTLET 5+

Climb two pitches of very steep ice (5+, 4+) left of the top pitches of Called on Account.

Alan Cattabriga, Ted Hammond, & John Mallory, February 7, 1999

FIVE MUSKETEERS IV M6+ 5+

This modern classic climbs a distinct independent line just right of Called on Account of Rains. Start at a short corner, traverse right on a narrow ledge to a left-facing corner (M5) and belay at a big cedar tree. Climb a steep left-facing corner and traverse left under roofs (M6 crux) past four fixed pins, to a set of double pins, downclimb seven feet left onto a slab, then up and left to a large cedar tree belay. The third pitch climbs up and right and then traverses right on an ice patch to a steep, narrow pillar (5+) and more steep ice to a ledge 20 feet below the top of the ice. The first

Greatly foreshortened here, Called on Account of Rains offers four pitches of the Lake's finest.
Luca Marinelli

ascent party rapped from here. It is possible to carry the route to the top via a short grade 4 pillar and then walk to the top of Called on Account of Rains.

This route was attempted prior to 2001 by Alden Pellett and John Abbott but they bailed due to warm temps and falling ice. In December 2001 Pellett and Doug Dillon returned, climbed the mixed crux free, then used a tension traverse after abandoning a more direct line to reach the upper ice (Pellett took a monster fall onto a #0 TCU when the moss he was dry-tooling on peeled off. A second attempt on the direct line was aborted because of bad gear.) Running out of daylight and with water pouring down the rock leading to the upper pillar, the pair decided to go down. The next day, visiting Canadian climbers Jean-François Morin, Bernard Mailhot and Mathieu Peloquin freed the mixed crux and the tension traverse after it and took the route nearly to the top. Pellet returned with Will Mayo the next day, repeated the tension traverse, but carried the route all the way to the top. After a discussion by Mailhot and Mayo, the conclusion was that Morin, Mailhot and Peloquin should get credit for the first ascent. In the spirit of good sportsmanship the Canadian's original name, Three Musketeers, was changed to Five Musketeers.

New England is tapped out. Yeah, right. The instant classic Five Musketeers found in 2001!
Bernie Mailhot

SUPER NOVA IV 4+ M4 A2

Left of Aurora by a few hundred feet climb to the top of a small buttress. On the next

pitch climb up a narrow ramp to its end then up to a bolt above a crack. Follow a line of bolts (not placed by the Super Nova FA party) and at the last one move left and up to a small ledge and a two bolt belay (these bolts were put in by the FA party). Pitch three aids up then left to a small right-facing corner. The next pitch goes up the corner, mixed free and aid, then left onto the start of the ice which is climbed to a large ledge. The last pitch climbs right and steeply to the top.

Jon Sykes & Nick Farley over three consecutive days from February 27 to March 1, 2001; they made the round trip from Franconia each day and the temperature was never above 5° (according to Sykes "the hike to the base was the crux").

AURORA IV 4+ 5.8 A2

This route and its neighbor Starman climb the central wall left of Brinton's Folly crossing at mid height. Begin left of Starman at a gully/depression; climb up and right and then up rock (5.8 A2) to reach a terrace above and the junction with Starman. Pitches 2-4 go up grade 4 ice to the right of the final pitches of Starman. Pitch 5 goes up and right surmounting an overhang at a fixed knifeblade and then to the top. The grade is listed as mixed although during at least one season the route was climbed on ice bottom to top.

FA Ted Hammond & Chris Rowins, February, 1986

AURORA DIRECT 5+

From the terrace below the upper part of Aurora traverse up and left passing the finishing pitches of Orion and continuing for at least 200 feet to one of the most sustained pillars at the Lake. This is a completely separate flow from the trio of flows mentioned in the Starman description (see cliff photo).

Guy Lacalle, late 1990's

STARMAN IV 5+ M4

Begin at a buttress near a large flake; climb up a chimney past a chockstone to a small snow field. Then go up the next tier to a belay at trees. Continue up a corner and easy ground to a major ledge system at mid-height on the face. Go left for a full pitch, crossing Aurora to reach the middle of three parallel flows at the top of the cliff. Up this for three more pitches of steep ice and hard mixed ground to the top.
An alternate start avoids the lower mixed pitches by going up an easy gully farther right (the approach gully for Brinton's Folly) and traversing left to join the route where it crosses Aurora.

Brad White & Chris Rowins, February 15, 1986

BRINTON'S FOLLY 4

To the south of the previous climb is a large open snowfield below a right-facing gully, running diagonally up to a narrow terrace. This climb is the short ice fall above the approach gully. It does not go to the top of the cliff. After one pitch of steep ice, rappel off from trees with two ropes.

FA: John Imbrie & Brinton Young, February 21, 1977

ORION IV 5.6 5

Climb the first pitch (snow gully) of Brinton's Folly, then traverse left on the narrow terrace passing under the upper good ice pitches of Aurora and Starman for two full pitches (5.6), to a tricky slab leading behind a prominent rock buttress. Here step onto a beautiful steep pillar and take it to the top.

Philippe Pibarot, Guy Lacalle & Bernard Mailhot, February 1994

STORMY MONDAY III 4+

Use the same approach as Brinton's Folly to reach the terrace, then traverse right to the base of a long, narrow ice flow. Three difficult pitches, involving thin ice in places, lead to the top. Rappel off trees down the northern border of the route to reach the terrace.

FA: Rainsford Rouner & Gustavo Brillembourg, February 12, 1977

CHINA SHOP IV 5+

Midway between Stormy Monday and Who's Who in Outer Space climb a narrow runnel of ice in an inside corner or gain a traverse ledge from the right and belay below a thicker ice flow. Five pitches of steep ice with the crux column on the fourth lead gain the top. The crux column is rarely in shape.

Dave Wright & George Hurley, January 18, 1991

CHOP SHOP 5+

This variation breaks left and finishes up steep pillars (what a surprise) dripping off a huge roof just below the top of the cliff

unknown

WHO'S WHO IN OUTER SPACE IV 5

This spectacular route climbs the flow immediately left of The Last Gentleman. The first pitch is usually the crux and climbs near-vertical ice normally just a couple of inches thick for a hundred feet. Above, follow thicker ice for two to three more pitches to the top.

FA: Mark Richey & Neil Pothier, January, 1984

THE LAST GENTLEMAN IV 5

This route ascends the left-hand of two immense ice falls in an amphitheater near the center of the west face of Mount Pisgah. Length, beauty, and an awesome amount of steep ice make this

Only at Willoughby would a route like Chop Shop be just a variation. Fred Bieber climbing fast to dodge the hanging cleaver.
Doug Millen

Ahh Willoughby; on a day like this there's no place better; the view toward Who's Who in Outer Space from The Last Gentleman.
Doug Millen

route one of the classic ice routes in New England. The climb is commonly done in either four or five pitches, depending on whether the direct start is in shape; it usually isn't. Most ascents begin by ascending the first pitch of The Promenade to the top of an ice column (bolt). Now traverse left on moderate mixed ground to the main flow. Overcome a difficult vertical section (the crux) past a cave. Two more very difficult pitches lead to the woods, with the usual finish up the right-hand column. Bring some blade pitons for the rock traverse.

Rainsford & Tim Rouner over several days, December, 1976

True alpine positioning on Willoughby's mega-classic The Last Gentleman.
Doug Millen

THE PROMENADE IV 5+

One of the most difficult and demanding ice climbs in the region. Long vertical sections, hollow ice, and frees-standing columns call for superior techniques and a mastery of the sport. The crux ice column takes a while to come into shape. Begin by climbing the initial ice flow to a ledge at its top, then continue up a difficult hollow sheet of ice to a cave belay. This pitch may be split. Above, persevere up a vertical free-standing column to easier ground. One final steep flow, with some stemming possible, leads to the woods.

Tim and Rainsford Rouner & Peter Cole, in two days in January, 1977

POWER TEST III M7+ 5+

This route and its variation climb a distinct section of cliff squeezed in between the Promenade and Reign of Terror. In the year of the first ascent there were two parallel blue ice streaks and this line tackles the right-hand streak. Just left of Reign

Up to the roof and scoot left on Patience; to the right is Power Test which traverses right under the roof at M7+.
Doug Millen

of Terror climb a steep slab on thin ice past four bolts (placed several days prior to the first ascent), or alternately, climb partway up P.1 of Reign of Terror and then head left. The second pitch gets on the right-hand blue streak and climbs to its top. The last pitch traverses right on rock (M7+) past three or four bolts to a steep right-facing corner which is climbed to the top.

Benoit Marion, Bernard Mailhot, March 14, 2001 (Marion drilled the P.3 bolts on the lead on aid and Mailhot did not second the pitch due to darkness)

PATIENCE III 5

This variation climbs the left-hand blue streak. Climb the previous route's first pitch or start up Reign of Terror then traverse left behind an ice curtain onto a steep, thin section. Continue left to reach the left-hand streak and climb it until a traverse left leads to a final column just right of the Promenade.

Benoit Marion & Martin Boiteau, December 2000

REIGN OF TERROR III 5

Ascends the steep ice flow on the right-hand side of the amphitheater where The Last Gentleman and The Promenade are located. Approach the amphitheater by way of an open avalanche scar from the roadside. Begin with about one hundred feet of relatively low angle ice which is followed to the base of a thin, steep runnel. Belay at its top up on the right off a tree. An alternate approach (the original first pitch is very rarely in shape) is possible by moving up and left from the top of the first pitch of Bullwinkle. Above, climb the very sustained vertical tower to the forest on the right.

Matt Peer & Tom Dickey, January 17, 1981

The 1980's testpiece Reign of Terror, not as terrifying as it once was, but still awesome. Antonio Pozzi nears the top
Luca Marinelli

BULLWINKLE III 5+

In terms of sheer verticality, this route epitomizes ice climbing at Lake Willoughby, ascending an unrelentingly steep free-standing icicle. Start to the right of Reign of Terror at a bulge. Either climb the bulge directly or walk up and around on the left. Continue up moderate terrain to a belay below the obvious, mushroomed, icicle. Then just tighten your wrist loops and go for it!

Ted Hammond & Dave Karl, January 27, 1984

ROCKY THE SQUIRREL III 5 M5

Walk to the right end of the snowfield at the base of Bullwinkle. Mixed climbing leads to a small overhang, traverse left and belay on a ledge in the center of the wall right of Bullwinkle. The long second pitch climbs thin, often candled and disconnected ice to the trees.

Jim Shimberg & John Mills, February 6, 1995 (Editors Note: there is a bit of confusion here as Guy Lacalle and Bernhard Mailhot also did a route here in February 2001 that has essentially the same description. We chose the party with the earlier date for the first ascent.)

THE WHITE STRIP III 5 M6

This new mixed line combines extreme difficulty with reasonable protection up a strip of ice just left of Float like a Butterfly. A mixed pitch with three bolts for protection leads to a two-bolt belay (when not buried) and a typical Willoughby pillar on pitch two.

Jim Shimberg and Jon Brown climbed the route in 2001 in scary (poorly protected) conditions. Two months later, Bernie Mailhot, thinking it was the first ascent, climbed the route (in really thin conditions) and added the bolts on pitch one. According to Shimberg, Mailhot called and "we talked, no big deal; now it will get done more often."

FLOAT LIKE A BUTTERFLY (LAND LIKE A TOMATO) III 4+

The often thin ice flow just left of Twenty Below Zero Gully. Climb diagonally left to reach typically thin and unprotected ice. Above, the flow gets thicker and steeper. Three pitches.

Bryan Becker, Peter Cole & Tad Pheffer, December 25, 1976

TWENTY BELOW ZERO GULLY
111 4+

The first route to be climbed at Lake Willoughby. The route is anything but a gully! Very popular. Take the line of least resistance for two pitches to a cave belay which protects the belayer from falling ice while the leader attacks the final and steepest section.

Henry Barber, Michael Hartrich and Al Rubin, January, 1974

GLASS MENAGERIE III 5

Located on the ice covered wall between Twenty Below Zero Gully and Extensive Homology. Delicacy combined with bravado is the preferred technique on this steep route, which is usually done in three pitches. Although the start is long and sustained, the top column is the crux.

Tim Rouner & Chip Lee, February 18, 1977

EXTENSIVE HOMOLOGY III 5

A formidable route, the last to be climbed on this section of the cliff. The first pitch is often nonexistent, but occasionally boasts thinly iced

The right end of Pisgah is festooned with 2-3 pitch routes that come in every year. Glass Menagerie would be a standout anywhere; here it's just another great grade 5.
Doug Millen

slabs and poor protection. The finish is also horrendous (i.e. unrelentingly steep).

John Imbrie & Dennis Drayna, January 31, 1979

INTENSIVE DRIPOLOGY 5 M5

To the right of the former route is yet another steep column at the top of the cliff. Though not as difficult as its neighbors the route makes up for it by offering a thin start and a few hard rock moves to gain the upper ice. If you don't like the looks of this, a traverse in from the midpoint of routes to the left is a reasonable way to reach the top column.

Jim Shimberg & Wayne Burleson, 1991

CRAZY DIAMOND 4+

The first major ice flow to the left of the three Tablets and just left of Zephyr. Climb moderate ice over bulges to a belay at the base of the upper vertical columns. Climb these energetically, stemming to reduce the pump factor, to the finish and the woods.

John Imbrie & Clint Cummins, December 27, 1977

ZEPHYR II 3 5.4

The flow between Crazy Diamond and the Tablet Left. Up the ice for a full pitch to a belay at trees. Move right to the buttress and up that to the top. Descend down the trail or rappel with two ropes.

Todd Swain & Ray Dobkin, March 5, 1983

THE LAST GENTLEMAN AMPHITHEATER

Who's Who in Outer Space	The Last Gentleman	The Promenade	Reign of Terror	Rocky the Squirrel
		Power Test	Bullwinkle	

Want to climb a half mile of near vertical to vertical ice? Look no further than the big routes in The Last Gentleman amphitheater. There is no greater concentration of steep ice anywhere in the lower 48.

Luca Marinelli

LAKE WILLOUGHBY DETAIL

MINDBENDER TO SHAKER HEIGHTS

A. Plug and Chug
B. Call of the Wild
C. Mindbender
D. Renormalization
E. Shaker Heights

SHAKER HEIGHTS TO AURORA

E. Shaker Heights
F. Called on Account of Rains
G. Five Musketeers
H. Super Nova

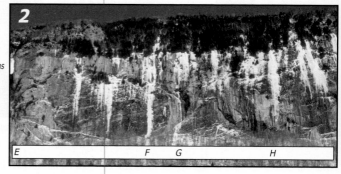

drawing by T.B.R. Walsh; photos by Bernard Mailhot

AURORA TO CHINA SHOP

I.   Aurora Direct (top only)
J.   Orion (starts as for Stormy)
K.   Starman
L.   Aurora
M.   Stormy Monday
N.   China Shop

CHINA SHOP TO FLOAT LIKE A BUTTERFLY

N.   Stormy Monday (top only)
O.   China Shop
P.   Who's Who in Outer Space
Q.   The Last Gentleman
R.   The Promenade
S.   Reign of Terror
T.   Bullwinkle
U.   Rocky the Squirrel
V.   The White Strip
W.   Float Like a Butterfly...
X.   Twenty Below Zero...

FLOAT LIKE A BUTTERFLY TO THE TABLETS

W   Float Like a Butterfly...
X.   Twenty Below Zero
Y.   Glass Menagerie
Z.   Extensive Homology
AA. Crazy Diamond
BB. Zephyr
CC. Tablet Left
DD. Tablet Center
EE. Tablet Right

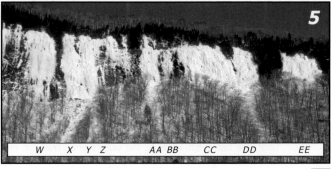

MT. PISGAH: The Tablets

In the first edition of this guide these flows on the south end of Mt. Pisgah went by the unfortunate designation of the Practice Slabs. In the second edition, and now in the third, we have chosen to give them the dignity they deserve by using the local designation for the area—The Tablets. Though these climbs pale in comparison with the likes of The Last Gentleman and other routes to the immediate north, if they were found alone any place else they would undoubtedly become destinations themselves. These big, fat flows vary in difficulty from grade 3 to 4⁺, have room for a number of parties, and offer a great place to climb if the big routes are too intimidating or the weather is too sketchy to stick your neck out. A good descent option is to do a 195' rappel from the trail just south of the routes. The tablets consist of the two flows on the far right side of Mt. Pisgah and they break rather naturally into three sections: the lefthand flow contains the routes traditionally called Tablet Left and Tablet Center, while the flow to the right has been called, well, Tablet Right.

TABLET LEFT II 3+/4+

The left side of the left flow consists of steep bulges that are climbed for two pitches to the trees. Immediately right is a very steep pillar (4⁺) that forms an independent line.

unknown

TABLET CENTER 3+

This true moderate (rare for Willoughby) climbs the right side of the flow for two pitches.

unknown

TABLET RIGHT 3

The easiest route in the region wanders up the right-hand flow over bulges for two pitches.

unknown

WILLOUGHBY: MT. HOR

Across Lake Willoughby from Mount Pisgah, stands Mt. Hor. If you're intimidated by the vertical ice of Pisgah the low angled ice slabs on this mountain may offer a suitable alternative. The following routes are good possibilities.

WOOBER GOOBER GULLY II 3+

On the road, a quarter mile south of Lake Willoughby, look to the left and you'll see a snow and ice gully running up the south side of Mt. Hor. Approach across the lake and up through the woods to the southern end of the face. After a short and steep first pitch, climb over moderate ice bulges on the second lead until one last pitch leads to the gully's end. Traverse left forty feet, then finish up thinly iced slabs. Descend down and left through the forest.

FRA: Wayne Domeier, Gene Popien & Tom Nonis, February 15, 1981. Henry Barber and Al Rubin did a route here in 1974 that may have followed the same basic line. Their ascent was before the first ascent of Twenty Below Zero Gully and their comment was that "it was very hard when we did it." Considering the gear available at the time, it must have been desperate.

THE BOISSONNEAULT-CATTABRIGA ROUTE 4

Several hundred yards north of Woober Goober is an obvious cliff band which diagonals up and left. Just past the bottom of this is a distinct short column.

Paul Boissonneault & Alan Cattabriga, February, 1991

In addition to these routes, there are other possibilities on Mount Hor including a steep route by Kurt Winkler between Woober Goober Gully and The Boissonneault-Cattabriga Route and a three pitch grade 4+ by Barry Blanchard.One of these routes reportedly climbs a very steep yellow icicle. Recent information has come in from Jon Sykes on some of the climbs here and the following will at least get you to good ice—even though the historical data is a bit foggy. Names were given to the routes to avoid the undignified designation of "unnamed," even though we all know they were climbed long ago. In the center of the steep east side of Mt. Hor are three long moderate ice routes worth the walk in.

ARCTIC CROSSING II 4

This is the center flow on the mountain. The crux is a steep pillar near the top of the first pitch. Pitch two heads up and right to the trees. Rappel the woods to get down. This may be the route climbed by Kurt Winkler.

unknown; on a subsequent ascent, the pitch one pillar was out of shape so Jon Sykes climbed a spruce tree and then stemmed over onto the upper ice; there is no rating for this sort of thing

TAKE BACK YOUR EMPTYS II 3+

The slabs far to the right of the former route offer two 350 foot routes. This, the left-hand route, climbs an extremely steep snow slope leading to moderate, thin ice.

unknown

TAKE BACK VERMONT II 3+

The even thinner companion to the right of the former route.

unknown

CRYSTAL LAKE

Crystal Lake is a small lake located a few miles due west of Lake Willoughby and offers a good alternative to Lake Willoughby if the weather or crowds are uncooperative.

CRYSTAL LAKE FLOWS 3-5

Crystal Lake is a small lake located a few miles due west of Lake Willoughby and is reached by bearing left onto Route 5 in West Burke and going north for twelve miles. The climbs are located on the far side of Crystal Lake on a short cliff band and are easily visible from the road. The ice flows which form here are typically much shorter and more mellow than those on Mount Pisgah. The main icefall is grade 3. A more difficult pillar lies to the left and there is also a wild grade 5 pillar that forms 20 fee to its right. There is more potential here.

unknown

JOBS POND

Jobs Pond is located east of Lake Willoughby and is reached by turning right off Rt. 5A onto Newark St. just north of West Burke and driving about nine miles to the pond. There is an obvious wall on the opposite side of the pond with a prominent streak down it. There are other possibilities here.

Jobs Pillar.
Doug Millen

JOBS PILLAR II 4

Park at the pond and walk across if well frozen. This two pitch route will be very obvious on the far side.

FRA: Chris Ellms & Mike Brochu, early 1980's

MOUNT WHEELER

Mount Wheeler is just west of Mt. Hor and is approached by turning north onto the Wheeler Mountain Rd. off Rt. 5 about five miles south of Barton. Follow the road north for several miles until you reach the end of the plowed section. Hike about a quarter of a mile and the cliff will be visible on the left. From the crest of the road hike north (passing a large boulder) and then right to the base of the cliff. The cliff faces south and cold conditions are required for good ice conditions. Avalanches are not uncommon on the open slabs so beware.

BEAUTIFUL DAY III 3+ 5.7

This mixed route starts at the base of the summer route VJ's (the largest expanse of open rock) and climbs a 200 foot pitch of low-angled rock and snow to trees at the obvious break in the slabs. This is a popular summer pitch so take care if you are wearing crampons—the FA party climbed the pitch without crampons. Traverse 100 feet right to a small tree belay below an obvious flow. The third pitch climbs snow to thin, detached bulges and then continues up the steeper, thicker flow above. Bring rock gear.

Dave Powers & Matt Elliott, February 9, 2002; crampons were only worn on the third pitch on the first ascent

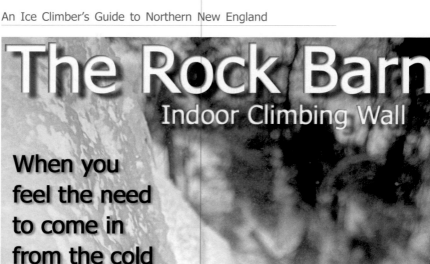

The awesome splendor of New Hampshire's Franconia Notch. From high on the big wall section of the cliff we look north toward Eagle Cliff.

Rick Wilcox

FRANCONIA NOTCH

Franconia Notch is one of the showplaces of New England climbing and home to some of its most serious and famous ice and rock routes. The notch is a desolate, windy, often bitterly cold place that doesn't treat visitors nicely. Cannon Cliff forms the west wall of the notch and is nearly a mile long and up to 1,000 feet high. It offers highly difficult and technical climbing on fractured granite and is considered an alpine wall even though its summit is just barely over 4,000 feet high. Catch it on a warm, sunny, calm day, and you might think Cannon's reputation isn't warranted. But on a day below zero, with two feet of fresh snow, a brooding sky, and a howling wind, you'll soon see why it has been considered one of the Northeast's greatest alpine training grounds for generations. Beside Mount Washington, Cannon is perhaps the most serious climbing venue in the state and climbers should not only be competent at the chosen grade, but also possess good judgment skills and the ability to self-evacuate in case of an emergency. The approach can be avalanche prone, the descent is long, and if caught out in the weather or the dark, the crag does not often offer an easy means of retreat. A generation ago a trip to Cannon was considered very demanding and dangerous and only the best climbers dared go. Today's technology, clothing, and the increased climbing ability of the "average" climber have tamed this reputation a bit. Nonetheless, good mountain sense is necessary: start early, be prepared both technically and mentally, consider not climbing beneath other parties, and be prepared to "get out when the gettin's good."

FRANCONIA NOTCH

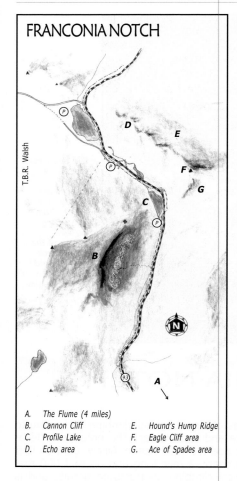

T.B.R. Walsh

A. The Flume (4 miles)
B. Cannon Cliff
C. Profile Lake
D. Echo area
E. Hound's Hump Ridge
F. Eagle Cliff area
G. Ace of Spades area

AREA HIGHLIGHTS

Location:	Rt. 93, ten miles north of Lincoln, NH
Routes:	Grades 3 to 5+; several long, serious ice and mixed routes, & shorter routes too
Access:	park near the top of the notch, 15-60 minute approaches depending on area chosen; not always packed
Descent:	rappel short routes, hike down from all else; can be long
Weather:	"Notch" (weather section); often windy and cold; east side sunny and warmer; late November through early March
Equipment:	standard ice rack, rock gear for big routes on Cannon, double ropes and extra gear in case of trouble
Superlatives:	roadside alpine climbing area is home to some of the most famous routes in the Northeast: Black Dike, Omega, Fafnir, and Whitney Gilman Ridge on Cannon, short hard and mixed routes on the east side
Amenities:	Lincoln has everything; Littleton, 15 miles north is a small city

Construction in the late 1980's has restricted traffic flow on Rt. 93 through the notch making access to the west side possible only when heading south. You can reverse directions at exit 34B at the Tramway at Cannon Mountain Ski Area at the head of the notch (when heading north) and at exit 34A, six miles south of the Tramway (when heading south). Parking for the routes on Cannon is at Profile Lake, just south of the north end of the notch on its west side. There is a sign-out/sign-in box at the south end of the lot; please use it. From the parking area head south on a paved bike path (it is usually well-packed) and continue for about 1/4 mile until an obvious (unless there's been a big snow the night before) climbers' path on the right leads up toward the left side of the face. If when you emerge onto the talus you're below a huge fin of rock that dominates the southern end of the cliff, you are on the right path for Cannon's classic route, The Black Dike. Even for other routes either side of The Black Dike this is usually the best approach trail. Climb through a short band of woods and then up what often feels like an endless talus slope (it can be avalanche prone).

Probably the most important action to take when climbing in Franconia Notch is to sign out and in at a box located at the south end of Profile Lake, stating your proposed climb and descent. Do not forget to sign back in after the climb! This check-in system is taken very seriously and if you appear to be overdue, rescue will be initiated.

While the major winter routes in Franconia Notch are located on Cannon Cliff, there are several other areas in the notch that offer great climbing. A popular toproping area, the Flume, is located several miles below the notch and is a great place to spend a few hours or even a day if the weather up the road is atrocious. In the last few years the east side of the notch has seen extensive development, led by the area's most prolific new-router, Jon Sykes. The routes he and his many friends have ferreted out of Echo Crag and the other cliffs on the Lafayette side of the notch have created wonderful opportunities to climb short, hard, often mixed routes—these are great alternatives if Cannon is in a nasty mood.

Winter ascents of summer rock routes are included here for historical value. Accurate route descriptions can be found in the rock climbing guides to the area, including Jon Sykes' new guide and Ed Webster's *Rock Climbs in the White Mountains* (out of print). First winter ascents of rock climbs are described with the initials FWA. Ice conditions vary so much that in some years crampons are necessary for the ascents, while in other years only rock shoes will be required. An ice or mixed grade may be listed for them if or when they can be done under normal or ideal winter ice conditions.

Our very special thanks to Jon Sykes for all his help in putting the Franconia Notch information together. His excellent guide, *Secrets of the Notch* (2001) is a great resource and includes information on all the rock and ice routes in this fantastic area.

FRANCONIA: THE FLUME

Located about five miles south of Cannon Mt., this spectacular gorge is a great sheltered place to toprope some very steep ice. It's a very handy alternative if you get to Cannon and find the weather conditions on the face atrocious. From Lincoln head north on Rt. 93 for about five miles to Exit 34A and take Rt. 3 north for about three miles then follow signs to the parking area for the Flume on the east side of the road. Follow a trail for about a half mile to the Flume itself where a walkway leads through the center bordered by steep rock walls. The right-hand wall is usually covered with hard ice varying from verglas to thick flows. Please be careful climbing here (helmets highly recommended) and take care to protect the resource. Don't trash the trees, place pins or bolts, and try not to scratch everything to death—this is a state park and summer folks might not appreciate the place looking like an active quarry. The stream through the Flume may be dangerous to cross in the early season. All the routes will be steep and anchors are easily found on top. Descend around either end or rappel. There are many possibilities here and few people have bothered to write up route descriptions. One notable exception is:

ONE PICKLE SHY (OF THE WHOLE BARREL) M7+ R

At the very back of the Flume corridor, near the back stairs, walk right to a frozen pool. Scratch up a 35' wall eventually getting on a tiny column. Hard to protect. On the first ascent Rob Frost had to start the route a number of times after losing all tactile adhesion with the ice while partway up.

Rob Frost, February 1998

SWAIN'S PILLAR 4+

Also in the vicinity is "The Pool," a huge pot hole in the Pemigewasset River that is home to a unique climb. Follow the bicycle path north into the notch until you see a warming hut on the right. Pick up another trail here and it will take you to the Pool. On the far side will be an obvious yellow free-standing column. You can rappel in to the right of the pillar. On the opposite side of the pool is another grade 3 ice gully and with short mixed lines on either side of it. This is a really neat place to climb.

FA: Todd Swain, solo, early 1980's

People lead this stuff? Rob Frost one pickle shy...
courtesy Rob Frost

FRANCONIA: CANNON

LA DEEPFREEZE III 2-4

This route is about 300 feet left of Omega, on the south side of the Henderson Buttress. Ascend a very easy 200 foot gully to a tree ledge. You can rappel from here or continue on. Several variations lead up the upper wall on mixed ground toward some final flows.

Todd Swain & Brad White, January 17, 1981

Swain's Pillar in "The Pool" is a great alternative to the crowded Flume (and there's other stuff here too.)
Mike Lee

HENDERSON II 5.5

A snow-packed rock climb. Probably safer to climb in winter than summer.

FWA: Ajax Greene & Rick Mulhern, 1974

OMEGA IV 5+

An extreme route which epitomizes the desperate nature of modern ice climbs with its thinly iced start, mixed climbing, and steep final columns. A classic of the region which rarely comes into shape. The route ascends the prominent icefall on the southern end of Cannon Cliff. A couple of hundred yards south of the Whitney-Gilman Ridge, past an obvious short buttress, is another rather vague buttress with a shallow amphitheater at its base. Even in the best of conditions this route is going to offer hard mixed climbing—bring rock gear (including pitons). Beginning on a verglas covered slab, mixed climbing leads to

Why is this man smiling? Perhaps it's because he's having a stellar day on one of New England's classic alpine routes—Omega. Occasionally seen as a series of yellow sabers dripping left of The Black Dike, Omega is on everyone's tick list. Rob Frost can check this one off now.

Mark Synnott

a belay near the base of the thicker flow coming down from above. Climb the upper flow for two more pitches, weaving up through overhangs on steep yellow columns. The crux is typically a sustained pillar a pitch below the top.The exact nature of this route varies considerably from year to year, and the best line and belay points depend on conditions.

After an attempt that failed just below the crux pitch a few days before with Rick Wilcox, John Bouchard returned with Rainsford Rouner to finish the climb in February, 1976

PROZAC IV 6R M6

This route climbs an independent line parallel to Omega that starts about 20' to its right. The first pitch climbs the buttress just right of Omega at M5. Pitch two climbs straight up a 5+R flow. The crux third pitch continues straight up over a roof at M6 and then climbs loose blocks (frozen in place after a night of -20° according to the FA party) to a final pillar that is separate from and about 40 feet right of the top pitch of Omega, early 2000's

Kevin Mahoney & Ben Gilmore

ABORIGINAL RHYTHMIC IMPLEMENT
III 3+ 5.9 A0 (a k a TOM TOM)

This new mixed route starts about 75 feet right of Omega at a small buttress. Depending on conditions the route may be a dry rock climb or plastered with ice. Start up a crack to a ledge and then gain the crest of the buttress. Pitch two angles right across a small snowfield to a series of left-facing corners and ledges leading to a fixed anchor on the highest ledge. A V-groove leads to another ledge with small trees then traverses 50 feet to the right. Step left to a block (piton) then aid up to a right arching crack and belay (short pitch). The last pitch weaves into a gully with trees, crosses back right on a small snowfield, then climbs straight up with difficulty finishing in an iced, right-facing corner. Bring rock gear to 4" and thin pitons.

Tom Nonis & Tom Callaghan
March 20, 2000

THE WHITNEY-GILMAN RIDGE
III 5.7

One of the best winter routes on Cannon, with superb mixed climbing and exposed situations. Highly recommended.

FWA: Leif Patterson & Henry W. Kendall, 1962

ACROSS THE GREAT DIVIDE
IV 5.7 A4

Climbs the somber wall to the left of The Black Dike. The first ascent of this difficult climb was done over several days in full winter conditions.

Peter Cole and Rick Wilcox

This must be alpine climbing. The Whitney-Gilman Ridge in nearly full conditions (it's not dark yet
Joe Klementovic

climbed the first pitch; Cole, Mark Richey and Rainsford Rouner did the second; and Cole and Wilcox finished the climb in November, 1975

THE BLACK DIKE IV 4-5 M3

Since its first ascent, The Black Dike has become a measuring stick for many aspiring ice climbers. Its length, sustained but not extreme technical difficulties, and tremendous atmosphere make it one of the most alpine of ice routes in New England. In poor conditions, below zero temperatures and with spindrift flowing, the route can feel (and be) very serious. Be prepared physically and mentally for the climb. John Bouchard soloed the first ascent on December 18, 1971, in subzero temperatures in a snowstorm. His account of the epic ascent (described in the history chapter) was doubted by many at the time. Because he was just a teenager with relatively little experience, the locals were

Peering down the void of the Black Dike—Chouinard's "filthy black icicle." Catherin Snead nearing the top of this all-time classic
Doug Millen

reluctant to buy his claim to New England's biggest plum. Bouchard returned the following winter and climbed the route with Rick Wilcox, Henry Barber, and John Bragg. Fixed gear high on the route, which matched Bouchard's description, confirmed his solo ascent and affirmed his honor. Initially considered solid grade 5, The Black Dike has lost some of its fearsome reputation (better equipment had a lot to do with it) and is now given a range of grades based on its moods, from 4 when fat and plastic to 5 when skinny and scratchy. To get to the start, hike up to the base of the Whitney-Gilman Ridge; The Black Dike is the immense gully on the north side of the ridge. Work up low-angled snow and ice, then trend right over bulges until reaching a belay stance below a pronounced rock wall. Climb the notorious rock traverse moving back left into the main inside corner (perhaps not as notorious as it once was; expect a short series of snowy rock moves with pretty good gear in typical conditions). In friendly conditions there is a narrow runnel of ice leading straight up to the main inside corner, making it possible to avoid the rock traverse. Fifty feet of this steep inside corner brings the climber to lower angle ice and typically a rock belay on the left. The next pitch is easier and climbs more bulges to one of several stances. Above, if conditions allow, follow the ice on the left to the very top of the route, or exit lower to the right into the woods (usually thicker). Hike uphill to the descent trail which leads down around the left (south) end of the cliff. This trail can be difficult to follow. Be careful to stay back away from the main cliff and do not head east until the cliff is safely passed. Turn north on the bike path to return to your car.

John Bouchard, solo, December 18, 1971

HASSIG'S DIRECT 5

Climb mixed rock and ice directly above the first belay on The Black Dike instead of the usual traverse to the ice ribbon. Rockfall has altered the original line (see next route) but climbing straight up is still possible at the grade.

Chris Hassig, February, 1979

DARK CRYSTAL III 5 M4

A new, nearly independent line between The Black Dike and Fafnir (recent rockfall may have blended this route into Hassig's Direct). Climb the first pitch of the Black Dike. The second pitch climbs immediately right of the Dike via thin mixed climbing to belay just above. The final pitch climbs right to thin flakes and corners and then up onto fat ice to the right of the right-hand finish of the Dike. The second pitch used to sport a bizarre cave—which has since fallen off (photo).

FRA Philippe Pibarot, Bernard Mailhot, Charles Laliberté & Jean Martel, late 90's/early 00's; the route had been done earlier by several parties

Dark Crystal was the only route to climb inside Cannon—a disturbing though
Bernie Mailho

FAFNIR IV 5

Descending in a series of steps on the right, this is the sister ice flow of The Black Dike. The difficult mixed climbing at the top is the crux. Wait for thick enough conditions. Climb the first two pitches, or one very long pitch, of the Dike to the right of the rock traverse. Belay on the right on a narrow, snow covered ledge at the base of the main flow. Step right, then climb a series of vertical steps to a good belay platform at the base of the final mixed portion. Take the line of least resistance straight up a fairly obvious weakness, stepping off right at the top—typically mixed.

John Bouchard, Steve Zajchowski & Roger Martin, December, 1975

Line of least resistance? Antonio Pozzi ponder. what looks like a lot of resistance near the top o Fafnir
Luca Marinell

BLACK DIKE AREA

A. Whitney-Gilman
B. The Black Dike
C. Fafnir
D. Lila

Luca Marinelli

LILA IV 4+ M6 (A2)

Ascends the thinly iced slab to the right of Fafnir, then the improbable upper headwall. The route requires good conditions to form, and even at that, aid may be necessary on the last pitch. Carry pitons, etriers, etc. Climb the verglassed slab to the left of the Cannonade Buttress for one long pitch. Thicker ice leads to a headwall. Follow the ice as high as possible up steep ground and dry tool (use small amounts of aid) to reach easier mixed climbing above. There is a fixed rock anchor at the top of the Cannonade Buttress that allows a quick descent after the first long pitch. A popular variation that avoids the upper route's hard mixed climbing is to traverse from the top of the Cannonade Buttress to the left and finish up the upper part of Fafnir.

Rainsford Rouner & Nancy Kerrebrock, March, 1976; Tom Nonis & John Courtney made the first recorded free ascent in February 1999

LILA VARIATION FINISH 4+ M3

Approach up Lila to near the top of the route. Twenty feet before the ice ends traverse left to a piton belay at a big right-facing flake. The next pitch climbs up a chimney for ten feet, then angles left and up to a ledge to a chimney, flakes, and a good belay ledge. The last pitch makes one hard move and then easier climbing leads to the trees. This route crosses over Lila Direct and finishes to its left. Kurt Winkler reports a great potential finish to the right of the upper part of this route. A knifeblade crack with nothing for the feet leads over a bulge. "When you fall your crampons will stick in the ice below, your ankles would break, and you'd fall head over heels down the cliff. I think that's what's holding people back," he said.

Kurt Winkler & Harold Hunt, February 14, 1990

LILA DIRECT IV 5+ M5 R

Joe Josephson and John Bouchard climbed a direct line to the right of Lila's normal first pitch, crossed that route above the top of the Cannonade Buttress and then took an independent line to the top.

Joe Josephson & John Bouchard, late 1990's

CANNONADE II 2-3 5.4

Mixed climbing on nebulous terrain. Not a popular winter climb.

FWA: Robert Hall, Jorge Urioste & Joe Boden, 1967

QUARTET ICE HOSE IV 5+ M6 5.10

A difficult mixed climb which ascends the two pitch ice runnel in the back of Quartet Corner, just left of Duet Direct on the left side of the Duet Buttress. From the top of the buttress there are many mixed options to the top of the wall. Carry a large variety of gear. A trend on recent ascents has been to climb the first two pitches and rappel.

Peter Cole climbed the first two pitches, then in January 1981, Ed Webster and Todd Swain made a nearly complete ascent, retreating from near the top in the dark in very cold weather. On December 9-10, 1989, Chris Dubé and Larry Sodano made the first complete ascent in full winter conditions. Jim Shimberg and Mark Davis made the first one day ascent in 1998.

DUET III 5.7

A rapid, six hour ascent in snowy conditions.

FWA: Andy Tuthill & Chris Ellms in 1977

ICARUS IV 5.8 A4 (11b)

The first new route to be climbed on Cannon in winter (by the calendar). One bivouac was made on the face. John Bouchard completed the route despite the fact that he broke his ankle in a fall near the top. Start on the north side of the Duet Buttress and follow steep corners right of Raven Crack and finish with the upper pitches of Duet.

John Bouchard & Rick Wilcox, with help from Jeff Pheasant, January, 1974

SAM'S SWAN SONG III 5.7

A very impressive winter ascent considering the year. Hard mixed terrain.

FWA: Robert Proudman & Mark Lawrence over two days in 1967

THE GHOST IV 5.7 A3

This arduous big wall climb also received its first winter ascent at an early date. A large ice flow was climbed to the top.

FWA: John Bouchard, Rick Wilcox & Henry Barber climbed the route over two days in 1973

ONE DROP OF WATER IV 5.9 A3 M4

This directissima of Cannon provides one of the most difficult mixed wall climbs in the Northeast. In winter conditions expect extreme difficulty on nearly every pitch. Start right of the arch on VMC Direct and left of the Direct Direct at a dike. Climb for two pitches, cross over VMC, aid under a huge overlap, pull over and continue on difficult mixed terrain for several more pitches.

Kurt Winkler & Chris McElheny climbed the route over four days in the early 1990's. They climbed and fixed ropes each day but did not bivy on the wall. Expecting hard free rock moves high on the route Winkler brought oversized rock shoes and electric socks. Unfortunately the team had horrendous weather (cold and stormy) during most of the climb and had to pendulum past the hard free moves so Winkler never got to try his custom footwear. At the top of the wall, while hiking off in the dark, a tiny mouse climbed up Winkler's leg then jumped off and ran into the pucker-brush, showing the climbers the easiest way down.

VMC DIRECT DIRECT IV 5.10 (5.7 A2)

A tour-de-force which took four days and one bivouac hanging in hammocks on the face.

FWA: John Bouchard, Jeff Pheasant, David Belden (France) & Jean-Claude Droyer (France) in 1975

LABYRINTH WALL V 5.7 A4

Rainsford Rouner and Peter Cole made the first winter ascent in warm weather in February, 1976. John Bouchard and Andy Embick followed a day later in worse conditions. Both ascents included a bivouac.

FWA Rainsford Rouner & Peter Cole, 1976

FRUIT CUP WALL V 5.8 A4

Another wall route that will feature hard aid and some mixed ground. The first winter ascent was done in moderate conditions. One bivouac was made on the face.

FWA: Mark Richey soloed all but the last pitch in 1975 (while still in high school). Mark Whiton, Bryan Becker and Alain Comeau climbed the first complete ascent in 1978.

MOBY GRAPE III 5.8

A superb free-climb done in rapid time; mostly rock climbing.

FWA: Andy Tuthill & Chris Ellms in February, 1976

UNION JACK III 5.9

Yet another cold rock climb following the summer route to the right of the Conn Buttress.

FWA: Chris Hassig & friend in 1978

VERTIGO III 5.9

A commendable two-day ascent. The climbers used nuts for protection and they used very little direct aid.

FWA: Chris Hassig & Dave Foster in 1976

NORTH-SOUTH-WEST III 5.8-9

A confusing enough route in summer without the added difficulties of winter.

FWA: Chris Elms and Andy Tuthill in 1976

Note: massive rockfall in this area may have altered or obliterated parts of the following routes (although, since it's Cannon, when the rubble is frozen you may still be able to climb here.)

CRACK UP III 4- 5.7 A1

The first winter ascent followed the summer line fairly closely to the Old Cannon Garden, a brushy, ledgy area about halfway up the cliff down and left from the Old Man of the Mountain. Several hundred feet left of Wiessner's Buttress climb three short pitches on thin ice to the Garden. Move right and climb a thinly iced slab left of Riddler for two pitches. Move left again to an old bolt, an overhang, and the top.

The first three pitches were climbed by Bob Baribeau and Gerry Handren in December 1989. Baribeau returned and rope-soloed the complete ascent in January 1991.

OLD CANNON III 5.6

A true winter adventure, provided conditions are good with a 300 foot ice slab at the top. The first winter ascent took four days.

Robert Hall & Jorge Urioste, 1971

UNNAMED III 3+/4+

A scratchy mixed route that rarely forms. Start at the corner at the base of Wiessner's Buttress and climb several pitches to the Old Cannon Garden. From the garden climb more difficultly between the huge rock scar on the left and the top pitches of Riddler on the right and continue to the top of the cliff finishing above the Old Man. Another route of about the same difficulty was climbed by John Bouchard and Mark Richey left of this around the same time.

Andy Tuthill & Jim Rossin, 1976; the complete line was climbed by John Bouchard and Mark Richey in 1997

WIESSNER'S BUTTRESS II 5.6

A long and worthwhile mixed route.

FWA: Joe Cote & Steve Arsenault in 1971

THE HORRIFYING EAR II 5.9 mixed

A couple of hundred feet left of the start of Lakeview is an obvious squeeze chimney. Hard rock climbing in mountain boots; highly recommended.

FWA Tom Coe, Chuck Graves, & Chris Derby, February 1987

LAKEVIEW II 2 5.5

The slabs were entirely coated in water ice and snow.

FWA: Tom Lyman, Rick Wilcox & A.J. LaFleur, Winter 1969

ADAMS' SLIDE II 2

A pioneering route from early in the last century by the Dartmouth Outing Club and led by Sherman Adams who would go on to become governor. Just right of Lakeview, climb the obvious snow and ice slabs to the big ledge below the Old Man then traverse right into the steep woods.

Sherman Adams, Ellis Griggs & D .W Trainer March 3, 1919

MAGICAL MYSTERY TOUR V M5 5 A0

This north-to-south girdle traverse includes over 6,000 feet of technical climbing and has rarely been done even during those long days in June. Begin at the right margin of the cliff and climb Lakeview for several pitches to ledges below the Old Man of the Mountain. From there head left for dozens of pitches and finish up the Black Dike. We only know of one winter ascent.

Mark Richey and John Bouchard climbed this route in winter in 1995 as part of their alpine training for lightning fast ascents in the Himalaya.

FRANCONIA: EAST SIDE

The Lafayette side of Franconia Notch is a maze of cliff bands, buttresses, gullies and walls. For years this area was home to just a handful of winter routes but in the last few years many routes have been put up here. Many of the routes found here are of the short, fairly hard, thin, or mixed variety and are a great place to round out the day, practice technique, or avoid an epic across the road. There are also some multi-pitch routes for the adventurous.

EAST SIDE: Echo Crag

This rambling crag is found at the very top of Franconia Notch and offers a nice collection of short routes just minutes from the road. When Cannon is howling or the talus looks like it's going to send a big load of snow down toward the bike path, Echo may be just the place to go. If there's a downside it's that the crag faces the afternoon sun which means the routes are rarely fat and they don't hang around long in warm weather. Routes will be described from left to right as you approach the cliff from the road. Please take care climbing here as many of the routes are also summer rock climbs and the use of pitons, or just a lot of bashing and scratching, can mar the rock.

To approach the cliff take Exit 34C (Rt. 18) off Rt. 93 and park at the Gov. Gallen Memorial or at the Echo Lake beach parking lot. Do not park along the curve or block the road or you may be ticketed or towed. The approach trail starts right at the curve in the road beside the off ramp from Rt. 93, ten feet to the right of a road sign for the viewing area and the Gov. Gallen Memorial. Follow the trail south for several minutes to reach the left end of the cliff. After a short wall you will come to a set of steps (if the snow isn't too deep) and the main cliff at Echo. The cliff is broken down into several sections.

Square Inch Wall: this is the first wall that you will come to on the trail. It is riddled with horizontal and vertical cracks (hence the name).

ROCK A BYE BILLY BOY 3

This is a seldom-formed runnel of ice 20 feet left of Hollow Hell. Climb a shallow right-facing corner up to and past a short, steep face to the top.

Jon Sykes & Bill Rzepa December 11, 1996

HOLLOW HELL 4

Hollow columns require rock gear for pro, with lots of hooking up this beauty. Another flow forms just to the right on occasion.

Jon Sykes, ope-solo January, 1994

SIDE STEPPING THE ISSUE 3+ 5.6

Just right of Hollow Hell is an ice-covered blocky slab leading to a steep face 15 feet up. At the base of the steep face traverse right with your hands in a horizontal crack until you come to a right-facing corner, mixed climb to top.

Jon Sykes & Brian Chartier February, 1995

MACK JAM 4

Climb detached columns through an overlap to steep sustained climbing above. A hard forty-footer.

FWA: Chris Marks and Jon Sykes January 29, 1998

ONE SWING AWAY 3+

This is the summer route avalanche. A rare thin drip that sometimes forms late season to make this a demanding lead. Good rock pro. At the first set of stairs climb a drip directly to the top. Rappel from trees.

Jon Sykes, rope-solo March, 1994

THREADING THE ALPINE NEEDLE 2+ 5.5

Start at the top of the first stairs. Climb up an easy gully and follow a wide crack to a ledge and white birch tree. Above finish up a crack, 5.5, through the center of the top overlap.

Jon Sykes, rope-solo January, 1994

TARDY BUT STILL FIRST 3 5.6

A rare mixed route forms on Skeletal Ribs (summer route), offering good protection and interesting, fun climbing.

Gareth Slattery, Mike Lee, & Jamie Cunningham January 30, 1999

SCOTTISH GULLY 3+ 5.4

Climb an iced gully to a small stance, then up thicker ice for thirty more feet to rock climbing above.

FWA: Jon Sykes, rope-solo December, 1993

FERRETT LEGGER 3+ 5.6

Thin ice climbing up bolt-protected slab with a vertical crack finish.

Jon Sykes, Chris Marks, & Gareth Stattery December, 1996

SACKLESS 3 5.7

Just past Cinch Sack is a right-facing corner leading to a rounded vertical crack system to the top.

Jon Sykes, rope-solo, winter, 1994

Fifty feet past the second set of stairs is the start of the next section; The Shield.

SPIRIT WITHIN 4 5.7

Climb thin ice on the face just right of the gully past trees to a large ledge 40 feet up. One can climb the gully as well. You are now under a large roof system. Step right on the ledge to a left-facing corner, climb it to a stance just right of the roofs, clip a bolt on a summer rock route (Ed's Weed Be Gone), and traverse right on a four- to six-inch ledge past another bolt on another rock route (Wesley's Aspiration); hard clip. Traverse

Eric Pospesil enjoying the sunny side of the street on Scottish Gully.
Jamie Cunningham

right until you reach steep ice leading to the top. Two rope rappel.
Jon Sykes January, 1994

LIP SERVICE 4 M7

The newest addition to Echo Crag, Lip Service has been attempted several times over the past few years. Chris Marks, with encouragement from "Team Bubba," finally pieced the puzzle together, creating the hardest mixed route to date in Franconia Notch. Start at the Spirit Within gully and, at the top of the gully, move up under the main roof and make a hard move to clip a bolt on an unnamed 5.10b rock route. With your remaining strength, pull through the hanging curtain and reach the top.

Chris Marks, Art Mooney, Jon Sykes, & Peter Ducette, December, 2000

ED'S WEED BE GONE TO SPIRIT WITHIN 4 5.6

Climb the vertical crack on Ed's and finish on Spirit Within.
Jon Sykes & Mike Lee December 10, 1996

WESLEY'S ASPIRATION 4+

Very thin technical ice and marginal pro make this a bold run for your money. Climb a runnel of ice up to a horizontal break, follow small columns (delicate) to an arch, then step right and climb the final ribbons of ice to the top and trees.
Jon Sykes & Chris Marks, January 29, 1996

CRUCIAL EVIDENCE 4

Look for a lone bolt on a slab. Tiptoe up 1/2-inch ice past the bolt to a horizontal crack and detached columns over an overlap. Pull over this (crux) to mixed climbing and the top.
FWA: Jon Sykes & Chuck Woodman February 20, 1996

SOCIAL EXPERIMENT 4+

Ten feet right of Crucial Evidence is the steeper and harder sister climb. A lone bolt protects the face start, then get natural gear through two overlaps and the face above. Rappel from trees.
FWA: Jon Sykes & Jamie Cunningham January 30, 1999

THE SHIELD 3+ 5.7

A ribbon of ice occasionally forms down this face. From a stance on top of two flakes, move up a 20-foot high buttress to a ledge below an overlap. Now step over the left side of the overlap into a thin vertical crack which splits the upper face. A final, small overlap leads to the top.
FWA: Jon Sykes, rope-solo January, 1994

Mr. Sykes at the office on new ground at Echo.
Jamie Cunningham

The Grunge Wall is the next section right of The Shield and is defined by its lower angle.

VAPORUB 3

This is the obvious, bushy ledge (stairway) system that separates The Shield from The Grunge Wall. Climb up thin ice to a thicker ice ribbon with some rock protection to trees.

Jon Sykes & Lois LaRock, January 22, 1996

CARPET PATH 3+ 5.6

 With good rock gear, the thin ice on this seldom-formed route makes this a real gem. Twenty feet right of Vaporub is a face with good horizontal edges/cracks throughout the climb. Ascend rock and ice straight up the face to a two-bolt belay.

FWA: Jon Sykes, rope-solo December, 1993

SWING EASY, CLIMB HARD 3+ 5.6R

 Fifteen feet right of Carpet Path is a mini-buttress with a left-facing inside corner. Start here with mixed climbing up this buttress to a stance, then step back right and up thin minimally-protected ice to fatter more protectable ice and the top. This climb forms every year and varies in condition.

Jon Sykes, rope-solo December, 1993

SLEEP IN THE DRY SPOT 3+ 5.6

This summer face climb on the right side of the wall sometimes ices up.

FWA: Chris Marks, winter, 1996

ALPINE GRUNGE 3+

Begin 30 feet to the right of Swing Easy, Climb Hard. Climb a small rib of ice, head straight for the top.

Jon Sykes & Chris Marks, January, 1995

AMPHITHEATER ICE 2-3+

 Continue right to this great practice area with 40-60 foot routes.

unknown

The Hermit Haven is the next area, which starts about 100 feet past The Amphitheater.

HELL BENT ON BIRCH 3+

Starting 10 feet left (north) of Syko's Pillars, climb the steep face up to a hanging birch at the top.

Jon Sykes & Chris Kratt March 13, 1998

SYKO'S PILLARS 4+

 Twenty feet left of Patella Swella Corner are two side-by-side freestanding pillars. Pins and natural pro are recommended.

Jon Sykes & Bill Keiler March 7, 1996

PSHYCHOTIC SATISFACTION (DIRECT FINISH) 4

This is the direct finish up a free-hanging pillar instead of the wandering line of Psychotic Reaction. There is also a bold direct start below the direct finish done by Chris Marks and Justin Melnick in the winter of 1999.

Jon Sykes, March 13, 1998

PSYCHOTIC REACTION 4 5.6R

Ten feet right of Syko's Pillars is a rock step to a corner leading up to a large ledge. Climb up to the ledge, step right past a pin to a right-facing corner (Patella Swella). Work your way up the corner ten feet, step right again into another right-facing corner and climb this to the top and the trees.

Jon Sykes & Tim Kemple, Sr., December, 1994

PATELLA SWELLA 3+/4

Follow the right-facing corner with thin pro and thinner ice to the top.

Chris Marks & Jon Sykes, February, 1995

SPANKING BILBO 4+

Five feet right of Patella Swella corner is a very steep thin runnel of ice going straight up. Mixed free moves at the start.

FA: Jon Sykes & Bill Keiler, March 7, 1996; FFA: Jon Sykes January 22, 1998

FINAL CONFRONTATION 4+

Climb a slightly overhung pillar system just five feet right of Spanking Bilbo. Very hard.

Jon Sykes & Chuck Woodman, February 20, 1996

THE HERMIT 4+

Rarely does this climb form fat ice. Delicate columns down low lead to fatter ice and the top.

Jon Sykes & Chris Kratt, March 13, 1998

EYE OPENER 5

This is a variation just right of the Hermit's second pillar. Rare to see it form in its original condition.

Will Gadd & Chris Marks, February 22, 1998

The Hone Wall is about 50 feet past Hermit Haven and is home to many excellent rock climbs; please minimize damage when when ice climbing.

ALPINE DIDDY 3+

Climb the mixed rock and ice ramp up and left to the upper wall and steeper more sustained ice. Many variations above. Two rope rappel.

Jon Sykes, rope-solo January 1994

THINSICLE 3+ R

Ten feet right of Alpine Diddy is a runnel that offers a vertical dance up thin to thicker ice with little protection to help the nerves.

Jon Sykes, rope-solo December, 1994

THANK GOD FOR TURF 3 5.6

Ten feet right of Thinsicle is a stepped wall leading to turf and more rock and ice above. Mixed climbing and tricky pro make you earn this seldom-formed route.

Jon Sykes, rope solo December, 1994

TOOTHLESS WONDER
4 5.7R

This is one of the bolder routes at Echo. Climb the steep, iced up ramp system leading to a prominent gully sixty feet up. There is a column of ice flowing out of the gully five feet long and one-foot thick. Tiptoe up this entering into the gully The climbing in the gully is awkward and scary with minimal pro. Bring a selection of pitons.

Jon Sykes & Bill Keiler, February 5, 1996 (Bill Keiler broke a tooth rappelling the route; hence the name)

Jon Sykes gnawing his way up the bold Toothless Wonder.
Jamie Cunningham

GOD, I LOVE THIS 4

Same start as for Toothless Wonder. Start up a ramp until you come to first columns, climb these to a stance and step left to more columns. These columns are much more delicate and hard to protect. Tiptoe your way up these detached columns for forty feet until the angle pitches back some (thin), then climb to one more column and the top. Rap from bolts.

FWA: Jon Sykes & Chris Marks, January 28, 1996

HURRY UP, I'M HUNGRY 4

Same start as for Toothless Wonder. Climb up the ramp to the first columns and follow columns straight up through a roof. One more column leads to the top, then rap off bolts.

FWA: Jon Sykes and Chris Marks, January 28, 1996

PRAYER GIRTH 4R

Starts just right of a big pine tree on a ledge. Climb thin to thicker ice for 60 feet until under a small overlap. Step left eight feet and surmount thin ice once again until under the final twenty-foot columns. Chug to the top and trees.

Jon Sykes & Bill Keiler, January 30, 1996

BONSAI GULLY 4R

Some thirty feet right of the pine tree is a runnel of ice that will humble even the hardest of the hard core. If you're lucky you'll even find two bolts from a summer rock route to clip (Ants in Your Lycra). Climb the runnel for sixty feet,

past the two bolts, until under the roof. Clip one more bolt (The Big Tweek) with a long sling and step left ten feet to the start of the gully. Climb up ten feet and step right onto a curtain of ice and climb it to the top and trees.
Jon Sykes, Bill Keiler & Chris Kratt, February 7, 1997

FEAR OF THE UNKNOWN   4R

Same start as for Bonsai Gully; climb the thin runnel for sixty feet to just under a roof. A ten-foot column of ice forms off the roof and barely touches down to create a very sustained climb from start to finish.
Jon Sykes & Bill Keiler, January 30, 1996

SWEET SECRETS 3+ 5.6

To the right of Fear of the Unknown is a small buttress—the climb starts at the bottom of it. Climb up the face with horizontal ledges and thin ice (rock pro), to a ledge with trees, forty feet up. A flow forms on the upper wall that is very enjoyable to climb. Rap from trees.
Jon Sykes & Bill Keiler, January, 1996

Dreamwall this is the next wall after The Hone Wall and the last wall at Echo.

THE ARETE 3+ 5.8

This is the prominent rounded arête on the left side of the Dreamwall. Climb the arête to the top and a two-bolt belay on left side of the arête.
FWA: Jon Sykes & Becky Smith, March, 1994

EAST SIDE: Profile Cliff

This is the dome of rock high above Echo Crag. Branch off the Echo Crag trail about 300 feet from the road (just before reaching Echo Crag) and hike uphill to the northern (left) end of the cliff. To date, one mixed climb has been done here. Traverse the base of the cliff and then turn up and to the right to reach the next route.

AZTEC WARRIOR II 3+ 5.6

Climb to the start of the ice and finish on an exposed dome at 5.6. Two rope rappel.
FWA Jon Sykes, rope-solo, February, 1997

EAST SIDE: Hound's Hump Ridge

This complex ridge wanders along the western flanks of Mt. Lafayette and is home to many winter routes. Greatly overshadowed by its famous neighbor across the street, most people never even knew the name of the formation until the publication of Jon Sykes' guidebook to Franconia Notch, *Secrets of the Notch*. For most of us this complex array of buttresses, gullies, and faces was just "all that stuff across from Cannon." In recent years this area has been developed steadily and now offers many fine alpine routes—great alternative to taking a number at the base of the Black Dike. Be prepared for complex approaches and descents, poorly packed trails, funky rock, and solitude. As with Echo, the area is spilt into a number of individual venues.

Eagle Crag Left

FLUSHOT II 4

To the left of the Eaglet Spire is a system of walls with one noteworthy climb, which can be seen from the Cannon Tram parking lot. Hike from the parking lot to the ice flow by walking a straight line into the base of the slabs and follow the trees separating the slabs until you are below the climb. Vertical columns hanging in space, attainable only by climbing a mushroomed stalagmite thirty feet to its top; continue by stemming against thin vertical ice to a small stance and the final curtain of ice. Rappel from trees.

Jon Sykes & Bill Keiler, March 3, 1996

DIGGING TO CHINA 3 5.6R

Just to the left of the Flatiron (the obvious buttress left of the Eaglet) is an indistinct gully named China Gully. In the summer, rock and debris constantly tumble down the gully but in winter it freezes to create a wonderful alpine climb. Approach by starting up the Greenleaf Trail on the east side of the road near the base of the Cannon Mountain Tramway and then branching up the Eaglet Trail. Hike up and left of the Flatiron to a distinct gully. Approach by wading up deep snow to a birch tree. The first pitch steps right onto a rock buttress where mixed climbing on rock, turf, and sometimes on ice will bring you to another tree belay. Move left to a steep ramp, then straight up to trees near the top. Rappel the route.

Jon Sykes and Mike Lee completed the ascent on January 10, 2001; an old, soft iron piton was found on the first pitch

Eagle Crag center

GARCIA-VEGA 4+

Looking from the highway up at the Eaglet you will see an ice flow a few hundred feet to the right (south) of the spire in a left-facing corner. Garcia-Vega occasionally forms here. Approach via the Eaglet trail and hike up past the Eaglet to the scree gully and head right to the start of the climb. Ascend delicate, thin, unprotected ice (crux) up a steep face for 80' and belay just left of the dihedral. The second pitch (140') climbs a chimney over a chockstone and finishes up lower-angled ice. To descend, hike up and left through the woods to the top of the scree gully and then back down to the Eaglet Trail. Rappelling is another good option. This is a serious route that rarely forms and has been called "the biggest sandbag in the whole book" (it used to be just grade 4).

Rainsford Rouner, Michael Hartrich & Peter Cole, January, 1975

FIRE AND ICE M6 4+

Climb the obvious chimney to the right of Garcia-Vega. This is an excellent, if scratchy affair, that benefits from rock gear (including pitons). Rappel.

FRA Charlie Lyon and Richard "Bubba" Parker, February 1979; Keith (Skeeter) and Alan Cattabriga also did an early ascent in the 1990's

The next climbs are found by hiking up to the right side of the Eaglet to a wall up and right of a prominent gully. Follow the wall south past Garcia-Vega and down around a buttress, up again, and hike up into a hidden amphitheater, with a few possible ice routes. In the middle of this amphitheater lies the main objective, a narrow chimney/dike with ice over one hundred feet high.

GRAVITATIONAL PULL 4 (mixed)

Climb very thin ice on a steep slab with some stemming for twenty feet until you come to a hanging curtain of ice flowing off an overlap. Natural gear and pins are recommended throughout the climb. Hook tools into the curtain, and pull up to more secure ice. Climb a thin, but fun, gully to trees and rappel with two ropes.

Jon Sykes & Gareth Slattery, December 2, 1995

A third class hike south up along broken walls brings one to a wonderful ice climb in a dramatic setting.

LATE NIGHT WITH YELLOW TOE II 3+

Climb the stepped gully with mixed pro to a lone hemlock. Rappel from the tree with two ropes.

FRA: Jon Sykes & Gareth Slattery December 3, 1995—Gareth followed the route in darkness and all that could be seen was the yellow toes of his plastic boots; this route was soloed by Tom Nonis in 1987/8 along with other climbs in this area

Access to these next five climbs is via the small slide down and to the left of Eagle Cliff. Ascend the slide until you meet a headwall, then traverse right a couple hundred feet to the climbs. There is an ice flow that starts at this headwall and follows an easy cleft for four pitches of fun grade II ice. Its history is unknown.

HEIGHTENED AWARENESS II 3+

This is the first climb you come to from the slide. A thin start can be avoided via a ramp on the right. Protection is found at the base of the final columns.

Jon Sykes, Gareth Slattery & Mike Lee, January 1, 1997

BURN STATION
II 3 5.6

Thirty feet right of Heightened Awareness is an

Gareth Slattery basking in the sun on Resolution Gully.
Jamie Cunningham

open amphitheater. Take the line of least resistance to the trees. Two rope rappel.

Jon Sykes & Steve Dupuis, February 1, 1998

RESOLUTION GULLY II 3+

This is a classic alpine route with grand views of Franconia Notch and fun, interesting climbing on a one-pitch flow. One hundred feet right of Heightened Awareness is a beautiful open gully with two starts. The right-hand start is unprotected for thirty feet. The left side has just a ten-foot, unprotected, thin start. The left side is the gully proper and the better of the two starts. Rappel from trees at the top.

Gareth Slattery, Jon Sykes & Mike Lee, January 1, 1997; left Start, Jon Sykes and Steve Dupuis, February 1, 1998

SLICE OF MEAT IN A ROCK SANDWICH II 4 R (mixed)

This is one of the most interesting climbs in Franconia Notch. Thirty feet right of Resolution Gully is a hidden cleft. An ice runnel forms on the right wall and leads to a mini amphitheater with one more wall with mixed climbing. Rap from trees at Resolution Gully with two ropes.

Jon Sykes & Mike Lee, January 8, 1997

EAST SIDE: Eagle Cliff

This is the huge green wall that you gawk at (and wonder about) when you're belaying on Cannon. And yes, there are lots of climbs here, mostly rock routes put up in the last ten years by Jon Sykes and company. One lone ice climb exists on Eagle Cliff, on the far left side. Access Eagle Cliff via Greenleaf Trail to Eagle Pass. Look for a trail on the left. If you come to the pass, you have gone too far.

EAGLE VISION 4 5.5R

Climb a blocky, loose rock gully on the left side of the cliff for 100 feet until you reach the base of a 50-foot pillar. Ascend the pillar to its top. There is a bolt and fixed wire nut for rappelling (two ropes).

Jon Sykes & Bill Keiler, January 31, 1996

LOST MIND 3 (mixed)

When you reach the cliff following the approach directions above, look up and you will see a nasty gully directly above. Ice only forms here after a rain and even then is never very thick. A mixed bag of tricks is required to safely climb this bowling alley.

Jon Sykes & Larry Boehmier, February 5, 2002

Several hundred yards north of the Big Slide, you will see an amphitheater with Ace of Spades and three other flows. Park at the climber parking lot on the southbound side of Franconia Notch Parkway (1-93) and hike the bike path under the highway to the eastern side of the Notch. Walk one hundred feet north from the underpass and look for a wooded gully leading to Ace of Spades. Hike about a half mile up the gully to an avalanche scar and the ice climbing. Routes will be described from right to left as one approaches the flows from the gully.

ACE OF SPADES 4

This is the best route here with an early season mixed start on the left and a more sustained direct variation via a pillar up the middle. Alternatively you can climb the original route up a steep first headwall to an ice cave, then move out right and up easier ice to the top. 150'

Rainsford & Tim Rouner, winter 1974-75

OVERBID 4+

 Occasionally just left of Ace of Spades, a 60-foot tall, free-standing pillar forms. This can be an arm pumping experience in thin conditions. The finish is the same as Trump Card.

FRA: Jose Abeyta & Dick Peterson December 14, 1980

TRUMP CARD 3

The start is ten feet left of Overbid up a ten-foot steep face. At the top of the face move up a ramp past trees to the top.

Rick Wilcox & Roger Martin, winter, 1976

SHORT TRICK 3

Fifty feet left (north) of Trump Card is another easy flow about 100 feet long with a twenty-foot headwall at the start and one final bulge at the top.

FWA: Jose Abeyta, Dick Peterson & John Dedenski, December 14, 1980

EAST SIDE: Big Slide

One of the more distinct features you will see on the eastern side of the notch is the huge avalanche scar just south of Ace of Spades. Big Slide has avalanched many times in the past one hundred years sending walls of mud, rocks, and trees onto the highway. The slide offers multi-pitch ice climbs from grade 2 to 4. This is a great area for teaching French technique. Warning: Do not climb in this area if avalanche anger is present in the White Mountains. The approach is the same as for Ace of Spades. Park at the climber parking lot and hike under the highway on the bike path. Walk south down the road a few hundred yards until below the slide. Hike in and take your pick.

SHORT STACK 4

This climb has one of the steeper approaches of any of the climbs in the Notch, and is a testament to the first ascentionists' determination. Follow the major slide path up and right to the highest ice flow one can see from the road. Climb a thin slab up to two 20-foot pillars, one on top of the other. A pumpy alpine gem.

Chuck Woodman & Tim Smith, February, 1995

EAST SIDE: Lafayette Ledges

WAIST DEEP AND A SNOWSHOE SHORT II 4R

This climb has the longest approach of any of the routes in the Notch. Don't forget the snowshoes. Park at the Lafayette Campground (accessible only southbound on Rt. 93; home to the trailhead for the Old Bridal Path and Falling

Waters trails). Hike about a mile on the Old Bridal Path and then bushwhack north to the base of the ledge. The climb starts on an iced-up slab (2) and climbs slabs for a hundred feet to four vertical tiers of ice. The first vertical section is the crux with thin ice, dry tooling, and no pro. The rest is fat ice to the top. Rap off trees to the right. The climb is over 200 feet long.

Jon Sykes & Mike Lee, January 29, 1997

FRANCONIA: LONESOME LAKE

Up above Lonesome Lake on the south shoulder of Cannon Mountain are many icy slabs and icicles. This climb ascends the most prominent line on the right or east side of this collection of short climbs. Park at the Lafayette Campground just south of Cannon. Approach the next climb by desperate bushwhacking up the hill from the packed trail at the east end of the lake. With luck, eventually you'll stumble upon this, or some other climb!

LEAP OF FAITH 3+

Scrape your way up an icy ramp for 40' to a good stance below a steep, right-facing corner. Climb the corner on good ice, and then make your way up steep but short headwalls to a belay in the bushes. Rappel the route with two ropes.

Chuck Woodman & Michael Kennedy, March, 1994

FRANCONIA: MT. GARFIELD

Mt. Garfield is the next major peak north of Mt. Lafayette and has several excellent climbs on its southwest face. The principle difficulty in winter climbing on Mt. Garfield is found in the approach, which involves a five mile hike, the difficulty of which depends entirely on trail conditions. The trailhead is reached by driving north from Cannon on Rt. 3 for about five miles to a road on the right just before the so-called "Five Corners" intersection (if you see the Trudeau Rd. on your left you have gone too far). Avoiding a right fork, follow the Gale River Loop Rd. south for 1.2 miles, then swing left and cross a bridge to parking on the right. Road conditions will vary depending on snowfall. Follow the Garfield Trail to a bushwack in to the flows.

THE BIG ONE II 5

The centerpiece flow on Mt. Garfield. Two pitches of hard ice climbing.

Bradley White & Jim Shimberg, winter 1987

POSTHOLE ALFONSO II 4+

Left of The Big One, up the slab to a belay ledge, then up the headwall.

Jim Shimberg & Bradley White, winter 1986

BAD DOG II 4

Climbs a flow at the far left end of the cliff.

Jim Shimberg & Bradley White, winter 1986

MAD DOG II 5

Flow to the right of The Big One.

Bradley White & Jim Shimberg, winter 1987

SICK PUP II 4+

Route description vague; it's in here somewhere, use your imagination.

Jim Shimberg & Bradley White, winter 1988

FRANCONIA: THE NUBBLE

THE NUBBLE FLOWS 3-4

This is the prominent shoulder on the north slope of North Twin in the Twin Mountain Range several miles east of Franconia. Approach as for Mount Garfield, pass the turn for that area, and then turn right at the "Five Corners." Stay straight and go as far as you can until a road leaves on the left (about 2.5 miles in), go left and keep looking up to the right. You should see the 200 foot cap of the Nubble and its flows. Bushwhack up to the routes. Allow at least an hour to approach the crag (more if the road isn't plowed; bring skis). There are two 130 foot routes here; a grade 3 and a 4. A trip to this crag demands an adventuresome spirit and the willingness to thrash around in the woods.

FRA Paul Cormier explored here in the early 90's

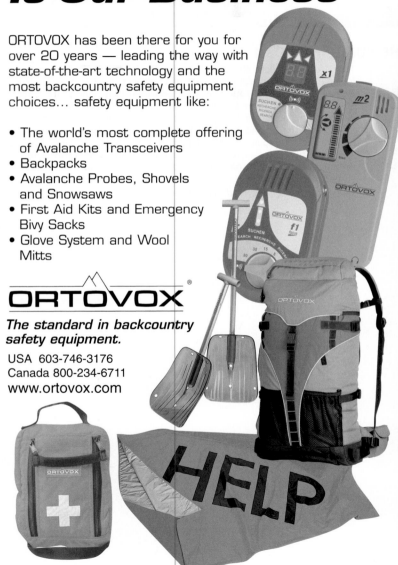

CENTRAL NEW HAMPSHIRE NOTCHES

There are several other ice climbing areas that are tucked away off the back roads of New Hampshire. Olivarian Notch, Kinsman Notch, and the Waterville Valley area are three such areas and because they don't fit in naturally with any of the other major climbing areas, we have decided to group them together here. Each area is just a short drive from the Town of Plymouth, NH and all offer secluded climbing way out in the woods.

Of the three areas, Kinsman Notch has the most ice, and as a result, gets the most traffic—but weekdays are still very quiet. A map of the area was logistically difficult, a state road map is all you'll need.

AREA HIGHLIGHTS

Location:	Olivarian Notch is on Rt. 25 about 18 miles northwest of Plymouth; Kinsman Notch is on Rt. 112 about 6 miles west of Lincoln; Waterville Valley is on Rt. 49 about 15 miles northeast of Plymouth
Routes:	Olivarian is home to two long moderate to hard routes on a big cliff; Kinsman is home to a number of short routes of all grades and has good toproping; the Waterville Valley routes are easy and very secluded
Access:	park below the crags, hike for 5-20 minutes (Olivarian and Kinsman), or an hour or more for Waterville
Descent:	hike down or rappel
Weather:	"Valley" (weather section), sheltered; December throuth March
Equipment:	a standard ice rack is fine
Superlatives:	quiet, high quality climbing; the Olivarian routes are real adventures; at Kinsman *Hanging by a Moment* provides extreme mixed fun and there are a host of moderates; the Waterville routes are far, far from the crowds
Amenities:	Lincoln and Plymouth, both off Rt. 93, have everything you'll need

CENTRAL NEW HAMPSHIRE: OLIVARIAN NOTCH

Olivarian Notch is located about 18 miles northwest of Plymouth, NH on Rt 25. From exit 26 off Rt. 93 take Rt. 25 west (lots of amenities in the first couple of miles) and go through W. Plymouth and Rumney (tiny villages). In W. Rumney (even smaller) Rt. 118 comes in from the left and joins Rt. 25. Continue on 25/118 for about three miles to the village of Wentworth (you guessed it, tiny). Here, Rt. 25A leaves on the left, but you continue on 25/118 for another three or four miles to the village of Warren (I guess they're all tiny). Here, Rt. 25C leaves to the left but, again, you stay on 25. In a mile Rt.118 will leave to the right; keep on 25 for another 4 or 5 miles to the notch and parking on the right near Olivarian Pond (not obvious). From the road head across a frozen swamp to reach the left side of the obvious cliff off in the forest. Owls Head is a large cliff with two rather obvious flows whose condition can usually be assessed from the road. While the cliff is in the National Forest, the land at its base is private so be considerate when climbing here. Descend off either side of the cliff (bushwhack) or it may be possible to rappel your route when finished.

SNAKE ATTACK III 4

Climb the large flow in the center of the cliff up and right to the trees. A 600 foot climb. The left end of the wall ices up but no additional information is available.

Chris Hassig, 1979

Adventure and solitude are virtually guaranteed on Owls Head's Snake Attack.
Brian Post (wildrays.com)

THE FEAR OF LIVING DANGEROUSLY II 4+

The left side of the cliff is characterized by two big flows. This route climbs the right-hand flow for four pitches. Very thin and delicate climbing is found throughout, with the crux being free-standing columns through overlaps on the second pitch. Bring rock gear.

Dougald McDonald & Carlton Schneider, January, 1986

CENTRAL NEW HAMPSHIRE: KINSMAN NOTCH

Kinsman Notch is located on Route 112 about five miles west of North Woodstock, NH. The climbing area is about a mile past the junction with Route 118, where a number of interesting climbs averaging 75'-90' high will be found on the south side of the road on the northeast side of Mt. Waternomee. Park on the east bound or downhill side of Route 112 near a yellow diamond-shaped road sign. Note: during snowstorms the Woodstock police department will tow your car if it interferes with snow plowing. The approach is obvious and takes about twenty minutes.

Kinsman Notch was a favorite haunt for a number of climbers living in the Plymouth area in the mid 1970's, some of them students at

Plymouth State College. Most of the routes in this area were climbed at that time by: Bob Pike, Ron Reynolds, Chris Hassig, Ted Hammond, Dave Karl, Mark Iber, George Lutz and others. Although lacking clear documentation, it is likely that most of the routes in this area were first ascended by members of this group. Climbs are listed approximately as you would approach them from the trail.

KILARNEY 2+

Forty yards west of Leprechaun's Lament is a one pitch flow consisting of low-angle ice bulges. Up the right-facing ramp for 50' to the top.

George Lutz & Tim Gotwols

POT 'O GOLD 4

Fifty yards right of Kilarney is a short climb which begins with a 50-foot vertical pillar.

George Lutz & Tim Gotwols

Short climbs of varying difficulty characterize the many routes at Kinsman Notch; the Pot 'O Gold area.
Brian Post

SHAMROCK   3+/4-

Start: 40 yards left of Pot Of Gold. Up the short (25') but steep first curtain and then follow ramp and hummocks to the top, 85 feet. This climb tends to ice in different each year—during good ice years there can be a steep second short wall at the top. Other years the right side of the upper ramp-like wall fills in making a nice variation.

Bob Pike & Ron Reynolds

HANGING BY A MOMENT 4 M6

Thirty feet left of the former route climb a narrow grade 4 pillar to a finger crack out a 15-foot overhanging headwall. This route has a very high pump-factor with a finish "hooking on packed dirt" according to local turf-master Brad White. Three pins help protect the crack; bring mid-sized cams as well.

Robert Adams & Eric Pospesil did the first recorded ascent of the lower pillar and finished left in the winter 99/00 naming it Irish Drool; Brad White and Jamal Lee-Elkin added the mixed crack in January 2002.

Contemplating the M5 finish and "packed dirt" of Hanging By a Moment.
Brian Post

LEPRECHAUN'S LAMENT 2+/3

Start 30 feet left of Hanging by a Moment. There are three variations possible on this flow, each about 70 feet high. The main route climbs the right side and the ramp directly up to the top. The second climb is up the first short ramp to the base of the ice curtain and straight up the curtain to the top, grade 3. The third climb follows the ice gully coming down from the left, grade 2.

Bob Pike & Ron Reynolds

Each season many minor ice columns and pillars form on the rocks between Leprechaun's Lament and Shamrock making for some entertaining mixed climbing. From Leprechaun's Lament, drop down over the rocks and follow a trail left (east) for 400 yards or so to a much larger and steeper flow. This is The Beast. In the older guide book this route was called "Luck O' the Irish." Traditionally that referred to the entire area, not any one route There are several climbs and variations in this area. Routes will be in relationship to The Beast.

COMPOSURE MAINTENANCE   4+/5-

Approximately 80 yards east of The Beast is a two pitch iced-up slab. The final bulge is the crux.

George Lutz & Tim Gotwols

THE BEAST 4+

Formerly called the Luck O' the Irish. Up the center of the main flow to the top of the headwall and belay, 100 ft. The second pitch goes up left to the upper ramp and the top, 65 ft.

Bob Pike & Ron Reynolds

WINDOW ROUTE 4+

A unique route requiring some "construction work." Up the left side of The Beast until you can get behind the main flow and belay in an alcove. Now climb the inside of the flow until you reach the top, then garden out a small window. Exit out the window and on to the main flow. Finish on the regular Beast route.

Tim Gotwols & George Lutz

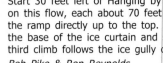

One of the main flows at Kinsman, The Beast provides two short pitches of dependable climbing.
Brian Post

RAMP ROUTE 3

Start down to the left of The Beast at the base of a yellowish colored ice curtain. The first short pitch is about 75 feet long and climbs the curtain to the base of a wide ramp leading up to the right. Pitch two climbs up the ramp for half a pitch to the top.

Ron Reynolds & Bob Pike

BLARNEY STONE 3

Approximately 60 yards left (east) of The Beast is a two pitch iced-up slab. The final bulge is the crux. Two additional grade 2/3 routes lie further left.

Bob Pike & Ron Reynolds

The following routes are located at the top of Kinsman Notch. Look for a pond with a talus slope rising up the slope from its far side.

HOLEY HELL 4-

At the top of this slope is a 50 to 70 foot ice flow. Park in the Kinsman Trail parking area. Follow the Beaver Brook trail for about 200 yards then turn right and follow the shoreline then the talus up to the flow.

Tim Gotwals & George Lutz , winter of 1980

BEAVER SCAT 4

Follow the Beaver Brook trail in a short distance then follow a drainage and line-of-sight to this grade 4 route with a short mixed start.

FRA Jon Sykes & Brian Whitfield, winter 99/00

STORE CRAZY II 4 5.7

About a mile west on Rt. 112 past the Beaver Brook Trailhead on the south side of the road is the Snake Skins Wall high up on the mountain. Look for a trail by a drainage. Store Crazy climbs the center mixed ice flow.

FRA Jon Sykes & Brian Whitfield, winter 99/00

CENTRAL NEW HAMPSHIRE: WATERVILLE VALLEY

Six or seven miles north of the Plymouth exit off Rt. 93 (exit 26), take Rt. 49 east toward the Waterville Valley ski area. Stay on Rt. 49 for about nine miles to the trailhead for the Sandwich Mountain and Drakes Brook trails on the right. Follow the Drakes Brook Trail (logging road) for .4 miles and continue straight where the trail goes right. Continue about 100 yards to the Fletcher Cascade Trail and follow this for 1.2 miles to a streambed. The trail follows the right side of the streambed steeply until you can see Fletcher Cascade.

FLETCHER CASCADE 2+

This is the obvious big flow and is reminiscent of Arethusa Falls on a smaller scale. The flow is about 50 feet wide with a forty foot headwall. There are many possibilities with easier options on the right.

Ron Reynolds & Boyd Allen, 1984

DIXIE CHICKEN 3

Up the largest of the pillars on the upper wall section of Fletcher Cascade.

Ron Reynolds & Boyd Allen ,1984

FELINE FLOW 2-3

Forty feet right of Fletcher Cascade is a 40-foot wide flow that varies in height and difficulty. Don't bother in a big snow year.

FRA Mike Arsenault & Anne Lepine, March 2, 1996

THE BAKER RIVER VALLEY

Short, steep, often mixed—that's Rumney. Ted Hammond on the first ascent of Reasons to be Cheerful.
Tim Gotwals

The Baker River Valley stretches northwest from Plymouth to Piermont, NH. Folks began ice climbing here in the early 1970's but the area remained off the beaten path until the 1990's, primarily due to the confusing approaches and a lack of published information on new routes. In the last decade or so, one of the areas, Rumney, has gained a reputation for being one of the nation's great sport climbing areas. With the increased popularity of the rock routes here, the ice climbs in the region have enjoyed more activity as well. With its south facing cliffs, the numerous small crags at Rumney are warmer than many of New Hampshire's other areas and it takes a prolonged cold snap for the routes to come in thick and stable. However, this also makes for some cool mixed stuff in the right conditions. The Newfound Lake area, south of Rumney, and overlooking the lake of the same name, faces east and is home to a number of thick, reliable climbs (as well as some more ephemeral stuff). Not as jammed as some of the areas to the north, Rumney and Newfound offer fun climbing in a quiet, relaxed atmosphere. Our special thanks go out to Jim Shimberg for helping us get all the information for this area right. Jim's enthusiasm and support were critical to our success and kept us smiling.

AREA HIGHLIGHTS

Location:	Newfound Lake is on West Shore Rd. about 12 miles southwest of Plymouth; the crags at Rumney are off the Buffalo Rd. about 8 miles west of Plymouth
Routes:	Newfound has a collection of moderate to hard routes on a cliff above a lake; Rumney has many short routes, often hard and thin
Access:	park below the crags, hike for 5-20 minutes
Descent:	hike down or rappel
Weather:	"Valley" (weather section), sheltered, often comparatively warm; January through early March
Equipment:	a standard ice rack is fine
Superlatives:	nice climbing away from the hotspots farther north; don't miss *Red Headwall* and *Duofold*; at Rumney look for the classics *Geographic Factor* and *Artificial Inteligence*
Amenities:	Plymouth has everything

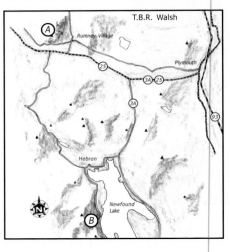

BAKER RIVER VALLEY

A. *Rumney*
B. *Newfound Lake*

Of all the areas in this guide, Rumney is perhaps the best example of climbers and land managers working together to protect the resource and the climbing experience. Thanks in great part to the Access Fund, Rumney will now be enjoyed by climbers for generations. Please climb responsibly here; and consider joining the Access Fund (accessfund.org)

your climbing future

BAKER RIVER VALLEY: NEWFOUND LAKE

Newfound Lake is located about eight miles southwest of Plymouth and is host to a number of reliable routes close to the road. From Route 93 take exit 26 onto Rt. 25 west. Follow Route 25 for about three miles and then turn south on Route 3A (traffic circle) and follow that road about four miles to the North Shore Road. Turn right and travel to Hebron Town Common. A general store will be on your right and Lake Shore Drive on your left (2.3 miles from the Rt 3A junction). Head left on West Shore Drive until the road meets the lake on the left (3 miles). The ice will be obvious on the right and there is a pulloff just before a "road narrows" sign.

The area is characterized by massive flows and very short approaches. Park wherever you can find room and approach the climbs up the scree. Descent for all routes is to the south (left) along the edge of the cliff and then down a wooded gully. Routes are listed left to right.

PILLAGE PILLAR 5

Left of Red Headwall climb out a cave to a free-hanging drip.

Jim Shimberg, solo, mid 1990's; J. Martin and Paul Boissonneault climbed a thin mixed route with a similar description here in 1996-97 calling it Thin Drip

RED HEADWALL 5

A headwall of steep pillars. Up the pillars to a slab leading to the top.

Chris Hassig, Brian Brodeur, 1977

GOOD KARMA ARETE 3+/4 (mixed)

Between Red Headwall and Bloodline is an aréte that is climbable after a heavy rain and freeze. There is a piton about 40 feet up.

Paul Boissonneault & Jay Martin, about 1986

BLOODLINE 3

Named for some developments in knuckle technique. It is 30 feet right of the Red Headwall. Climb up the apron to a corner. Exit the corner on the right and continue up ramps to a belay in the trees.

Ron Reynolds & Mark King, 1977

PIKE LINE 4

Right of Bloodline and 50 feet left of Duofold a small steep ribbon of ice drops out of rock slabs above. Climb the ice and rock above to the trees.

Tim Gotwals, Chris Hassig & Bob Pike, 1977

SLIM JIM 3+/4 5.6

Right of Pike Line, start near the road and climb a verglas slab to a short pillar and overlap. Bring rock gear.

Jim Shimberg, solo, January, 1990

DUOFOLD 3+/4-

One hundred feet from the right edge of the cliff, begin in a large corner with a headwall at its top. Climb ice leading left and up the headwall.

Bob Pike, Jim Cummings & Chris Hassig, 1977

NEWFOUND LAKE

A. Red Headwall
B. Good Karma Arete
C. Bloodline
D. Duofold

Brian Post

BAKER RIVER VALLEY: RUMNEY

This famous sport climbing area, home to hundreds of routes, is home to several good ice climbs as well and the potential for mixed climbing (especially with so many bolts nearby) is high. Seven miles west of Plymouth, N.H., on Route 25, turn right at the junction with Stinson Lake Road. Follow this for .6 miles to the center of Rumney village. From the town common, take the first left onto Buffalo Road and drive just under a mile to a parking area on the right; this is The Meadows. Although there are additional pullouts along the road climber's are urged to use the lot—you may be towed if you park along the narrow road and interfere with snow plowing. The climbing here, on the flanks of Rattlesnake Mountain, is complex with many short cliff bands scattered over the hillside. Even with the leaves off the trees it can be a hard place to navigate. Areas and routes will be described from right to left (approximately) beginning at The Meadows. Unless otherwise noted, you can easily walk off or rappel from all the climbs.

THE MEADOW FLOWS 2-4

This area combines easy access with a high concentration of short routes on a large group of pillars and bulges. From the parking lot walk back and slightly right (east) to the obvious cliff band—the Parking Lot Wall. The original line climbs the cleft in the center. This is a great area for toproping and ice bouldering and the descent is a straightforward walk-off.

John Rankin, Chris Hassig & Dave Foster, 1972

G3 GULLY 3

Eighty feet left of the main flow a small snow gully leads to an ice headwall. Belay in trees. Descend to the right.

Chris Hassig, John Rankin & Dave Foster, 1972

SCOTTISH GULLY 3

This is the obvious slab to the right of Centerfold. Highly Recommended.

unknown

CENTERFOLD 3+

Left of the center of the wall a steep ramp leads up the middle of a short face. Climb the wall to the trees (70'). Descend by rappel or downclimb left.

Chris Hassig & Dave Foster, 1972

SHAELYN'S WAY 5

This route climbs the corner just above the trail and just left of the obvious chimney. Climb a slab to a free-hanging icicle with bolts; cool. This and other routes in the immediate vicinity provide some great mixed climbing (thanks in part to to the nearby bolts).

Jim Shimberg & Jay Sterner, February 2002

GALAPAGOS 5

About 40 feet left of Centerfold locate the route Franky Lee on an obvious steep wall. Galapagos and Barbados form infrequently just to the right. Galapagos climbs very thin ice right of Barbados and loosely follows the rock route Red Sea Pedestrian. Bring nuts and thin pitons (you may also be able to clip bolts.

Jim Shimberg & Gary Heath, February, 1991

BARBADOS 5

Climbs the flow just right of Franky Lee following the sumer line Dead Sea Equestrian. Often thin (you may be able to clip bolts).

Bradley White & partner, 1987

FRANKY LEE 4+

Located 75 feet left of the Centerfold. A steep wall of pillars and hummocks provide some unique and sustained climbing (90'). Belay in trees. It is usually in questionable condition. It is best to rappel

Chris Hassig & Brian Brodeur, 1977

PRIVATE EYE 4+

Located about 200 meters left of the previous routes in the meadows. Take the left fork in the approach trail and head uphill for about 150 feet. Private Eye climbs a 40 foot sheet of ice. Rappel from a fixed anchor or walk off right. There is also a grade 2+/3 gully to the left of Private Eye, which is recommended (see below).

Jim Shimberg, solo, January, 1991

PARALLEL GULLY 3

Located in the gully that splits the Captain Fingers and Bad Seed sport climbing area left of the Parking Lot Wall. Left of Private Eye are two short gullies; the left usually harder than the right. There are several other gullies and smears in this area.

unknown, about 1980

The next climbs are located on the Orange Crush Cliff and the Main Cliff. From the parking lot walk west on Buffalo Rd. for several hundred feet to the next trail on the right. This trail heads uphill toward the right side of the main cliff. There is a gully that separates the two cliffs providing an easy means of descent. The Orange Crush Wall is on the right.

MANDIBLE 3+

This climb is located on the right side of the Orange Crush Wall. Climb a verglased slab to a short headwall of ice. Descend to the right.

Jim Shimberg, solo, Winter, 1992

JAWS PILLAR 5

A rarely formed route to the left of Mandible. Even when formed expect very hard and poorly protected climbing.

Bradley White & Tom Bowker, late 1980's

LEARNING DISABILITIES 4

This route is located on the right end of the main cliff, up and to the left of the previous route. It is 75 feet left of a 200 foot overhanging wall. Climb through the two headwalls to the trees. There is usually a fixed rope in the descent gully to the right. Highly recommended.

Chris Hassig & Bob Pike, 1976

VENEER 4

Located 50 feet left of Learning Disabilities, it is never more than 1 inch thick when it does come into shape. Climb the thin slab to a bulge and belay on a ledge. Climb the ramp to the headwall and belay in the trees. Descend as for Learning Disabilities.

Brian Brodeur & Chris Hassig, 1977

ARTIFICIAL INTELLIGENCE 5 M5

This route is located 80 feet left and downhill from Veneer, just before the ground begins to rise. It consists of a group of occasionally connected ice hummocks and runnels and provides an interesting mixed route. Climb up steep rock on mixed ground to the left end of a corner leading to a belay ledge on the edge of a prow. Climb the rock and ice above to the uppermost pillar on the headwall and the top. Descend as for Learning Disabilities.

Chris Hassig & Mark Iber, 1978; Jim Shimberg and Joel O'Connel climbed a harder, more direct start in 1994

The next four routes are located west of the Main Cliff where a large flow drops out of an enclosed gully. From the parking lot walk west on the Buffalo Rd. to the second trail on the right; the ice should be visible through the trees. Follow the easiest path straight up through the woods.

THE CAVE ROUTE 3

Climbs the ice inside the gully for 75 feet to the trees. Rappel.

Chris Hassig & Bob Pike, 1976

DANDRUFF 4-

This rarely formed route climbs verglas between The Cave Route and Selsun Blue. Rock gear needed. Descend as for the previous route. The creation of the rock route Dirtigo makes the route less scary than on the first ascent (you can clip bolts).

FRA: Jim Shimberg & Jim Hagan, February, 1989

SELSUN BLUE 4

This is the broad flow consisting of a series of steps just left of Dandruff. Descend left or rappel The Cave Route.

Bob Pike & Chris Hassig, 1976

Tom Coe at the start of a bad hair day on the steep start of Selsun Blue

Jim Shimberg

PSORIASIS 5

A separate icicle left of Selsun Blue which has only formed once.
Chris Hassig & Tim Gotwols, 1977

To access the next group of climbs, walk west up the road until just before it takes an obvious turn to the left. There will be a trail on the right that leads up through the Blackjack Boulders (you can't miss them). Continue straight ahead and then steeply uphill through scree and trees until you see a prominent hanging icicle (Fangmanship) This is the Triple Corners area. The first two routes are located several hundred feet to the right.

LONG BOARD 4+ 5.7

Formerly Hula Hoop. Above the Blackjack Boulders, head east (right) past the Fangmanship wall to the left end of a cliff called the Waimea Wall. At times there are three ice flows in this area. Hula Hoop climbs the left-hand flow and offers excellent, sustained mixed climbing. Bring thin pitons, rock gear and short screws. Some bolts low on the route may be available. Descend right.
Jim Shimberg & Mike Johnson, February, 1991

MOLAR 4

This route, formerly called Polar Pile, is located in the Triple Corners area above the Blackjack Boulders and between Long Board and Fangmanship. It climbs short, steep headwalls.
Chris Hassig

K-9 4

Two hundred feet right and uphill of Fangmanship there is a corner with an ice ribbon dropping down. Climb the ice ribbon (typically mixed ground) to trees and the top. The easiest descent is by rappel.
Chris Hassig & Bob Pike, 1977

REASONS TO BE CHEERFUL 5+

Left of Fangmanship climb the inside corner of the rock route of the same name.
Ted Hammond & Alan Cattabriga, 2001

LOG JAM 3

Climbs the rock route of the same name in the next corner left of the former route.
George Lutz & Tim Gotwols, 2001.

TWIT 5+

Climb the next corner left and then out onto the exposed pillar.
Ted Hammond & Alan Cattabriga, 2001

FANGMANSHIP 5

A route rarely in suitable shape. Climb the wide left-leaning ramp to a large platform at the base of the pillar. Climb the pillar slab above to trees (180 foot pitch). Walk off up and left to the northwest and down a gully. The headwall to the right of the normal route has also been climbed.
Chris Hassig & Bob Pike, 1978

THE DAGGER 4+

This route climbs the free-standing pillar left of Fangmanship.
Jim Shimberg & Jon Brown, 1999

ICE-OLATOR 4

This climb is located between K-9 and Fangmanship. Go up a snow ramp to a short headwall. Typically thin. Descend the woods on either side.
Ted Hammond, Dave Karl & Jed Collary, 1982

For the next collection of climbs, hike up and left from the bottom of the Triple Corners area. A steep gully will lead for a couple of hundred feet to the base of the next big cliff band. This is the Hinterlands area. The right side of this cliff is split by a gully. The first routes to be described here are located just left of the gully. To descend from these routes, either head down and to the right using the gully (difficult, there may be a fixed rope) or rappel with two ropes off large trees above The Geographic Factor.

THE GEOGRAPHIC FACTOR 5

This is Rumney's most spectacular ice climb. A series of steep, stacked pillars flowing out of an overhanging basaltic dike create unique, airy climbing conditions.
Brian Brodeur & Tim Gotwols, 1978.

PRESTOR JOHN 4

Immediately right of The Geographic Factor, ascend a steep series of steps to the trees.
Chris Hassig & Tim Gotwols, 1977

JOHN'S PILLAR 5-

Climb the rare column between Prestor John and Prestor Pillar.
Jim Shimberg & Joel O'Connell, winter, 1992

PRESTOR PILLAR 5-

This is the farthest route to the right. Climb the continuous pillar to a ledge just below the trees.
Tim Gotwols & Chris Hassig, 1977

Spilling out of a huge basalt dike, The Geographic Factor is one of the most consistent hard routes at Rumney
courtesey Dave Karl

The next three routes are found about a hundred yards farther west from The Geographic Factor. Traverse left passing three gullies to a final snow gully capped by an overhang and with an ice wall on its left.

DUSTBOWL 3+ 5.6

Climb frozen turf to a short, steep headwall and then up to the top.

FRA: Jim Shimberg & Pete Gamache, winter 1989.

SASQUATCH 5-

Start on the lower left side of the flow and diagonal up to and over the headwall; continue on slabs to the trees.

Bob Pike & Ron Reynolds, 1978

SOFFIT BREATH 4

Up the gully 50 feet to a ribbon of ice which flows down the corner of the gully. Climb ice to the trees just below the gully's top.

Chris Hassig, 1982

The following route is found high on the hillside near The Prudential.

VERY NICE ICE 4 M5

To find this route follow the trail that leads out west from the Black Jack Boulders to the Northwest Territories Cliff. Hike past the NWT and the Prudential Cliff. This route is found on the rock buttress that forms the left (west) side of the gully and climbs a pillar and then a rock corner left of the rock climb Very Nice Crack. Bring rock gear.

Brady Libby & Ted Hammond, February, 2001

This last area us right off the road west of the 5.8 Crag.

THE JOBSITE 3-4

Three small flows sometimes form on a small roadside crag located one half mile west of the Black Jack Boulders area. There is a short grade 3 flow on the left, a grade 4 to its right that climbs up to a ramp/shelf and then launches up a short headwall, and then the namesake route of the area (and most consistently formed) that climbs an aesthetic pillar on the right.

Ted Hammond & Brady Libby, February 2001

KANCAMAGUS HIGHWAY

Where there's a will, there's a Way in the Wilderness. Bernard Mailhot on this Kancamagus classic.
Jean-Pierre Danvoye

Stretching west to east from Lincoln to Conway New Hampshire, the scenic Kancamagus Highway contains a variety of secluded, high quality ice climbing areas. Ranging from the moderate Rainbow Slabs, to backcountry classics like Way in the Wilderness and On the Drool of the Beast, to the quiet beauty of Champney Falls (at least mid-week), "The Kanc" has something for everyone. Since many of the climbs here don't get the volume of traffic that the more popular areas do, climbs along the Kancamagus typically involve some bushwhacking on skis or snowshoes on the approaches. But the solitude and beauty found here make all the effort worthwhile. Please note: there are no services of any kind between Lincoln and Conway (32 miles). The information here is just a start and many other cool routes are waiting to be discovered in this scenic area. Climbing areas will be described from west (Lincoln) to east (Conway).

AREA HIGHLIGHTS

Location:	The "Kanc" stretches west to east for 32 miles from Lincoln to Conway and is one of the most scenic drives in the White Mountains
Routes:	Everything from short toprope areas to classic backcountry hard routes scattered among a bunch of crags
Access:	park below the crags, hike for 10 minutes to over an hour depending on the area
Descent:	usually hike down but be prepared to rappel at some crags
Weather:	"Valley" (weather section), typically sheltered; late December through late March
Equipment:	a standard ice rack is fine; exceptions noted
Superlatives:	great toproping at *Champney Falls*; *Way in the Wilderness* and *On the Drool of the Beast* are backcountry classics; *Rainbow Slabs* offer wonderful easy routes and *The Mongul* is an extreme mixed route
Amenities:	Lincoln (west) and Conway (east) have everything

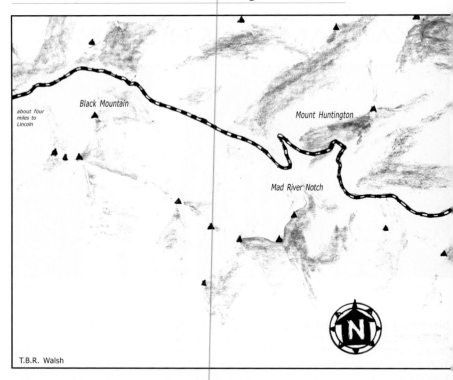

about four
miles to
Lincoln

Black Mountain

Mount Huntington

Mad River Notch

T.B.R. Walsh

THE KANC: BLACK MOUNTAIN

LONG WAY HOME III 2-3

The center of the three gentle, broad ice flows on Black Mountain opposite the Wilderness Trail trailhead. About two miles east of the Loon Mountain ski area and just 5 miles from Lincoln, park as for the Wilderness Trail and bushwhack south to the flows. After a two to three mile approach, climb six to eight pitches of enjoyable, low-angled ice.

Brad White & Doug C. Burnell, February, 1978

THE KANC: MAD RIVER NOTCH

This dramatic cleft in the hills east of Lincoln on the Kanc is home to several spectacular backcountry routes. From Lincoln head east for about 11 miles to the Greeley Ponds Trail parking area on the right (if you go around the obvious hairpin turn you've gone a half mile too far). Hike or ski in the trail heading southeast for about 1.5 miles to the climbs.

KANCAMAGUS HIGHWAY CLIMBING AREAS

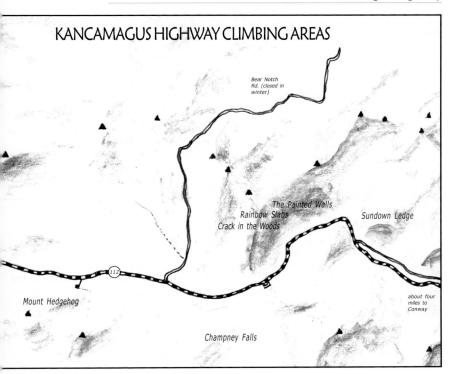

Bear Notch Rd. (closed in winter)

The Painted Walls
Rainbow Slabs
Crack in the Woods

Sundown Ledge

112

Mount Hedgehog

about four miles to Conway

Champney Falls

ON THE DROOL OF THE BEAST
II 5-

This dramatic ice-choked chimney will be found on a cliff on the flanks of Mt. Osceola. Follow the Greeley Ponds trail (or the ski trail that starts below it) for about a mile until the trail begins to climb steeply. As you near the top of the steep section you will see the cliff up and right. The climb will be obvious.

Kurt Winkler & George Hurley, January, 1982

AYE KARUMBA M5 4+

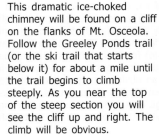

This severe one pitch route is located to the right of Drool.

Jim Shimberg, Ted Hammond & Dave Rioux, 1997

Catching some Drool in Mad River Notch
Joe Klementovich

The following two climbs are located on the far left end of the Drool of the Beast cliff.

BEAUTY AND THE BEAST 3+

Start in a right-facing corner and climb a narrow flow to a short headwall.

Ken Grinnell & Brad White, February 21, 1997

THE BEAST WITHIN 4-

Start twenty feet right of Beauty and the Beast and climb stacked pillars to an awkward step left around a block to the final 20' headwall.

Brad White and Ken Grinnell, February 21, 1997

THE KANC: MT. HUNTINGTON

SHEER ELEGANCE II 4+ 5.6

This climb is located on the very obvious wall facing the Kancamagus on the southeast face of the lower summit of Mt. Huntington. Park at the Pemi Overlook parking area just west of the height-of-land at Kancamagus Pass (and just east of the hairpin turn) and walk straight in to the cliff. Begin in the middle of the cliff in a right-facing corner. The first pitch is mixed, up a column to an overhang, escape right on rock, then back left to ice, then up the gully to belay on left. Then follow the gully up and right to thin ice and the top. On the first ascent protection was so bad on the second pitch that there was groundfall potential from 200 feet up!

Brad White, Todd Swain & Jack Wenzel, January, 1985

THE KANC: MT. HEDGEHOG

CHOCKSTONE CHIMLEY 3 5.6

Named for a speech impediment, this is a one hundred foot mixed route in Helms Deep Gully on the south face of Mt. Hedgehog. The description is old and the area is fairly complex (lots of cliff bands) so consider a trip into this area to be an adventure where actually finding the climb will be a bonus. Drive 14.5 west of Conway to the trailhead for the UNH Trail. Follow the trail (take the left fork just a few hundred yards in) for 2 1/2 miles to the first open ledges. In a gully to the east of the summit ledges, about a hundred feet further along past the open ledge, is an obvious steep-walled gully descending into the woods; scramble down this then climb a steep slab to a chockstone in a chimney, bypass it on the left to a ledge with a small tree, and rock climb up a corner (5.6) to the finish. Combined with other routes on the same cliff this is potentially a worthwhile undertaking.

Todd Swain, January 8, 1981

THE KANC: CHAMPNEY FALLS

Formerly called "Pitcher Falls," this dramatic chasm has become one of the most popular toprope practice areas in the White Mountains. If you plan on heading in here on a weekend day you can expect crowds so consider yourself forewarned. The area can comfortably keep about a dozen climbers occupied as long as everyone is polite and considerate. Often there is a spider's web of ropes hanging down and sharing ropes is common—use good judgment. And if you see lots of cars in the parking lot, consider going somewhere else. The trailhead is on the south side of the Kancamagus Highway 10.8 miles west of Conway. The 1.5 mile approach hike (40 minutes) is pleasant and usually well-packed. When you reach the area of the falls take the spur trail to the left into the obvious chasm (this is likely to be the most well-packed trail). While some of the routes can be led (in particular, the main flow in the back) most people toprope here from trees. Take care when scrambling above the cliff to set up anchors.

CHAMPNEY FALLS
3-5 M5-8

Champney Falls; left side of the main wall.
Brian Post

Along the right wall of the chasm, in the back, is usually a big blue flow (3+) that makes for the best moderate lead here. To its left are a series of candled curtains that offer a good grade 5 workout. To the right of the main flow is a steep wall and a two-tiered grade 5, then a steep face usually covered in yellow ice with more grade 3-4+ topropes. To the right of this are a lot of sick little drips in the M5-M8 range that are fun to play on (more fun with a rope from above) including at least one tiny pencil on the far right. Some of this stuff has been led. An interesting two pitch girdle traverse is also possible at about grade 4.

FA: George Hurley, Bradley and Philip Platt climbed the main flow on December 30, 1979. Hurley returned on February 3, 1980, and climbed an upper section (Grade 1) with Chap Fischera, Jim Saybo, and Bill Zelop. Peter Yost and Jim Graham did the girdle traverse on February 24, 1983, and John Tremblay and Joe Lentini visited the area in the mid 1980's and led some extremely steep and thin climbs and others followed in the 90's.

CHAMPIN' AT THE BIT M8+

On the left wall of the corridor a series of horizontal cracks and dubious drips lead up vertical rock. A testament to the skill of the late Alex Lowe who blew in one year for an ice festival and proceeded to open everyone's eyes. Lowe did another hard mixed route just to the right of this one.

Alex Lowe, February 1995

CRANKIN' IN COTTON M5+

This is the very distinct groove to the left of the former route. Long before

anyone knew you could dry tool stuff like this, Jerry just did it.
Jerry Handren, late 1980's

THE KANC: CRACK IN THE WOODS

This hidden cliff is a favorite getaway for rock climbers and has a couple of worthwhile ice routes as well. It is located in the woods just west of Rainbow Slabs. Park at a pullout 7.7 miles west of Conway, cross the Swift River, turn right on the Nanamocomuck Ski Trail for a short distance, and then turn left and head up into the woods for about fifteen minutes to reach the crag.

COLUMN IN THE WOODS 4
Left of the obvious corner is a steep icefall. Rappel the route.
Kurt Winkler & Chris Hassig, March 4, 1982

BOSSANOVA 3
The next ice flow to the left. Rappel the route or descend left.
Chris Hassig, solo, March 4, 1982

ANGELS DON'T SHATTER 3
Left of Bossanova is a thin ice wave. Descend left.
Kurt Winkler, solo, March 4, 1982

THE KANC: RAINBOW SLABS

RAINBOW SLABS 2-3 (3+ 5.4 A0)

This sunny practice area offers many possibilities for beginning and intermediate ice climbers. The slabs are easily seen from the road as a wide, rectangular cliff band and are usually covered with blue ice. Many flows will be found here giving one to three pitches of forty to sixty degree ice. To descend, rappel off trees with two ropes. Just west of the parking lot for Lower Falls the Rainbow Slabs are visible across the river from a convenient roadside turnoff (7.3 miles west of Conway). Cross the Swift River, turn right for a short distance along the Nanamocomuck Ski Trail, then angle left on overgrown logging roads to the base of the cliff. In addition to the main face, there are a few more short, moderate ice flows on the slabs between Rainbow Slabs and The Painted Walls. A right to left girdle traverse has been completed to the central flow (II 3+ 5.4 A0).
unknown; Kurt Winkler, Shraddha Howard and Drubha Hein climbed the girdle traverse in February 1992.

THE KANC: PAINTED WALLS

High above and to the right of Rainbow Slabs is a striking cliff lined with vertical stripes, The Painted Walls. Park as for Rainbow Slabs. On the left side of the cliff is a distinct dihedral that in a good season will be choked full of ice. The approach is a long uphill bushwhack,

Kurt Winkler inundated on Way in the Wilderness. The climb can get quite drippy on a bright day.
Charles White

but fortunately the condition of the route can usually be determined from the road.

WAY IN THE WILDERNESS II 5

One of the most beautiful climbs in the White Mountains. Park at the Lower Falls parking lot. Cross the Swift River and head up a very steep hill to an amphitheater at the climb's base. Because of its south-facing location, the route needs optimum conditions to form and there is a constant danger from falling ice. Ascend a series of vertical sections on occasionally candled ice to a secure rock belay on the left with fixed anchors. Step out onto a steep pillar, climb into a V-groove, and finish up the final lower-angled gully. Rappel the route with two ropes, or walk around the cliff to the left end.

Jim Dunn, Michael Hartrich & Peter Cole, February, 1978

LEFT OF THE WILDERNESS 4

Between Way in the Wilderness and Stormy Monday is a 40 foot slab that leads to a 25 foot pillar. The route is reported to be excellent.

FRA Brad White, mid 1980's

STORMY MONDAY 4 5.7

This route climbs an inside corner 300 feet left of Way in the Wilderness via lots of "rock, turf, thin ice, and one section of good ice" according to first ascensionist George Hurley. The second pitch is very short. Rappel.

George Hurley, Ed Ewald & John Cederholm, February 8, 1997

THE KANC: SUNDOWN LEDGE

The next bunch of routes are found in the vicinity of Sundown Ledge, a big rambling series of crags on the north side of the Kancamagus highway near the Albany Covered Bridge. Good practice climbs, some obscure stuff in the woods, and a pair of hard mixed climbs on Sundown's Main Cliff will be found here.

THE COVERED BRIDGE ICE FLOWS 3-5

A convenient practice area right next to the road as well as some harder options on neighboring crags make this area attractive. Drive the Kancamagus Highway west from Conway for 6.4 miles to the covered bridge. Park at the bridge, walk through it, hike east on the Dugway Rd. for about 200 feet, then turn left onto the Boulder Loop Trail. You'll soon see a few ice flows on your left off in the woods. These offer good bouldering and toprope problems.

unknown

Mark Synnott on what he considers his best creation in the region, The Mongol.
Courtesy Mark Synnott

THE MONGOL M7

This awesome route, called by first ascentionist Mark Synnott "the best mixed route I've ever done in the Mount Washington Valley" is located on the Main Cliff at Sundown. Follow the directions for the Covered Bridge Ice Flows and continue on the Boulder Loop Trail for 5-10 minutes (depending on snow pack) to a trail junction with a sign that says "Ledges" and points left. Continue to the right for a couple of hundred feet to a sharp turn in the trail and a drainage. In another 100 feet turn left and climb up through the talus (you're in the right spot if you climb past a huge boulder just at the base of the talus) to the cliff. Head right for about 100' to the old climb Grave Digger (just right of the sport climb Romper Room). Climb an overhanging groove to a roof and reach up to a hanging icicle. "The hanging icicle at the top was full on M7 with small TCU's tucked under the roof for pro," said Synnott. With work, the climb protects well. Lower from slings above the roof.

Bob Parrott climbed partway up the route in 1986 with Bill Holland; Mark Synnott and Eric Siefer completed the line in February 2000

PIMPSICKLE M6

Just to the right of the Mongol climb overhanging mixed ground to reach ice and then continue into a moderate ice gully.

Eric Siefer and Kevin Mahoney, 2002

The next routes are found on the other side of the Kancamagus Highway on a prominent hill about 4/10ths of a mile east of the covered cridge.

WINTERLUDE II 3+

From the covered bridge, walk back towards Conway on Route 112 (the Kancamagus Highway) for .4 miles or so and you will see a flash of blue in the trees to the south. Cross a small stream and walk uphill 200 yards to a small crag. Winterlude is the most prominent flow on the crag, ascending the 100 ft. high cliff near the left hand end.

Kurt Winkler & Joe Perez, February 22, 1979

ICE CAPADES 3

Approximately 75 feet left of Winterlude, go up an ice ramp to a tree, then climb up and left in a mixed groove to a ledge and continue to woods.

Todd Swain & Jim Frangos, January 17, 1983

QUALUDE (IT'S WORTH THE TRIP) 5

About 300 feet right of Winterlude look for an easy icy groove heading up and left which is climbed to a ledge. The second pitch climbs verglass to the woods. Descend by rappel.

Todd Swain & Jim Frangos, January 17, 1983

ICE FALLIES 4

Further to the right is another poorly protected route that begins up a short corner and finishes up a short, steep column to a slab.

Todd Swain & Jim Frangos, January 17, 1983

SACO RIVER VALLEY

The Saco River Valley is one of the most scenic areas in New Hampshire. In the twenty-five miles from its head at the top of Crawford Notch the Saco River changes character from a rushing brook spilling over boulders in the narrow notch, to a wide, gentle stream that meanders through the farmland underneath the cliffs of North Conway. Years ago, to boost tourism in the area, the local chamber of commerce adapted the designation of Mt Washington Valley for this area and unfortunately it stuck. For this guidebook, however, we will return to the more appropriate designation of Saco River Valley.

Some of the best known, and hardest ice climbing in New England is found in the lower stretches of this valley on Cathedral and Whitehorse Ledges. Streaked each winter with ice, these dramatic granite cliffs are an unforgettable sight. Short approaches, the relative lack of objective danger, and generally more hospitable weather only add to the attraction of this popular ice climbing area.

Considering the equipment, Bryan Becker shows great poise on the crux pillar during an early ascent of one of the regions's finest routes, Remission.
Ed Webster

Running north from these major cliffs, Route 302 parallels the Saco River, and good ice climbing is to be found all along this beautiful valley. Areas in this section will be described from south to north.

The town of North Conway, with its many amenities, is a convenient center only a few miles from Cathedral and Whitehorse. Lodging, food and drink, bargains at the factory outlet stores on the infamous strip and the latest information on climbing conditions are all readily available. Three major climbing retailers: International Mountain Equipment (IME), Eastern Mountain Sports (these two across the street from each other at the north end of the village), and Ragged Mountain Equipment (three miles north on Rt. 16), offer full lines of gear and route information. Routes in the Saco River Valley will be described from south to north, beginning with three easy climbs on the flanks of Middle and South Moat Mountains, just south of Whitehorse Ledge.

Winter ascents of summer rock routes in this section are noted for historical value only. First winter ascents of rock routes are designated FWA. Accurate route descriptions can be found in the rock climbing guides to the area.

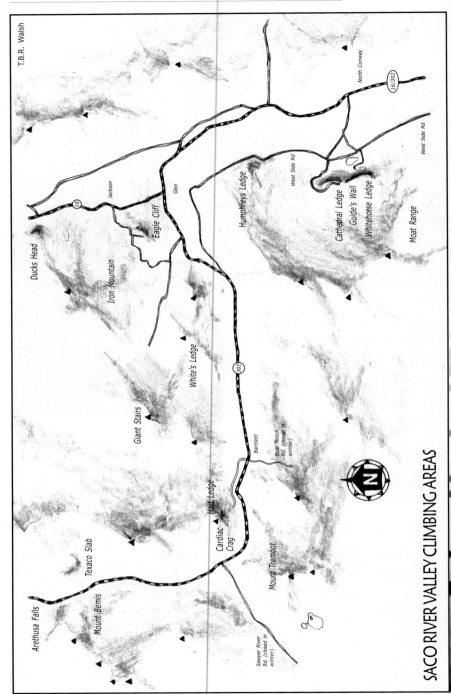

T.B.R. Walsh

North Conway

16/302

West Side Rd

West Side Rd

Jackson

16

Glen

Humphreys Ledge

Cathedral Ledge

Guide's Wall

Whitehorse Ledge

Moat Range

Ducks Head

Eagle Cliff

Iron Mountain

White's Ledge

302

Bartlett

Bear Notch Rd. (closed in winter)

Giant Stairs

Matt Ledge

Cardiac Crag

Mount Tremont

Texaco Slab

Mount Bemis

Arethusa Falls

Sawyer River Rd. (closed in winter)

N

SACO RIVER VALLEY CLIMBING AREAS

SACO RIVER VALLEY: MOAT RANGE

RED EAGLE BROOK ICE FALL II 1

This brook starts high on the east side of South Moat Mountain and provides a longer and easier climb than Willey's Slide in Crawford Notch. It is a place for a beginner to practice French technique in absolute privacy. Trees beside the brook provide all needed belays. Even a few inches of snow will obscure the ice. From the north edge of the gravel pit on High Street (off the Passaconaway Road, also called the Dugway Road), follow a logging road west to Red Eagle Brook (1 mile); the road ends at the brook. Follow the brook upstream to the ice fall. The approach takes about a half an hour from the gravel pit.

George Hurley & John Bickford, February 9, 1980

MOAT MOUNTAIN ICE FALL II 2

This climb is about 300 feet of easy to moderate ice. The ice fall is on the east side of Middle Moat Mountain and can be seen from the center of North Conway. To reach the climb, drive south on West Side Road to the Passaconaway (or Dugway) Road; then west until near the Conway/Albany town line; turn north on High Street to the end of the road. "End of the road" may be at the end of the plowed and inhabited part of High Street, or at a Forest Service barrier (.2 miles farther) just east of a gravel pit, or .8 miles farther at the actual road end. From an old clearcut logged area where the road ends, bushwhack northwest to a stream bed. Follow this west to the ice fall. With good conditions the walk takes about 30 minutes from the clearcut to the ice fall. If you must walk the maximum distance the approach would take about an hour. If there is deep snow, don't bother with this route.

George Hurley & Chris McElheny, December 17, 1979

HANCOCK FALLS 1

This ice fall is in a hidden basin midway between the summits of Birch Hill and Middle Moat Mt. on the stream which starts just east of the top of Middle Moat Mt. The easiest approach is by skis from Ledge View Dr. in the N.W. end of the Birch Hill housing development off West Side Road a mile south of Whitehorse Ledge. Snowmobiles usually pack out the trail to within about one hundred yards of the falls.

George & Jean Hurley, January 22, 1982

AREA HIGHLIGHTS

Location:	This area stretches for 15 miles from North Conway to Bartlett at the bottom of Crawford Notch
Routes:	Many areas: toproping, classic hard routes, multi-pitch aid and ice routes, new mixed routes
Access:	Parking is always close; most approaches under 20 minutes
Descent:	Usually hike down but be prepared to rappel at some crags
Weather:	"Valley" (weather section), late December through late March
Equipment:	A standard ice rack is fine for most routes; exceptions noted
Superlatives:	Great practice and long classics on Whitehorse and Cathedral (*Myth of Sisyphus, Repentence, Remission, Mordor Wall*); thin classics at Duck's Head and Eagle Cliff (*Cold, Cold World, Eagle's Gift*)
Amenities:	North Conway and Bartlett have everything

SACO RIVER VALLEY: WHITEHORSE LEDGE

The varying terrain characteristic of Whitehorse Ledge offers the climber two types of winter climbing. The east facing slabs occasionally ice up enough in the middle and upper sections to give a long and fairly committing mixed route. Poor protection and wind slab avalanche conditions add to these routes a degree of seriousness which other areas such as Willey's Slide usually lack. Slab avalanches of three to four feet thick are not at all uncommon during heavy snow years.

The South Buttress of Whitehorse presents an entirely different profile. Here steep rock faces up to 500 feet high infrequently ice up to form ice routes of 3-4 pitches in length. These routes are only possible after prolonged spells of subzero weather and on cloudy, cold days. A sunny day in February with temps in the 30's is a really bad time to be climbing here. Climbs are described right to left beginning with the slabs.

To get to Whitehorse turn west on River Rd. at a traffic light one block north of International Mountain Equipment in North Conway. Follow the road over the Saco River to a left turn onto the West Side Rd. About a mile down this road turn right at a sign for the White Mountain Hotel and follow signs to the hotel's lower parking lot. DO NOT park in the hotel's upper lot. The folks here are very friendly toward climbers but they ask us not to clog up their upper lot. Hike to the upper lot and take a trail from the northwest corner to the base of the cliff. All the routes from the slabs left are best accessed by thrashing along the base of the cliff with the exception of The Myth of Sisyphus. For that route follow a trail to the south that parallels the cliff just beyond the parking lot for the hotel. This trail will follow the cliff all the way to its left-hand end and then turn sharply right and uphill to reach the base of the cliff just 50 feet left of the start of The Myth of Sisyphus.

BEGINNER'S ROUTE II 2-3 R

A poorly protected, snow-covered rock climb, that climbs straight up about a hundred feet left of the right-hand margin of the slabs. Summer belays are all from bolts, but don't count on finding them.

FWA: unknown

STANDARD ROUTE III 3-4 R

A classic mixed route and probably the best climb on the slabs in winter. Follow the thinly iced and snow-covered slabs up to the arch, and climb this to Lunch Ledge. Then climb any of the several ice flows through the final overlaps depending on which one is in condition. Some aid may be necessary here.

FWA: David Bernays & Andrew Griscom, February 7, 1954

SLABS DIRECT III 4 R

A poorly protected mixed route in the center of the slabs. Climbs two pitches up Whitehorse Slabs Direct (the summer route between Standard and Beginner's) to the Standard Route Arch. Climb over the arch on steep verglased slabs and connect with a prominent blue ice flow on the final dike of Sliding Board. Climb a short vertical pillar to the upper slabs.

Ed Webster and Butch Constantine made the direct route over the arch in March, 1982; the start and upper pillar had been climbed before

SLIDING BOARD III 4 5.7 R

Another difficult and poorly protected mixed route. Climb to the base of the arch and then follow the summer route, paralleling the arch for two pitches to an obvious left facing corner, then straight up to the final headwall.

FWA: Jeff Pheasant, 1978

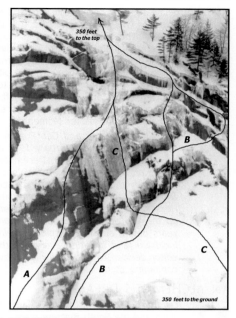

WHITEHORSE SLABS

A. *Sliding Board*
B. *Standard Route (with possible variations)*
C. *Slabs Direct*

WEDGE III 4 5.6 R

In the same category as Sliding Board. Wait for thick conditions. Ascends the smooth face left of Sliding Board eventually traversing left on a tree ledge to the final upper slabs.

FWA: unknown

MOMENTO III 5.4 R 3-4

This route shares some terrain with Dreams of Regurgitating White Horses . About 50 feet right of the two dikes mentioned in the description below, climb the smooth slabs of Sea of Holes for two pitches (good snow on the first ascent; may be scratchy rock) and then angle over to the tree island. Traverse left to trees just before the big corner system (Mistaken Identity). Continue up the corner to a grade 4 slab and then climb a steep bulge to a belay beneath the left end of a big, right-facing roof. Step left through a weakness (good rock gear) and continue up a diagonaling, left-facing corner. Easy climbing leads to a large amphitheater; take any of several grade 3-4 lines to the upper slabs and several hundred feet of easy climbing. Descend by hiking north and then down the Bryce Path between Whitehorse and Cathedral Ledges.

Dave & Dee Dee Kelly, March 1999

DREAMS OF REGURGITATING WHITE HORSES III 4 5.6 R

This fun, full-length climb and its neighbor above wander up the junction between the Whitehorse Slabs and the South Buttress. About 200 feet from the left edge of the slabs (the obvious groove of Mistaken Identity clearly delineates this), climb the left-hand of two dikes for two long pitches to a tree island (5.6 R). The next pitch works its way left to Mistaken Identity. The 4th pitch climbs up and left to a big right-facing corner below an obvious ice flow. The 5th pitch climbs the huge right-facing corner to a step left (crux) and trees. Finish left and up the final pitches of An Alchemist's Dream. Descend as for Momento.

FRA Steve Weitzler and Gen Popien climbed the route in February 1982 and called it Regurgitation. On December 15, 1995 Kurt Winkler and Marty Wolons did what they thought was the first ascent and called the route Dreams of White Horses. Research for this edition turned up the Weitzler & Popien ascent many years before and in the spirit of being inclusive (and irritating everyone) the editor decided to ruin both names by combining them.

ALCHEMIST'S DREAM AREA

A. Alchemist's Dream
B. Dreams of Regurgitating White Horses
C. Momento
D. Whitehorse Slabs (top)

AN ALCHEMIST'S DREAM III 4

On the right of The Ceiling, a large horizontal roof seen just left of where the slabs and the South Buttress meet, is a long, multi-pitch ice climb with a tenuous, freestanding ice column at the start. Ascend low-angled ice to the ceiling, belay, then move out right onto the column, the crux. Work up easier slabs to trees and follow the ice flow to the top of the cliff, over a steep step on the fourth pitch. Descend as for Momento.

Clint Cummins and John Imbrie climbed the column in January, 1978, before the leader took a very serious fall; Ken Andrasko and George Reiser completed the route the following weekend.

SLEEPING BEAUTY 5 M5/6

The delineation between the slabs and the South Buttress of Whitehorse is quite clearly defined—a rather dirty right-facing groove marks the boundary. About 100 feet left of this look for a very distinct V-groove with a small tree growing in it near its base. This is the initial section of the rock climb Sleeping Beauty. Scramble up the steep slope to a tree belay below the groove. Jam and stem up the steep, verglased corner and then climb a series of cracks leading up and right. The first ascent party found some of these cracks filled with ice while others were clear and offered good rock protection—an excellent combination for spectacular mixed climbing. The first ascent party rappelled from fixed anchors at the end of the pitch. Although there is a second very short pitch that could be dry-tooled, it would damage a nice rock pitch so rappelling is recommended.

Steve Larson & Henry Barber February 2002

"It would be even more fun if there was less ice," says Henry Barber. Steve Larson on the FWA of Sleeping Beauty.
Henry Barber

ENDANGERED SPECIES III 4+ 5.7-8

Due to poor protection, this is a serious mixed route. Climb the isolated ice flow right in the center of the South Buttress, just to the left of the Children's Crusade dike, about fifty feet left of the obvious 5.4 dihedral start to Beelzabub. Pitons and Friends may be helpful. Face climb up the Eradicate dike for two pitches, making the transition to ice on the second lead. On the third pitch, ice climb out right past moderate bulges, then climb verglas and rivulets of ice diagonally right to the traverse ledge of the Girdle Traverse. At this point, the first ascent party traversed right and rappelled off.

Ed Webster and Kurt Winkler made the first ascent in January, 1982; EB's were worn on the first pitch and the crux ice lead was done in the dark.

THE ELIMINATE IV 5.8 A3

A long and demanding artificial climb. Richey was just 16 years old when he accomplished this important ascent.

FWA: Mark Richey, solo, January, 1975

SOUTH BUTTRESS DIRECT IV 5.8 A3 (5.11 A0)

A long and difficult mixed route in winter. Rarely repeated.

FWA: Jeff Pheasant made the first ascent of the climb, solo, over a period of several weeks in the winter of 1976.

THE MYTH OF SISYPHUS III 5

Rarely in shape due to a southern exposure, The Myth is the prominent vertical ice ribbon to the right of the Inferno route on the left side of the South Buttress. It is climbable only after sustained periods of very cold weather. See the approach info in the intro to this section. Three pitches of delicate, sustained, poorly protected ice climbing lead to the top. After each pitch you can escape left. Carry pitons and nuts.

Rainsford and Tim Rouner made the first ascent of the first two pitches and traversed off right in February of 1976; the direct finish, the crux, was completed by Kurt Winkler and Ed Webster in January, 1982.

THE GIRDLE TRAVERSE OF WHITEHORSE IV 3-4 5.9 A0

A very long mixed climb across the entire cliff. Over 2000' of alpine conditions from the slabs around to the South Buttress.

FWA: Doug Madara & Bill Kane, February, 1977

Marc Chauvin on an early attempt to repeat the Myth of Sisyphus in December 1981. It was so fat but we didn't finish it; boo hoo.
S. Peter Lewis

SACO RIVER VALLEY: GUIDE'S WALL

Between Whitehorse and Cathedral is a small cliff called the Guide's Wall. The following climbs are hidden in the woods between the Guide's Wall and Whitehorse, closer to Whitehorse. Approach as for Whitehorse and bushwhack up right from the lower right edge of the slabs.

ON THIN ICE 2-3

This is the first climb you will come to up and right of Beginner's Route on Whitehorse and left of Season's Greetings. Up low-angled slabs and thin ice to below a steep bulge. Traverse right to a hemlock tree.

Todd Swain & Ed Keller, January 3, 1983

SEASON'S GREETINGS 3

An obscure but well worthwhile route that begins on a low-angled slab, climbs to a bulge at ten feet and then finishes up a 70 degree slab for a full pitch.

Tiger Burns & Butch Constantine, December 18, 1982

SOLDIER OF FORTUNE 3

Below the Guide's Wall and slightly left, but still to the right of Season's Greetings. Climb the obvious thin flow from the bottom to the top with marginal protection. The first ascent party literally came under live fire when someone below the cliff began shooting off tree branches with a high powered rifle!

Todd Swain & Ed Keller, January 3, 1983

5.12 PILLAR 4

This obscure route is located several hundred yards to the right of the former routes. The easiest approach is from the Cathedral Ledge road. As the road curves right to run parallel with the cliff a dirt road leaves on the left. Follow this past an old parking area and continue into the woods for several hundred feet. Hike 200 feet past a large boulder on the right then turn right on an old woods road. In a hundred feet the woods road curves up and right to a short cliff band with a 30 foot pillar near its left end. This short approach isn't easy to follow in the winter but the tiny cliff should be visible up in the woods from the boulder. Only the curious mind of Todd Swain could ferret out a route such as this.

FRA Todd Swain, early 1980's

SACO RIVER VALLEY: CATHEDRAL LEDGE

Cathedral Ledge offers easy access to some of the most challenging ice climbs in the Saco River Valley, and in fact in all of New England. In a good year, the cliff will be streaked from one end to the other with water ice, such as the year in which Thin Air was done entirely as an ice climb, but these years are rare. Each year, most of the cliff's finest ice routes are formed by mid-January. The summer tourist road is still the best approach in winter, except that it is not plowed beyond the second turnoff into the chalet development. Therefore, climbers normally park in the southwest corner of the development where there is ample room for many cars. The unplowed summit road offers quick access to all climbs on the cliff. Descend north along the trail skirting the cliff's edge to the North End or hike down the auto road. The climbs on Cathedral will be described from left to right, beginning with the upper left wall. For routes on this part of the cliff, the best approach is to ascend the auto road to the summit, then follow a climber's path south, skirting the cliff edge to a snow gully that leads to the very left-hand edge of the upper left wall. Traverse the ledge north to reach your intended climb.

5¢ CIGAR 5

This is the first ice climb that you will find when you traverse the tree covered ledge from the left end of the cliff. About 25' left of Alpha Corner climb a short, steep pillar to the woods.

FRA Steve Larson with Becky Bisagni, 1992

ALPHA CORNER 5

Just right of a shallow right-facing corner climb a pillar to a steep, sometimes hanging curtain.

unknown

DRESDEN 4 M6

Twenty feet right of Alpha Corner is a steep slab that ends under a roof. Above the roof a steep wall is split with a crack. Climb the fat flow that seeps out from under the roof and then dry-tool the finger crack to the top.

Doug Madara 2000/01

NUTCRACKER 5

This steep climb follows the summer crack climb of the same name. Start on the right side of the Dresden flow and climb up and right to another

Kevin Mahoney scratching for fun near Nutcracker on Cathedral's upper left wall. In a good winter this wall will be covered in vertical sheets like this.
Rob Frost

CATHEDRAL LEDGE UPPER LEFT WALL

A.	5¢ Cigar	C.	Dresden	E.	Nutcracker variation	G.	Layton's Ascent
B.	Alpha Corner	D.	Nutcracker	F.	Chicken Delight	H.	Nomad Crack

flow that drips down the crack from the top of the cliff. A separate thin flow sometimes forms just to the right offering scratchy fun.

FWA: Peter Cole, Bryan Becker & Mark Whiton, January, 1977

DOUBLE VEE 5

Similar to the other ice flows which infrequently form on Cathedral's upper left wall, a steep sheet one hundred feet right of Nutcracker (look for two V-grooves stacked on top of each other).

FWA: Mark Whiton, 1977

OFF THE HOOK 5

Between Double Vee and Chicken Delight climb another thin sheet of ice that oozes down the vertical wall. This is the summer line of Off The Hook. On the first winter ascent the ice was thick enough so that only ice gear was needed.

Steve Larson & Henry Barber, February 1994

CHICKEN DELIGHT 5

Another vertical pillar fifty feet right of Double Vee. Look for a left leaning finger crack. If you can see it the climbing will be scary but you may get rock gear; if you can't, the climbing may be easier but the pro may be sketchy.

FWA: Kurt Winkler & George Hurley, 1982

LAYTON'S ASCENT 5

Start as for Chicken Delight and follow the summer line along a handcrack trending up and right. Thuggish, cold and scratchy in the winter.

Steve Larson & Paul Boissenneault, winter 1992/93

NOMAD CRACK 5+

Beginning just right of Chicken Delight , seventy-five feet of unrelenting vertical ice call for the proper mental attitude. Finish here or step out right and climbs another short vertical flow up to the woods.

Kurt Winkler & Jim Tierney, February, 1982

REFUSE II 3 5.5

The bottom of the ramp on upper Refuse occasionally ices up. A worthwhile and moderate mixed route with good protection. A rappel approach is recommended; see the following route description.

unknown

BLACK CRACK II 5 M7 5.10R

At the right end of the tree covered ledge is a huge right-facing corner with a low-angled ramp (Refuse) to its right. In the very back of the corner is an offwidth crack with a notorious reputation as a rock climb and now an equally notorious reputation as a mixed route. Both this route and the previous route are most easily approached by rappel (two ropes) from the tourist lookout at the top of the cliff. Descend a gully to the right of the fence (looking out) to a ledge system that leads under the lookout. Rappel from trees to a piton anchor 40' down at the top of Refuse (or, if buried, continue another 40' to a pine tree on a ledge), rappel again to the tree covered ledge. Climb the initial Refuse ramp for 20 feet then straight up the ominous offwidth of Black Crack. Stem, chimney (5.10 in the summer; hard to imagine in the winter), and generally grovel passed a lone bolt then step out right to a hanging flow coming down the wall, climb it for a while, then step back left and finish up the main chimney. Bring rock gear (including huge cams), screws (some stubbies), and a whole lot of chutzpah for this long, demanding pitch

George Hurley & Mike Kahn, March 25, 1997 (George was 62 at the time, Mike was young enough to know better)

Climbs will now be described left to right beginning at the lower left end of the cliff. Approach the first routes from near the State Park kiosk and traverse left below the cliff until you can turn uphill and intersect the cliff near Three Birches.

THREE BIRCHES II 4 5.8

Approach from directly below following faint paths to the lowest point of rock. A twenty foot right trending arch marks the start of the route. Exciting climbing up verglased slabs just right of the arch, followed by mixed climbing to a clump of trees. Rappel, or follow a long, cold layback flake to the tree covered ledge.

FWA: Bill Kane & Mack Johnson, January, 1978

FUNHOUSE 5.7

POOH 5.7

Both Funhouse and Pooh provide good exercise in snow-covered rock climbing. Fifty feet right of Three Birches, Funhouse begins in the right-hand of two parallel right facing corners, face climbs to a good ledge and then finishes up a steep face just left of Pooh. Pooh climbs just right of Funhouse into a chimney with a hanging block, up to the ledge, and then moves left to finish up an obvious steep crack and face directly above the first pitch of Funhouse.

FWA: Kim Smith, et al, January, 1978

For the next three routes hike straight up the talus above the kiosk for 100 feet, bear left and up into the woods then climb up and right (you may see stairs if the snow is light) and then back left until directly below the prow of the cliff. You are now directly under the next two routes.

RECOMPENSE III 5.9

Another worthwhile winter ascent, primarily rock. Begins at the lowest point of rock below the tourist lookout just left of The Prow buttress. Follow cracks up and left to an obvious chimney and finish up the striking right facing corner just

left of the top of The Prow.

FWA: Henry Barber & friend, 1974

THE PROW III 5.6 A2 (5.11+)

A recommended winter aid climb. Much of the route is fixed with pitons; please do not place any additional pins. A large selection of wired stoppers and some small Friends will be all you'll need. Follow a direct line up the very prow of the buttress using disconnected crack systems aiming for a triangular roof near the top of the cliff.

FWA: John Bouchard and Ajax Greene, December, 1974

YELLOW BRICK ROAD III A2

A long, dark, cold aid climb with mostly bolts and some scary stuff. The start is uphill and to the right of The Prow.

FRA: Dave Rose & Peter Lewis, over two days, January 1984 (the second ascent party was starting up as the FA party finished—the route has probably not been done since)

The next several routes are best approached by walking north on the road for about 200 feet and then turning into the woods on the left. After passing a huge boulder you will be directly under the Mordor Wall. Traverse up and left along the cliff base to reach the nasty looking gully that is The Big Flush.

THE BIG FLUSH II 4+

The large tree-filled corner which divides Cathedral Ledge in half provides an excellent mixed climb in winter. The route consists of ice flows separated by rock steps and trees and is harder than you might think.

FWA: Chris Noonan and Jeff Butterfield, Winter 1978

GOOFER'S DIRECT II 3

Although the first forty feet can be thin and awkward to protect, Goofer's is one of the most popular routes of its grade. In one long pitch, or two short ones, climb the obvious sustained ice fall to the left of Thin Air, near the base of The Big Flush. The route ends in a prominent cave. Rappel with two ropes from the cave, or traverse left and head down to the trees with one rope.

John Bragg, John Bouchard & Henry Barber, Winter 1972-73

SUPER GOOFER II 5-

The difficult direct finish. Climb one pitch of Goofer's and belay on the left at a tree. Continue up easy ground to the base of a prominent steep ice column with a protection piton at its base. Ascend the strenuous forty foot pillar to a belay ledge on the left. The crux involves delicate, thin ice above. When the ice ends, climb over moss and leaves to a tree belay. Finish up a steep groove to the fence at the top of the cliff.

George Hurley & Les Gould, January 31, 1982

THIN AIR III 5 5.6

On occasion, Thin Air ices up providing a mixed route of a superb nature. In February of 1976, the ice covered the entire face; not a single rock move was made! These conditions have never returned since. Most climbers settle for a thin ice smear at the start, rock climbing to the two bolt belay above the traverse, and continue up the moderate ice flow at the top. Two hundred feet right of The Big Flush climb straight up for fifty feet to an obvious traverse line leading right. At its end climb straight up the face to the right facing corner and a good ledge. The last pitch goes straight up to the top of the cliff. Descend by walking off to the right and then up left through the woods to reach the road.

FWA: Michael Hartrich & Mark Whiton, February, 1976

STANDARD ROUTE III 4 5.6

A true alpine classic whose severity in winter depends entirely upon the conditions. Should the cave wall be verglased, the ascent can be very difficult. Climbs the obvious chimney system that splits the center of the cliff right of Thin Air. After a narrow smear of ice at the start, mixed climbing leads to the cave. Climbing the notorious "cave wall" is the crux. Above, work up mixed snow and ice in the upper chimney to the top.

FWA: Hugo Stadtmuller & Henry W Kendall, January 19, 1964

DIAGONAL III 5 5.6

The crux of the summer rock climb, the final bulge, overflows with ice each winter to create a fifty foot vertical pillar. Climb up Standard until a dike on the right is reached that runs diagonally up and right across the blank wall. Rock climb for two pitches up the poorly protected dike at the start, then go for all the marbles up the column. A bit on the serious side. Two ropes are needed to retreat from this section of the cliff.

FWA: Chris Rowins & Tiger Burns, Winter 1977-78

GRAND FINALE IV 5.8 A3

A winter wall climb with little ice. Begin about fifty feet downhill from Standard.

In Tolkien's trilogy the author describes Mordor as a frightful place. Dave Kelly, Craig Taylor and Uwe Schneider claimed they just had fun on their ascent of this mixed rock/aid/ice classic on Cathedral Ledge. The equally serious Diagonal is to the left and Cathedral Direct is to the far right.

courtesy Dave Kelly

Dowels mark the start of this route which climbs mostly on aid for two pitches before crossing Diagonal and finishing over a steep bulge left of that route's chimney.

FWA: Alain Comeau, climbing solo, came very close to climbing the first winter ascent of the route before Steve Larson and Paul Boissonneault completed it in the winter of 1978-79

MORDOR WALL IV 5 A4

An arduous combination of difficult aid and steep ice. Start right of Grand Finale at an obvious flake and shallow left-facing corner. Aid (nuts only please) the corner to a hanging stance. Hook right across the blank wall to hard aid up a bashie ladder leading over the crest of the wall. From here aid up until the ice is reached and climb the massive ice flow to the top. There is a sustained vertical curtain near the top.

FWA: Bryan Becker & Alain Comeau over three days in January, 1979

MORDOR/DIAGONAL LINK IV 5 A4

An intriguing link that breaks up and left from the end of the second pitch of the Mordor Wall to reach the lowest drip coming out of the Diagonal's crux chimney. The connecting pitch was just a couple of inches thick on the first ascent and involved a completely unprotected run-out for 80 feet directly above the hanging belay. Finish up the column on Diagonal.

FRA: Pat Hackett & John Tremblay, winter 1986/87

BONGO FLAKE/PENDULUM LINK-UP IV 4+ A3

Start up the Bongo Flake 75 feet right of the start of the Mordor Wall and aid climb to the sidewalk belay below the Pendulum Roof; finish up that route's hanging curtain. This is a serious and committing winter route.

Brad White & Jose Albeyta (day 1); Brad White and Jim Ewing finished the climb, winter 1986/87

MINES OF MORIA IV 5.7 A2

Another hard wall route up the center of the cliff. Mostly rock.

FWA: Bryan Becker, Alain Comeau & Eric Engberg, January, 1977

PENDULUM ROUTE IV 5.8 A2 (5.11) 5

A long and intricate winter climb, with an ice curtain hanging down off the roof.

FWA: Chris Hassig & Mark Whiton, winter 1977

FOREST OF FANGORN IV 5.7 A3

A long mixed aid and free route.

FWA: Steve Larson & Paul Boissonneault, winter, 1979-80

PENDULUM/CATHEDRAL DIRECT/OPTION 9A IV 5.10 5 M4

A hard mixed climb that starts by front-pointing up the huge tree at the base of Pendulum Route and then gets more bizarre above. After climbing the crux (10.b) traverse on the second pitch of Pendulum, head right and down into the Cathedral Direct chimney. Climb this for 40 feet or so and then climb out onto the left wall of the chimney to reach ice dripping down the wall. Climb the ice-clad face (following the approximate summer line of Option 9A) to the top. Expect consistent mixed difficulties throughout.

Steve Larson & Doug Madara, early 00's; the climb was done entirely free on the first ascent, including the 5.10b undercling in plastic boots—be fore-warned, these guys are really good.

CATHEDRAL DIRECT III 3-4 5.7 A2

This is the next full length chimney system two hundred feet right of Standard Route. Begin beneath the huge cathedral-like cave, aid left along a horizontal crack to the back of the cave. The second pitch takes the wild thirty foot roof directly with much fixed gear. Above, follow the ice choked upper chimney for at least four more pitches to the top of the cliff.

FWA: Alain Comeau & Tony Trocchi, Winter 1976-77

SUBMISSION 5

This route climbs an iced up water groove left of Repentence's first pitch.

Kevin Mahoney & Ben Gilmore, February 1999

REPENTENCE III 5

The classic hard ice climb in the East with steep and sustained difficulties. The line ascends the left hand of two prominent ice-filled chimneys on the northern end of Cathedral Ledge, and is commonly done in either three or four pitches. The crux on the second lead can take a considerable amount of time to form and even then can be exceedingly hard if the column is candled or detached. Finish over an awkward chockstone just below the top. The first ascent of this route was a major breakthrough in difficulty for New England ice climbers.

FWA: John Bragg & Rick Wilcox, Winter 1973

ANGEL'S HIGHWAY III 5.8 A2

The aid route that climbs the blank wall between Repentence and Remission.

FWA: Peter Cole & Jeff Pheasant, Winter 1974-75

REMISSION IV 5+ 5.8

One of the most difficult routes on Cathedral Ledge, it ascends the right hand chimney (forty feet) right of Repentence. An awkward mixed pitch (5.8) up a left-facing corner gains the base of the ice flow and a large belay ledge on the right. Continue up thin ice to another stance on the right below the crux column. Swing onto the vertical pillar which is followed into the upper chimney and a ledge on the left. A short pitch

Kurt Winkler styling pitch three of Cathedral's classic grade 5, Repentence; the infamous chockstone looms 50' above.
S. Peter Lewis

159

leads to the woods.

FWA: Rainsford Rouner, Peter Cole & Timothy Rouner made the first winter ascent in January, 1976, using etriers on the crux column.

REMISSION DIRECT START 5+

Instead of climbing the first rock pitch, climb straight up the sheer wall below the first belay up a terribly thin and steep smear.

The history of this amazing variation is quite muddled. Jim Shimberg, Dan Lee, and Bob Baribeau have all had their names put forth as candidates for the first ascent with an ascent by Shimberg, Ted Hammond and Alan Cattabriga in early February 1996 being the likely winner. One interesting story was told to the author by Kurt Winkler. He said that Dan Lee told him that when he first did the pitch on or about February 10, 1996, he found tool and crampon tic-marks in the ice. It turns out that Bob Baribeau, in town and with a couple of hours to kill, wandered over to see what was in at Cathedral. He later told Winkler that he had seen that the Direct Start to Remission was in, started up it just to check it out, and soon found himself committed. Finishing the pitch but not up for soloing the rest of the climb, Baribeau said he downclimbed the Direct Start. This a remarkable example of climbing in control. Also making early ascents in mid February of 1996 were Jeff Fongemie, Peg Immel, Jeff Lowe, Alex Lowe, Brad White, Steve Larson, Kurt Winkler and Charles White. Murky history and all, this is an awesome pitch.

WARLOCK II 5.8 A4

Hard aid climbing to the right of Remission.

FWA: Paul Boissonneault & John Drew, Winter 1981-82

DIEDRE III 5 5.9 M4

One of Cathedral's most challenging winter mixed climbs. This is a steep, difficult route and aid was used on the first winter ascent. It is an outstanding mixed climb yet has seen few winter ascents. To the right of Remission by about 150 feet and halfway up the cliff, is an obvious right facing corner with a birch tree near its top. Climb up triple ledges via short ice columns to a large belay ledge. Pitch two is very short and traverses right under a small roof (M4) onto another belay ledge below the dihedral. Pitch three climbs the icy dihedral (M4) and then a short easy pitch gains the huge terrace on the right via a giant flake. The crescendo finish is the final pitch up the overhanging crack near the left side of the terrace and the steep face

Doug Madara on the first winter ascent of one of Cathedral's best hard mixed routes, Diedre.
Paul Ross

above it. Climb the steep hand crack (5.9) to its top and then make the crux transition onto the thinly iced slab above which is followed to a final steep wall and finishing turf shots. On the first ascent this pitch was sheathed in verglas and dripping with icicles. On the first free ascent the pitch was similarly sheathed but the climbers were over a quarter-century wiser (and better equipped).

FWA: Doug Madara & Tony Trocchi, Winter 1975-76; FFA Doug Madara & Steve Larson, early 2002

ACK THE RIPPER A3 (5.11)

This and the following routes are found just left of the left end of the Practice Slabs at the North End.

FWA: Todd Swain, Winter 1980-81

HE POSSESSED A2 (5.12)

FWA: Ed Webster & Ken Nichols, February 1974

CATHEDRAL LEDGE CENTER

A.	Whitehorse Ledge Slabs (.5 miles away)	D.	Mordor Wall	F.	Repentence
B.	The Big Flush	E.	Cathedral Direct	G.	Remission
C.	Diagonal				

CATHEDRAL LEDGE: The North End

The North End of Cathedral Ledge has become increasingly popular over the years as a place for beginners to get their first taste of ice climbing and for experienced climbers to get in some practice. The area is easily accessible, sheltered, often warmer and less windy than the mountain areas, has great toproping from low-angle to steep and has a little something for everyone. With all these positive attributes the area can become very crowded, especially on weekends. Please be conscientious when you climb here and don't hog routes. To reach the North End park at the end of the plowed road and follow the summit road north along the base of the cliff. A hundred yards before the road turns sharply left and uphill there is a steel gate and the climbs will be easily visible up to the left. The approach takes about ten minutes. Many short climbers' trails approach the climbs from the road and the easiest descent from the top of all the routes is to traverse the cliff's top to the right (north) and then back down to the right of the main slab or further right around the pillars—it will be obvious. Routes will be described in relationship to the main slab.

JUST LAUGHING 4+ M6

Just right of The Possessed and left of the 80' high Practice Slab is an obvious groove capped by a roof. The left side of the roof is Black Magic while the right side is The Roof. Zig left up a ramp then zag right to a poor stance and then continue up to hanging icicles at the right side of the roof, up and around these to a belay on a ledge. The second pitch climbs an overhanging mixed groove (pitch two of the summer route They Died Laughing) to a large terrace at the left end of a steep, weepy wall of yellow ice (The Unicorn climbs the right side of this flow). The third pitch climbs up a series of ledges and hummocks to a seam that goes up and then sharply left to the top. This is an excellent, if rarely done, mixed route.

Tom Callaghan climbed the first pitch in the 1990's; Henry Barber and Duncan Ferguson swapped leads on the complete line on January 9, 1997

YELLOW PERIL 5

This pitch of mixed climbing parallels the third pitch of the route above about 40 feet to its left. Approach either by doing the first two pitches of Black Magic or hiking up around the North End and then traversing the ledge system below The Unicorn (technical), or by rappelling down from above. Once there, climb a series of vertical steps to a groove leading into and then out of a big hole.

Jack Tackle & Henry Barber, February 1998

THE UNICORN 4+

A steep, rather obscure, ice corner and face located above the summer climb They Died Laughing, about 250' left of The Thresher. It is best approached by ascending the snow gully just right of the North End Slab at the North End and then following the trail along the top of the cliff. Rappel to start or traverse carefully in from the right.

Paul Boissonneault, Chris Noonan & Jeff Butterfield, January, 1978

THE THRESHER SLAB 3/3+

Walk left along the base of the cliff for about 150' and you will see a flow above you on a steeper wall. A short pitch leads to a large terrace and a small tree. Above the tree climb either straight up (steeper) or slightly to the right to the woods. Between The Thresher and the North End Slab are lots of short toprope climbs on a steep little wall; approach (carefully) via a ramp that diagonals up and left from the base of the North End Slab. There is also a short, easy chimney below and just left of The Thresher; and above the terrace and to the left is a vertical yellow drip (4+) that can be toproped (be very careful setting it up).

unknown; George Hurley has led the yellow drip (such courage)

NORTH END SLAB 2

This is the obvious central flow. It is about 50' wide and 160 feet high and has room for two or three parties to climb comfortably. It can only be toproped from the top of the cliff (climb an easy gully immediately right of the slab) or from an intermediate anchor set by a leader.

unknown

NORTH END PILLARS 3-4

A hundred feet to the right of the North End Slab are a series of about five short, steep pillars that drip down a cliff band. They are about 40 feet high and easily led or toproped from trees at the top. Saturdays here are like visiting the zoo.

unknown

SACO RIVER VALLEY: HUMPHREY'S LEDGE

Humphrey's Ledge, 1.7 miles north of Cathedral and Whitehorse Ledges, is complex and has several areas of interest to ice climbers. Under optimum conditions, there are several ice flows on the main face; farther north, hidden around the corner, lies Black Pudding Gully, and farther yet are still more flows on the steep hillside in the Barking Dog Icicle and Cemetery Cliff areas. In addition, there is a hidden practice area in the hollow up and left of the main face. Descriptions will begin at the practice area and continue north.

To reach Humphrey's Ledge continue north on West Side Road past the entrance to Cathedral and Whitehorse. Humphrey's main cliff will soon come into view straight ahead. Take care in parking on the road below the cliffs, and do not park at the Lady Blanche house on the right. The best descent from most routes on and around Humphrey's is via rappel (there are many trees) as the bushwhacking can be horrendous. If you complete a climb on the main cliff the easiest rappel line is down the center of the face in the vicinity of the summer route Soul Survivor (the obvious diagonalling dike in left-center). With two ropes rappel once to a two-bolt anchor at the birch tree at the top of the second pitch of Soul Survivor, then to a tree ledge, then to the ground.

HUMPHREY'S LEDGE: Humphrey's Hollow

This is an odd little area that has been rumored to be good for years—although few people have actually been in here. This is the place to go if you feel like a little exploring.

HOLLOW FLOWS 2-4

Hidden in the woods in the distinctive hollow to the left of Humphrey's main face is a good practice area that offers an uncrowded alternative to the more popular areas at Cathedral Ledge. Approach around the left side of the main cliff, and walk for about fifteen minutes to reach the ice. Several moderate flows and a short, steep route characterize the area. Descend to the sides.
unknown

HOLLOW TIERS 3-4

Farther up in the woods there is another route that ascends the obvious, broken, three-tiered cliff that forms the very back wall of the amphitheater. Continuing past the practice area for another fifteen minutes up a very steep hill will get you to the base of the bottom tier.
Unknown

BOISSONNEAULT-PHILIBERT ROUTE 3+ 5.7

In the center of the cliff climb grade 2 ice for sixty feet to the first tree ledge, traverse right thirty feet or so and climb 5.7 rock (well protected) to the second tree ledge. A full pitch traverse (walking) will get you to the right-hand of two flows that ascend the third tier. Seventy feet of grade 3+ ice takes you to the top. The left-hand flow is about a grade harder. Descend by rappel.
Paul Boissonneault & Kevin Philibert, January, 1992

HUMPHREY'S LEDGE: Main Face

The big cliff at Humphrey's faces south and catches sun most of the day. This makes the following routes rare at best and in most seasons they never make it past the wet streak stage. If they do form, get an early start and climb fast.

THE SENATOR II 5

Southern exposure makes the formation of this climb a rare event. In fact, since the first ascent it has never been seen again. The route ascends a thin and poorly protected ice slab just left of the obvious dike that splits the main face. The main flow begins from a tree covered ledge that can be accessed by several routes. The easiest option is to walk toward the left end of the cliff until a gully/groove leads up and right to the tree ledge, then traverse the ledge to the right until under the flow. An alternate (M5) approach is to climb the obvious corner (rock gear) that leads to the right end of the tree ledge. From the ledge, two hard pitches lead to the top. Rappel the route.
Mark Richey & Rainsford Rouner, February, 1976

SOUL SURVIVOR II 5 M5

This is an ice climb of considerable stature involving a fine natural line and high technical difficulties. Pitons and a rack of cams make the ascent easier. The route follows the prominent dike that bisects the face. The first lead is an exercise in bridging in crampons up a right-facing corner (M5, the same as the right-hand approach pitch to The Senator) that leads to the end of a large tree ledge. The second pitch, the crux, ascends the free-standing column over the large overlap to thinly iced slabs above. Belay at bolts at a prominent white birch. Finish up a steep ice column in the dihedral above.

Kurt Winkler & Dennis Ellshon, January, 1982

SUNNY SIDE OF THE STREET 3

Climb the ice flow just to the right of the start of Soul Survivor for one pitch. When the ice suddenly ends at a seep, rappel off the route. An appropriate finish is needed to complete the ascent.

Ed Webster & Butch Constantine, February, 1982

WIESSNER ROUTE II 3 5.8

To the right of Soul Survivor by about a hundred feet is a huge left facing corner with a chimney/offwidth in the back that runs the full height of the cliff. Two difficult pitches of chimneying gain the upper ice-choked groove. The rock climbing on this route will probably be harder than the ice.

FWA: Kurt Winkler

THE DESCENT CHIMNEY 3 5.4

Ascend a thinly-iced 60 foot chimney at the extreme right-hand side of Humphrey's.

Todd Swain, January 1982

HAGGIS SLAB 2

The low angled ice slab to the right of the Descent Chimney.

Todd Swain, January, 1982

HUMPHREY'S LEDGE: Black Pudding Gully

Continuing north past Humphrey's main face, West Side Road curves to the left and in a couple of hundred yards a large broken cliff is seen high on the left. This cliff is home to several hard routes; the most obvious is Black Pudding Gully, a free-standing pillar high and left in a dark groove. Park along the road beneath your intended route and bushwhack up the steep slope. Continuing north for about the next quarter mile is a rather featureless hillside characterized by short cliff bands and shattered buttresses. In a good year a number of climbs in the grade 2-4 range will be found here.

BLACK PUDDING GULLY LEFT 4+

Seldom in shape. The line is completely separate from the main line of Black Pudding Gully and about 50 feet to its left. Climb the increasingly steep ribbon of ice for one pitch.

Mark Whiton & David Belden (France), February, 1976

BLACK PUDDING GULLY 4+

The prominent ice-filled gully on the east face of Humphrey's Ledge. A two-pitch route, the first lead giving some extremely strenuous climbing up what is often a thin and candled vertical pillar. Finish diagonally right up a gully or to the left for a steeper ice flow. The best descent is to rappel the route from trees using two ropes.

A.J. LaFleur, Rick Wilcox and Peter Cole made the first ascent in January, 1973, using etriers on the initial pillar. Note: the first ascent party found the climb in unusually good condition (several feet thick) and it has never come in as well again.

The crux pillar on the rarely-forming Black Pudding Gully. When it does touch down, expect poorly bonded candled icicles with the best protection being a big sling around the base.
Doug Millen

BPG VARIATIONS M4-5

To the immediate left of Black Pudding Gully are two thin mixed lines up a steep wall. They are reported to be Kevin Mahoney routes. On February 17, 1996, Kurt Winkler watched a man and woman climb a hard mixed route 25 feet right of Black Pudding Gully. The route was never reported by the first ascent party. Our best guess is that these one pitch routes are about M4-5 in difficulty.

most likely Kevin Mahoney (left routes); unknown (right)

TRIPECICLE II 5

Ascends the ice slab and obvious column to the right of Black Pudding Gully. Two easy pitches up snow and ice slabs get you to the column's base. Climb a verglased slab to the column and then strenuously up it to the belay at a hemlock tree at the base of a snowy chimney. Struggle up that to a ledge, traverse left under an overhang, and finish up a large ice-filled dihedral facing left.

Mark Whiton and friends, winter 1977

HUMPHREY'S LEDGE: Barking Dog Icicle Area

Extending for about a quarter of a mile past Black Pudding Gully are a series of brushy buttresses and short cliff bands that gradually diminish in height and culminate in a very prominent blue bulge behind the second house (they used to have an obnoxious dog) beyond the prominent roadside boulder. This bulge is The Barking Dog Icicle (3-).

Most of the climbs are in the 2-4 range, do not follow obvious lines and tend to go from tree to tree. Nonetheless there have been at least six routes put up here by the ever prolific Todd Swain and although short, this area makes for a good change from the North End (Cathedral) since there are no crowds. It can be a really fun area to explore.

DOG TIRED 4+

Perhaps the most significant hard route in the area, this is the second major flow to the left of the obvious shallow cave (Pitman's Arch) and a couple of hundred feet left of the Barking Dog Icicle. Steep icicles connected by very thinly iced walls make for a spectacular and dangerous route.

HUMPHREY'S LEDGE: Cemetery Cliff

Continue north on West Side Rd. for about a half mile and there will be a steep hill with a brushy cliff up and left in the woods. Similar to the Barking Dog Icicle area, there are a number of somewhat nebulous routes on the cliff. Park along the road at the top of the first rise and head left into the woods (you'll see the old cemetary). The most obvious routes will be described below; other stuff exists.

BARNABUS COLUMN 3+

The left side of the cliff has two distinct flows. Barnabus Column is on the left and begins directly between two hemlock trees. Climb a steep flow to a gully and the woods. Rappel off.

Butch Constantine and Jim Tierney approached the upper part of the flow by traversing in from the left in the winter of 1981/82. In January 1983 Todd Swain and Mike Hannon added a direct start.

DARK SHADOWS 4 5.6

The sister route to Barnabus Column climbs a thin ribbon below an overhang; traverse right and up on rock to join the former route. A knifeblade and a medium cam will be helpful.

Todd Swain & Mike Hannon, January 26, 1983

SACO RIVER VALLEY: DUCKS HEAD

This little crag in the village of Jackson, seven miles or so north of North Conway, is home to a number of thin ice and mixed routes. Drive about five miles north of North Conway on Rt. 16/302 and bear north when Route 16 turns in the village of Glen. Drive two miles to Jackson Village. Directly opposite the covered bridge is a steep cliff on the west side of Rt. 16. This is Ducks Head. Park either in Jackson Village or on Rt. 16 about a half mile south of the covered bridge at an obvious pullout on the east side of the road near the Ellis River. Do not park anywhere on the west side of Rt. 16 or at the power substation or on Green Hill Rd. At the time of this writing ownership of the land and legal access to the cliff was uncertain so specific approach information will not be given. As with any area where access is tenuous, please be respectful of property owners; park legally, ask permission to cross private land, go somewhere else if permission to climb is denied. There was huge rockfall here in 2002.

WHEN LIGHT MEETS NIGHT 4

This is the last major flow on the right-hand side. The climb is one pitch long and usually thick. There are other short routes farther right.

FRA: Kurt Winkler, March 18, 1981

LUNAGLACE 3+

To the left of the previous climb is an ice flow in a right-facing corner. Poor ice and protection are characteristic, although a better winter may make thicker ice conditions than were present on the first ascent. It is suggested that pitons and medium cams be carried.

FRA: Kurt Winkler & David Stone, on the night of March 24, 1981

OVERLOAD 5+

On the left side of the crag is a steep wall that is typically encrusted with verglass. To call these next two routes ice climbs is somewhat misleading since most of the time the ice is thin enough to read a book through. Protection will be found to be purely psychological on these serious routes. Overload climbs the obvious central drip on this part of the wall. A hundred feet of extremely thin and technical climbing with little protection (pins needed) will finally get you to the safety of the trees. These routes stand as a testimony to the skill, control, and sheer nerve of John Tremblay.

John Tremblay & Dave Rose, January, 1987

John Tremblay skating away on the thin ice of a new day on the first ascent of Overload.
Joe Lentini

THE LAMINATE 5

The equally thin but shorter neighbor just to the left.
John Tremblay & Joe Lentini, January, 1987

SACO RIVER VALLEY: EAGLE CLIFF

This small cliff just west of the village of Glen, 5.5 miles north of North Conway, is home to two spectacular (if rarely formed) routes. Just west of the intersection of Routes 16 and 302 in the village of Glen is a convenience store/post office on the south side of the road with a

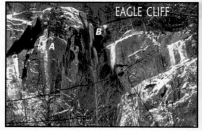

Joe Klementovich
A. Eagle's Gift   B. Cold Cold World

restaurant across the street. Just east of the restaurant a dirt road heads north toward the obvious crag. Park where you can and hike in the dirt road. In a few hundred yards you will come to a gravel pit. From the very back and highest part of the pit follow an old overgrown logging road that leads toward the crag. Follow this for a couple of hundred yards then break left into the woods and head up to the cliff. The cliff consists of a steep wall on the left and a low angled slab on the

Visiting master Jared Ogden grappling with a cold, cold climb on the first ascent.
Mark Synnott

right. The next two routes are found high on the right end of the steep wall. Approach up a steep, brushy gully.

COLD COLD WORLD M8+

This difficult mixed route, one of the hardest in New England, is located around the corner to the right of Eagle's Gift. There is one bolt and additional rock gear will be needed. Climb a short grade two ice gully to a large cave with a small ledge and a fixed pin. Above, climb through a first roof via an iced-up one inch wide crack to a second roof, swing out onto a hanging icicle, surmount the roof and then climb vertical, poorly bonded ice to the top.

Jared Ogden, Mark Synnott & Randy Rackliff, February 1999

EAGLE'S GIFT 5+

One of the more elusive routes in the region. Though frequently seen from the village of Glen as an inviting drip down the steep wall of Eagle Ledge, it is rarely thick enough to climb. An extreme exercise in thin ice climbing. Sixty feet of verglass will get you to the heart-stopping drip above. On the first ascent, the climb's second pitch was about two feet wide, only a couple of inches thick and detached. After Winkler's lead there was not enough ice left to follow the pitch. Even in the best of condition the climb will be very technical and hard to protect. Bring pins and cams.

Kurt Winkler with Joe Lentini & Alec Behr, January 1985

SACO RIVER VALLEY: IRON MOUNTAIN

Iron Mountain is a big, rambling hill northwest of the village of Glen, five miles north of North Conway. Climbs on Iron Mountain are reached by turning north onto Jericho Rd., 0.8 miles west of the intersection of Routes 16 and 302 in Glen.

FRIENDSHIP ROUTE II 3

From Jericho Road take the first right on Glen Ledge Road following it through a chalet development. Follow this up and back left until almost level with an ice flow dropping off the side of Iron Mountain on your left. Bushwhack along a red-blazed property boundary to a hill, then trend slightly left up this until the ice climb is visible through the trees. There are two pitches, the first thin, the second short.

Kurt Winkler & Joe Perez, January 26, 1980

MISGUIDED 3

To the left of the former route by about 50 feet is a 60 foot flow. The first ascent was done in lean conditions; it may be a lot easier when thick.

George Hurley & Marc Chauvin, December 18, 1982

SACO RIVER VALLEY: GIANT STAIRS

ACROSS THE RIVER AND INTO THE TREES II 4

Follow the Jericho Road 4.4 miles to its plowed end in the Rocky Branch Wilderness. Hike for 2 1/2 miles to the Stairs Col Trail. At the Giant Stairs Cliffs, but below the actual col, bushwhack about 250 yards along the base of the lower cliff to its right-hand end. Depending on snow conditions, this approach could take three hours or more. The 125 foot icefall is climbed in two pitches. The initial section is thin and unprotectable. The steep and sustained finish, is considerably thicker. At the top, hike uphill 100 yards, then head down and right to a snow gully and the base of the route.

Kurt Winkler & Joe Perez, January 6, 1980

SACO RIVER VALLEY: WHITE'S LEDGE

The next climb is located on the large cliff that forms the south face of Mt. Stanton. When it's in shape it is easily seen from Route 302 by looking north from a point on the highway just east of Attitash ski area. To get to the cliff, drive about two miles west on Route 302 from the intersection with Route 16 in Glen and turn right into a housing development called Birchview by the Saco. Take the first left and park off the road where it curves to the right. A dirt road goes straight ahead into the woods before the curve. Follow this for a half a mile until White's Ledge is visible through the trees on your right and then follow vague trails and bushwhack uphill to the base. Allow about an hour in good conditions.

WHITE'S GULLY II 3+ 5.5

This route begins a couple of hundred feet uphill and left from the lowest toe of rock. Move up and right to a tree; then up straight before you traverse left to the gully proper (5.5). Follow the gully up and over a short vertical pillar. Two more pitches up the stepped ice flow above lead to the summit. The easiest descent is made by following the Mt. Stanton trail which leads east from the summit back down to the north end of the chalet development.

Bill Kane & Kim Smith, February, 1978

The following route is found on a tiny cliff several miles west of White's Ledge.

STALACTITE 3+

A short ice climb is found on the right-hand cliff of Cave Mountain north of Bartlett, NH. Turn north at the main intersection in the center of Bartlett (7.2 miles west of Glen), cross the Saco River, turn right and park at the end of the road opposite a farmhouse. The crag is clearly visible as a long broken rectangle and takes about a half hour to approach. Climb a thin, detached ice curtain to ice bulges and a steep rock wall. Traverse left carefully until an exit can be made to the top. Medium cams make the ascent easier. Rappel down a corner to the left of the route.

Todd Swain & Jim Frangos, January, 1982

SACO RIVER VALLEY: HART LEDGE

The ledge, which is on the north side of the Saco River, is easily viewed from Rt. 302 a mile or so west of Bartlett village in the vicinity of the Silver Springs Campground. However, to reach it, you must turn north in the center of Bartlett (6.3 miles west of Glen), crossing the Saco River at a bridge. Turn west (left) and follow a road up the far bank of the Saco, crossing railroad tracks, and continuing along the river to a cluster of houses. Turn north on the road, crossing the tracks again, and in a couple of hundred yards the dirt road will end and there is room to park. Hike straight in toward the base of the cliff. The cliff is composed of three distinct tiers culminating in a summit cap of orange granite. Due to its south facing exposure, ice climbs at Hart Ledge are seldom in shape, but in a good year there are at least six flows on the cliff.

Dual Hearts climbs a pitch each of rock and ice— typical scratchy work for this south-facing crag.
Doug Heroux

HART OF THE MATTER II 3

A three-pitch route ascending the entire height of Hart

Ledge. The first pitch is up a moderately hard flow on the left side of the lowest tier. An easy ice slab follows in the center. The upper tier is climbed via an ice flow to the right of a prominent cleft on the right side of a large, rocky buttress.

Brad White & friend, winter 1977-78

DUAL HEARTS II 4 5.8

To the right of the former route and about 150' left and downhill of Ice Tears, climb ice curtains to low-angled ice in a gully. Rock climb up a crack to a traverse right to a tree belay, 100'. The second pitch climbs a right-facing corner to the top for 75 feet. Bring rock gear to 3" (including a bugaboo and standard angle piton) in addition to your standard ice rack.

Kurt Winkler & Doug Heroux, February 10, 1997

ICE TEARS II 5-

A two pitch climb up steep ice on the lowest band of Hart's Ledge. Located in approximately the middle of the cliff. It is an excellent, steep route.

Jim Dunn & Dick Cyrs, February, 1978

SACO RIVER VALLEY: CARDIAC CRAG

This is a small south-facing crag located on the east side of the Saco River about a quarter mile north of Hart's Ledge. Drive in as for Hart's Ledge but at the cluster of houses after the first railroad crossing, instead of bearing right, continue paralleling the river past about five houses to the end of the road. Park and walk in almost due north, intersecting a logging road which is followed to the left to reach the crag. Allow about a half hour. Though only a pitch high, this crag is densely packed with moderate routes and the location almost guarantees solitude. Due to its south-facing exposure, routes here never get that thick, or stay around for long. It is possible to get a brief glimpse of the crag from Route 302, and if you see white, then you'll know there is at least a skim of ice. The routes are all easily top roped and descent is around either side (easiest to the right). Routes will be described from left to right.

PACEMAKER 2-4

The farthest left flow. Rappel off from an oak tree at mid-height, or continue on hard mixed ground.

George Hurley & Todd Swain, January 22, 1983

CORONARY BYPASS 4-

The thin, detached runnel to the right of Pacemaker. No protection for 100 feet.

Todd Swain & George Hurley, January 22, 1983

HARTLESS 3-

The thickest flow in the center of the crag.

George Hurley & Todd Swain, January 22, 1983

CARDIAC ARETE 3+

Another thin detached route; unfortunately there is no protection this time.
Todd Swain & George Hurley, January 22, 1983

EKG 3

The last flow on the right. Thin and (you guessed it) poorly protected.
George Hurley & Todd Swain, January 22, 1983

EMERGENCY ROOM 1-2

The wide, easy flow above and to the right of the crag.
Todd Swain & George Hurley, solo, January 22, 1983

SACO RIVER VALLEY: MOUNT TREMONT

CASPER THE FRIENDLY GHOST II 2

This obscure route is on an unnamed shoulder of Mt. Tremont on the south side of Route 302 across the river from Hart's Ledge. It is easily seen above a set of tourist cabins about 1 1/2 miles west of Bartlett Village.
Bryan Becker & George Stevens, Winter 1979-80

XANADU FALLS II 3

An easy ice climb which makes a worthwhile route in lean snow years. Four miles west of Bartlett and just after the bridge over the Sawyer River, the Sawyer River Road leaves to the south. Depending on whether there is logging activity in the area, the road may or may not be plowed. Drive, hike, ski, or snowshoe up Sawyer River Road for one mile to a house on the left. Across the river lies a large slab or scar on the slope above. Xanadu Falls follows an ice flow immediately right of this feature. Cross the river and follow a stream bed, then a ridge to an open area. Bear right until the original stream bed is reached again. A large leaning oak tree marks the climb's start. After a fifty-five degree, thin, first pitch, four more rope lengths lead to the top. Descend the climb. About six hours, car to car.
Kurt Winkler & Jim Tierney, January 22, 1980

SACO RIVER: TEXACO SLAB

This sunny little area is found just south of Crawford Notch State Park and offers a variety of fun ice climbs from easy to hard. On bitterly cold days its sunny nature makes it a good alternative to the east and northeast facing climbs at Frankenstein. A little over six miles northwest of Bartlett and just a 2.3 miles south of Frankenstein is a large parking lot on the east side of the road, the trailhead for the Davis Path. Park here, cross the suspension bridge over the Saco River, and then follow the river upstream to reach the crags. The first area to be reached will be the Texaco Amphitheater up into the woods on the right, and a few hundred yards farther will be the obvious flow of the Texaco Slab itself. The approach to the amphitheater takes about thirty minutes and the slab itself is another fifteen minutes away. Routes will be described as they would be encountered on the approach from the Davis Path.

TEXACO SLAB: Texaco Amphitheater

Several hundred yards to the south of the obvious Texaco Slab is a sheltered amphitheater with a number of short (100 feet) climbs that vary from grade 3 to desperate and are consistently thick and in shape each season. It is a sunny sheltered place to climb away from the crowds. Descend around either end of the cliff or rappel.

John Tremblay and Mark Arsenault on Ankles Away—note the vintage hardware
S. Peter Lewis

THE DUNKING 3

The right-hand end of the crag consists of three obvious routes on a steep wall. The Dunking is the farthest right, shortest route and was named after a failed attempt by a subsequent party to shortcut the approach by crossing the (almost) frozen Saco River.

Most likely Todd Swain, Curt Robinson & Maxine Train, February 7, 1983

THE IMPASS 3+ 5.8

The central route about fifty feet left of the previous climb. Up a steep blue column until blocked by a large roof. Traverse left around the roof to the top.

FRA: John Tremblay & Mark Arsenault, Winter 1984/85

ANKLES AWAY 3+

The next route to the left, Ankles Away climbs up a steep curtain to a ledge and then easier terrain at the top. The name implies the flying style of the leader on a subsequent ascent.

FRA: A little sketchy, but

Visitor Barry Blanchard high on The Lowe Down, one of the first fixed-gear mixed climbs put up in New Hampshire.
Doug Millen

probably Todd Swain, Curt Robinson & Maxine Train, February 7, 1983

ANKLES AHEAD 4

Just left of Ankles Away is a nice chimney.

unknown

THE LOWE DOWN 6- M5

This and the following routes are two of the steepest in the region. About a hundred feet left of Ankles Away is a steep wall with a three-tiered overhang, each tier with its own hanging curtain. Extremely technical dry-tooling and ice climbing past a pin and two bolts will get you up this stunning line. The first ascent was rather controversial (fixed gear pre-placed) although the din soon quieted as folks just started having fun on the route.

Alex Lowe first toproped the route during an icefest in 1997/98; Arthur Haines placed a pin and two bolts on rappel and led the route the following winter with Dave Anderson and Brad White; Rob Frost subsequently climbed the route via a harder direct start and without the fixed gear.

A confident Tom Callaghan on the FA of The Doubting Thomas.
S. Peter Lewis

EUGENE'S WOODY 6

To the right of The Lowe Down climb a short pillar to a roof (pin) and dry-tool over it to gain cauliflower ice that leads to an upper smear.

After at least one roped attempt, Kevin Mahoney soloed the route in January, 2000.

DOUBTING THOMAS 4

Fifteen feet left of The Lowe Down are several pillars that drip off the gently overhanging wall. Doubting Thomas climbs a steep smear until an exciting step right onto the frees-tanding pillar can be made.

Tom Callaghan & Peter Lewis, February, 1986

TEXACO SLAB: Texaco Slab

This popular slab is easily seen as a blue streak down a big slab on the east side of the valley just before you enter Crawford Notch State Park. Approach as for the Texaco Amphitheater and continue upstream along the river until you see the obvious slab. The slab can also be approached by parking in the vicinity of a defunct gas station (it used to be a Texaco station; get it?) and heading directly toward the slab. Crossing the Saco River may be the crux (see the description for The Dunking). Descent for the following routes is via rappel.

TEXACO SLAB 2-3

This is the big blue flow that is easily seen directly across the river from where the old gas station used to be. If thick, several lines are possible, each being one long pitch.

Dave Walters, Bill Ryan & Bill Adamson, Winter 1972-73

EMBARGO 2-3

To the left of the slab it is possible to piece together a line that runs for several pitches up and over a series of cliff bands ending in an obvious narrow gully on the extreme left end of the Missing Wall, the cliff above Texaco Slab.

unknown

SACO RIVER VALLEY: MOUNT BEMIS

Mount Bemis is the rather lumpy looking mountain that lies to the west of Route 302 and is just south of Frankenstein Cliff. There are two areas here of interest to the ice climber. High on a shoulder directly across from the Texaco Slab are two wide, gentle flows that are harder to approach than to climb. Park near the defunct convenience store and bushwhack straight up to the flows.

OPEC ICE FALL 2

The left-hand of the two mysterious flows. Two or three pitches — which may not be worth the effort in a heavy snow year.

Todd Swain & Jim Frangos, January 5, 1983

GASOLINE ALLEY 2 5.4

The easy mixed climb up the flow to the right.

Todd Swain & Jim Frangos, January 5, 1983

About a half mile farther north, just before entering Crawford Notch State Park, you will just be able to spot the top of a yellow icicle on a small isolated cliff on the northernmost hump of Mt. Bemis. Park as for Frankenstein Cliff. Walk south on the tracks for 15 minutes, then bushwhack up to the ice climbs. The approach from the tracks is steep and takes about 45 minutes. Routes will be described from right to left. Descent for all routes is easiest by rappel.

CYNICAL CIVILIAN 3

The farthest right flow.

George Hurley & Kurt Winkler, March 11, 1988

DANCING AT THE RASCAL FAIR 3+

The next flow to the left.

Kurt Winkler & Peter Quesada, March 6, 1988

ENTREPRENEUR 4

This is the first route to the right of the obvious yellow flow.

Kurt Winkler & Peter Quesada, March 6, 1988

VISION THING 4+

Climbs the yellow pillar that is just visible from the road.

Kurt Winkler & George Hurley, March 11, 1988

There are several more mixed lines to the left of these routes in the M4 3+ range that Brad White and company scraped around on in the 1990's.

SACO RIVER VALLEY: ARETHUSA FALLS

This wonderful area is between Mount Bemis and Frankenstein and can be a nice quiet place to climb (at least on weekdays). Park as for Frankenstein Cliff. The trail is marked and leaves the railroad tracks just a few feet left of the house at the top of the dirt road. Hike along the Arethusa Falls Trail to a secluded amphitheater at the base of the falls. There are many possibilities here and room for about four parties. Descend around either side of the falls.

MAIN FLOW 3

Climb the center of the main flow for a long pitch to the top. This route typically comes in early in the season and gets really thick as the winter goes on.

unknown

MAIN FLOW LEFT 3+

Up and left of the Main Flow by about 50' is a steep wall typically covered in ice. Several lines can be easily toproped from trees.

unknown

ARETHUGGISH 3+/4 M4/5

This route climbs a steep wall to an obvious offwidth/chimney crack to the right of the main falls.

FRA Ray Rice, Brett Taylor, & friend, 2002

DRIPETHUSA 3+/4

Forty-feet right of the former route and just left of the descent gully climb a steep slab to an obvious yellow drip.

unknown

CRAWFORD NOTCH

S. Peter Lewis

T.B.R. Walsh

CRAWFORD NOTCH AREAS

A.	Frankenstein Cliff	C.	Mount Willey
B.	Mount Webster	D.	Mount Willard
		E.	Mount Avalon/Tom

The varied terrain of Crawford Notch offers many routes which encompass the full spectrum of ice and alpine climbing challenges, from beginners' slabs on Willey's Slide, to short, hard icefalls at Frankenstein Cliff and Mount Willard, and backcountry routes on Mount Tom and Mount Avalon. In addition, longer snow and ice routes are found on the south face of Mt. Willard and the west face of Mt. Webster. The latter offers long gully climbs comparable with Huntington Ravine with up to 2,500 feet of vertical rise from the base of the notch to the summit and an equally long descent to follow. The setting in Crawford Notch, though not as alpine as you'll find on Cannon Cliff, is nonetheless a great ice and alpine area in which to climb. On a cold winter day, with the wind howling down through the notch it can feel very alpine indeed. The routes are generally easily accessible and of high quality. Each different area will be described in the order in which it is encountered when driving northwest from North Conway N.H. on Route 302.

179

AREA HIGHLIGHTS

Location:	This area stretches for about 10 miles from just west of Bartlett Village to the headwaters of the Saco River at the top of the notch
Routes:	Many areas containing a huge variety of routes and grades; roadside classics, long gullies
Access:	Parking is always close; most approaches under 20 minutes
Descent:	Usually hike down but be prepared to rappel at some crags
Weather:	"Notch" (weather section), early December through early April
Equipment:	A standard ice rack is fine for most routes; exceptions noted
Superlatives:	sunny pure ice and hard mixed routes at Texaco (*Doubting Thomas, The Lowe Down*); seclusion at *Arethusa Falls*; awesome moderate and hard classics at Frankenstein (*Chia, Pegasus, Standard, Fang, Dracula, Dropline* plus sick mixed routes in the *Hanging Gardens*); long alpine climbs on Mt. Webster (*Shoestring Gully, Central Gully*); one of the region's greatest long easy routes (Willey's Slide) on Mt. Willey; lots of classics on Mt. Willard (*Gully #1, Great Madness, Cinema Gully, Hitchcock Gully*)
Amenities:	The village of Glen, five miles east of Bartlett Village on Rt. 302 has most things, N. Conway, five miles farther has everything

CRAWFORD NOTCH: FRANKENSTEIN CLIFF

No other ice climbing area receives as much winter traffic as Frankenstein Cliff, which has many excellent ice flows concentrated within a small area. Climbers of all abilities will find routes to their liking here. Most of the climbs are one to two pitches with simple descents through the woods. Drive north on Route 302 out of North Conway for just over 20 miles and take the first left a couple of hundred yards after entering Crawford Notch State Park. Park in the large lot at the bottom of the hill. A short road leads uphill to the site of the old Willey House post office, now replaced with a private home. Although there is room for additional cars along the road just below the house, please respect the rights of the owners by being courteous and by not blocking their driveway. All the climbs are approached by hiking north along the railroad tracks (not in use in the winter). Routes will be described from south to north.

FRANKENSTEIN: South Face

The following routes are found on the big, south-facing wall that you will see in front of you immediately after turning north onto the railroad tracks. Many of Frankenstein's best (and some of its most elusive) routes will be found here. This cliff can be dangerous on sunny, warm days. Approach routes on this face by walking just a few minutes north on the tracks and then heading uphill. There will be a packed trail most of the time; expect a workout if you're the

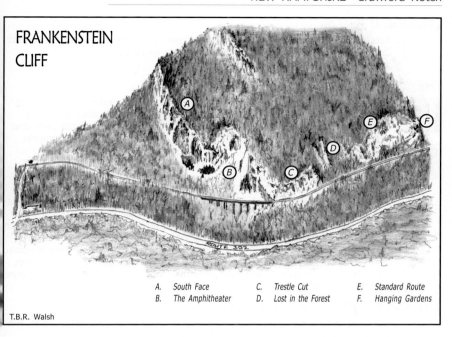

FRANKENSTEIN CLIFF

A.	South Face	C.	Trestle Cut	E.	Standard Route
B.	The Amphitheater	D.	Lost in the Forest	F.	Hanging Gardens

T.B.R. Walsh

first party in after a big storm. There are two possible descents: either walk north and then east to intersect the climbers' trail from the top of Smear and then hike over and down the right side of Chia (easy when packed) or rappel your route (two ropes will probably be needed).

FIRST ASCENT GULLY II 4

The farthest ice climb to the left at Frankenstein, up the steep ice gully in the back of a pronounced recess to the left of the Main Cliff. Approach as for the main cliff and continue traversing left from Young Frankenstein for at least twenty minutes. The route received its name because three separate groups of climbers claimed the route as a first ascent within two years!

Chris Noonan & Jeff Butterfield, Winter 1978

YOUNG FRANKENSTEIN 2-3

The route follows a right diagonally running gully to the left of Silver Heels, the farthest left continuous ice flow on the Main Cliff. The first pitch climbs an ice slab and rock corner to trees and the base of the gully. Easy mixed climbing and snow plodding lead to the top in two more pitches. Rappel the route.

Todd Swain & Jim Frangos, January, 1982

SILVER HEELS II 4

As with the other routes on this face, this steep and typically thin ice climb is rarely in shape. Climb the two pitch ice flow on the left margin of the face and rappel off.

Mark Richey & Alain Comeau, Winter 1977-78

COCAINE II 4+

Ascend the sustained ice flow just to the right of the former route. A two-pitch climb, it is rarely in good condition and seldom repeated.

Peter Cole & Jay Wilson, February, 1978

THE WRATH OF THE VALKYRIE II 4+ M5

A difficult ice flow with a mixed finish make this a stout undertaking. The first ascent used aid up high but the route is now all free. Climb steep ice to dry-tooling past two poor bolts on the blank wall above. (Bring nuts and cams and expect to be scared.) This climb has received rave reviews since its multiple first free ascents (see below).

Franck Vernoy and Jack Hunt climbed the initial ice pillar in January of 1977. Stopped by a blank wall, it's unclear how they finished the route. On the second ascent, by John Drew, Todd Swain and Brad White in the winter of 1981, the blank wall was overcome by Drew who in desperation threw a cluster of pitons over the top which amazingly snagged in a birch tree. He then made a very scary jumar to the top. Paul Boissonneault, with Ted Hammond and Alan Cattabriga, climbed the route on January 20, 1991 with only one pull on a stopper (just before dark). The FFA was made by Jim Ewing and Evan Sanborn on December 22, 2000 (after Ewing and Sanborn's free ascent Steve Larson, Doug Madara and then Brad White all climbed the route and thought they were making the first free ascent!).

THE SWORD AND THE STONE 4+

This is a slender ice ribbon about one hundred and thirty feet left of Fang, the largest ice fall on the south-facing Main Cliff.

Jeff Butterfield & Chris Noonan, Winter 1978

FANG II 4+

One of the most spectacular ice climbs in the region, Fang is unmistakable when in shape, a wide stream of icicles that drip all the way down the main face. Rarely reaching all the way to the ground, the upper ice can sometimes be reached from the left. When in, the climb offers three short pitches of very steep ice. Hike north down the tracks for just a couple of hundred feet then bushwhack up through the woods to the base of the climb. Start in a huge, right-facing corner and climb the ice just to its right. At the top of the corner, belay from trees on the left. The second pitch climbs up and right on the left side of the flow up a steep column (crux) and the third pitch continues to the top. The easiest descent is via rappel (two ropes).

Peter Cole & Alain Comeau, Winter 1977-78

direct 4+

Start about 40 feet right of the normal start and carry the line straight up the entire flow.

FRA Joe Josephson and his wife Margo in one super-long pitch on February 13, 1996

BRAGG-PHEASANT II 5

Perhaps the most ephemeral route on the face, it ascends a series of steep, thinly-iced corners to the right of Fang. The start offers poorly protected mixed climbing. For almost thirty years this climb has been one of the most coveted in the region. Many climbers with much harder ascents to their credit absolutely beam when they return from an ascent of this historic route.

John Bragg & Jeff Pheasant, January, 1974

FRANKENSTEIN SOUTH FACE

A. Young Frankenstein	F. Fang	K. Shooting Star
B. Silver Heels	G. Bragg-Pheasant	L. Ice Rock Café
C. Cocaine	H. Diamonds and Rust	M. Cosmonaut
D. Wrath of the Valkyrie	I. Cloak and Dagger	N. The Cossack
E. Sword in the Stone	J. The Spaceman	

DIAMONDS AND RUST 4+

To the right of Bragg-Pheasant is a sheltered wall with four very short, steep, one-pitch ribbons of ice. Occasionally they are thick enough to climb. Ascend the sustained left-hand ice flow. Rappel off a convenient tree.

Jim Dunn & Franck Vernoy, January, 1977

CLOAK AND DAGGER 4

Thin ice and a small overlap at twenty feet make this slender ribbon to the right of Diamonds and Rust fairly unprotected.

Todd Swain & Ed Webster, January, 1977

THE SPACEMAN 4+

Climb the second ribbon to the right of Diamonds and Rust.

Jim Dunn & Franck Vernoy, Winter 1977

SHOOTING STAR 4

After a difficult ice curtain, climb an easy dihedral and runnel to the top of the right-hand of the four flows.

Ed Webster & Todd Swain, January, 1982

ICE ROCK CAFÉ 3+

Start to the right of Shooting Star and below an obvious left-facing corner that starts 25' up. Climb 3+ ice to a fixed pin, step left into the short corner and climb it to a belay tree at 50 feet. The second pitch climbs over a 40 foot wall to the top.

Kurt Winkler & Andrew Surbur, February 13, 1996

Down in the woods below the previous four climbs are several short ice flows of varying difficulty. If you're on your way up to the Diamonds and Rust area from a point before the trestle, and well left of The Amphitheater, you'll run across the following routes. Each route is eighty to one hundred feet high.

COSMONAUT 3

The farthest left flow, fifty feet left of The Cossack and one hundred feet right of the left margin of this small cliff band. Climb steep ice to small trees, a bulge, and the woods.

Todd Swain & Ed Keller, January, 1982

THE COSSACK 2

A large mass of ice lies hidden in the woods 150 feet right of the left-hand end of the cliff band. Move up a slab to a steep bulge and the top.

Todd Swain & Ed Keller, January, 1982

WHITE RUSSIAN 3

On the lowest cliff band, three hundred feet left of Smear, is a left-facing corner which fills with ice.

Todd Swain, Dave Saball & Brad White, January, 1982

THE STEPPE 1-2

Climb the left-diagonaling snow covered ramp one hundred feet left of SMEAR. The easiest approach to the Banshee or Diamonds and Rust areas.

unknown

RUSSIAN ROULETTE 4

A mixed climb on the low cliff band two hundred feet left of Smear. Ascend a left-facing corner, past a chockstone at the bottom, to some ice bulges. Move over them to a snow slope capped by a final bulge.

Paul Boissonneault & Todd Swain, January, 1982

FRANKENSTEIN: The Amphitheater

The Amphitheater at Frankenstein has one of the highest concentrations of moderate ice climbs in the region. It is a sunny, sheltered, friendly place with lots of thick ice and everything from practice bulges to free-standing pillars. Prior to heading in it is wise to walk out onto the railroad trestle to see what lines are open. The best and safest access is to leave the tracks just before the trestle and follow a well-packed trail uphill to Pegasus. From here you can go either left to reach Smear and the routes to its left or head right to reach the other routes. This approach is recommended for every route in the Amphitheater except Brown Recluse, Widow's Run, and Bob's Delight, the farthest right-hand routes, which are quickly and safely approached from the far end of the trestle. It is wise, especially on sunny days, to avoid traversing under the cliff-band that Widow's Walk drips from—this wall frequently calves off refrigerator-sized chunks. Six major frozen waterfalls descend from the rim of The Amphitheater with several minor routes as well. The descent for most routes is to hike through the woods at the top of the cliff,

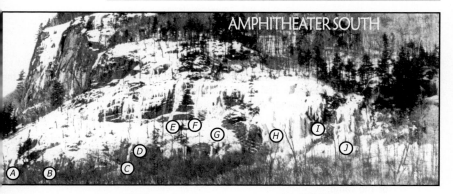

AMPHITHEATER SOUTH

A.	White Russian	F.	Wild Thing
B.	Russian Roulette	G.	Banshee
C.	The Step	H.	Smear
D.	Slim Pickens	I.	Double Barrel
E.	Brocken Spectre	J.	Bow Saw Buttress

either right or left, to a descent trail between Chia and The Blobs. It is easier to rappel from Bob's Delight. During good ice years, several ice flows form on the slab immediately left of Smear, the large ice flow on the far left side of The Amphitheater. They are approached from the right starting up Banshee until a traverse left is possible on a big ledge.

SLIM PICKEN'S 5

The flow farthest left of a rare ice area just left of Smear. One pitch of very delicate climbing up a lacy curtain.

Kurt Winkler & Paul Boissoneault, 1982

Slim Picken's Direct 4

Forty feet above the top of Slim Picken's climb a 20 foot overhanging column.

Kurt Winkler & Ed Mullen, February 18, 1990

BROCKEN SPECTRE 4+

The thin ribbon of ice in the center of the slab features particularly delicate climbing with poor protection. Ascend up a verglased slab to a stance, then climb the upper flow.

Todd Swain & George Hurley, January, 1982

WILD THING 4

Ascends the small ice smear fifty feet left of Banshee. Begin just right of two trees growing against the cliff.

Todd Swain & John Powell, January, 1982

BANSHEE 3+

The smaller ice fall to the left of Smear. Depending on conditions, the first pitch is often mixed, but the upper lead is generally good ice. Start just left of the base of Smear and climb a ramp up and left to a ledge and big tree. The second pitch climbs straight up a wall and then slabs to the top.

Alain Comeau & Jack Hunt, Winter 1977-78

SCREAMING M5

A difficult mixed pitch climbs a corner and finger crack (piton) directly below the tree at the top of the first pitch.

Alain Comeau & partner, late 1990's

SMEAR 3-4

This is the big flow about 250' left of Pegasus. Overcome the initial steep wall and climb up and left along a ramp to an obvious tree belay. The second pitch climbs steeply for a short distance and then finishes straight up the upper slabs. A direct and harder ascent (4) forges straight up the climb to the right of the ramp.

John Bragg & Rick Wilcox, Winter 1972-73

DOUBLE BARREL 4+

Begin 50 feet right of Smear, up a detached, hanging curtain to traverse up and right to a bushy belay. Step left to the upper column and finish up bulges.

Mark Grant & Dave Kelly, January 17, 1990

BOW SAW BUTTRESS 3-4

Climb the icy buttress between Smear and Pegasus past bulges.

Todd Swain & Dave Saball, January 6, 1981

A soft day on one of Frankenstein's perennial favorites, Pegasus. Nick Yardley finds the going plastic.

S. Peter Lewis

PEGASUS 3-4

A beautiful and very popular ice climb, the wide flow in the back of The Amphitheater to the right of Smear. The standard line climbs the first steep bulge (3) then a low-angled slab to a belay at the base of the upper column on the left. The second pitch climbs this column (4) to the top.

Dennis Merritt & Sam Streibert, Winter 1970-71

ROCK FINISH 3+ 5.6

This is an excellent alternative that takes a parallel line up a short column and then rock thirty feet right of the left-hand column. There are two starts. Climb the initial wall on Pegasus and then angle up and right on the slab to reach a two-bolt belay to the right of the right-hand column, or climb the first 75' (easy) of Hobbit Couloir and then angle left and up to reach the same belay. The second pitch climbs the short, steep column left of the bolted belay to a big ledge and then the short rock corner and wall above. It is very well protected with fixed pitons and small rock gear.

WINGTIP 5.6

After the column on the rock finish, instead of heading into the corner, traverse out left for about 15 feet on slopey holds to a crack and then climb delicately to the top.

FRA Paul Miller & Jon Harris, January 1999

HOBBIT COULOIR 4+

Climb the narrow and recessed couloir on the right side of Pegasus to a vertical corner filled with a bulging, awkward pillar. The vertical chandelier at the top is the crux of the route. The route can be done in one pitch or you can belay from the two-bolt anchor mentioned in the previous route.

Bryan Becker, Winter 1978-79

GANDALF THE GREAT 4

This route ascends the right-hand wall of the Hobbit Couloir via a steep ice smear. Climb the first half of Hobbit Couloir until the ice can be reached on the right.

FRA: George Hurley & Vince Wilson, February, 27, 1986

CHIA PET 3 5.7

Climbs a narrow V-groove to the right of the former route. Begin up Hobbit Couloir until a mixed traverse right on a ledge can be made to reach the groove. Climb the groove up and over a chockstone near the top.

FRA: Charlie Townsend & Dave Auble, Winter 1989/90

HARD RANE 4

An excellent line that unfortunately doesn't form that consistently. When it does come in, belay just left of Chia. Climb a very thin smear to a belay on a shelf, then head up and left on steep ground for two more short pitches. A harder, direct start is also possible 25' left of the bottom of Chia.

Dave Walters & Jeff Lea, February, 1979

CHIA 3+

In the very back of The Amphitheater lies the large icefall, Chia. It is easily identified by a distinctive ramp system running up on a diagonal from left to right. A moderate, and yet spectacular route, usually done in two short or one very long pitch. Chia was among the first plums picked upon discovery of

Frankenstein in 1970. An alternate line (4+) stays left and climbs a narrow runnel all the way up the cliff left of the upper column on Chia Direct.

standard line: Sam Streibert & Dennis Merritt, winter 1970-71

CHIA DIRECT 4+

Climb a steep, strenuous curtain on the right side of the fall. Then cross over the normal ramp system and continue up the upper central column.

unknown

ANGEL CAKE 5-

A severe, one-pitch, free-standing column on the Upper Tier of Frankenstein Cliff. Approach uphill above and right of Chia.

Jim Dunn & Franck Vernoy, January, 1977

Taking the direct line on Chia, Kitty Calhoun finds long sections of vertical ice.
S. Peter Lewis

FALLING ANGELS 3-4

Just left of Angel Cake begin on the right side of a small buttress, up thin slabs to a belay at trees above an overlap. Step left and climb a twenty foot column to slabs and the top.

Alain Comeau & Kurt Winkler, January, 1986

CHOCKSTONE CHIMNEY 4

Climbs the left diagonaling chimney line on the Upper Tier to the left of Angel Cake by a couple of hundred yards. After difficult and poorly protected mixed climbing, pass under a chockstone near the top.

Jeff Butterfield & Chris Noonan, December, 1978

THE BLOBS 2-3

Downhill to the right from Chia but before Cave Route are a series of blobs in the woods that offer short leads and topropes. To toprope, approach from part way up the descent trail to the right of Chia.

unknown

The rarely climbed free-standing column of Angel Cake.
Doug Miller

AMPHITHEATER CENTER

A. Pegasus
B. Pegasus Rock Finish
C. Hobbit Couloir
D. Hard Rane
E. Chia
F. Chia Direct

A. Pegasus
B. Chia
C. The Blobs
D. Cave Route
E. Widow's Walk
F. Widow's Run
G. Bob's Delight

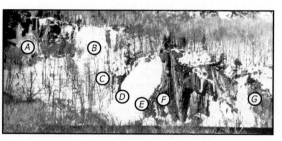

AMPHITHEATER NORTH

THE CAVE ROUTE 3+

On the north wall of the amphitheater is an overhanging wall. On the left side of the wall, 75 feet left of Widow's Walk and 50 feet right of The Blobs, climb a thick flow to a ledge beneath a broken wall. Traverse carefully left over The Blobs or rappel to descend. This is an excellent route.

Al Rubin & Oriel Sola-Costa, Winter 1970-71

THE WIDOW'S CAVE 4+

In a good season a completely independent pillar will form right of Cave Route and left of Widow's Walk.

unknown

WIDOW'S WALK 5

This spectacular route forms as a nearly freestanding column dripping off the center of the overhanging wall 75 feet right of Cave Route. When in shape it offers a long pitch of very strenuous ice climbing with little chance of a rest. DO NOT WALK BENEATH THIS ROUTE ON SUNNY DAYS—chunks of ice the size of walruses regularly fall off it.

Alain Comeau & Jack Hunt, February, 1977

WIDOW'S RUN M7

To the right of Widow's Walk look for three ice tiers that drip off overhangs. There is a bolt near the top.

Eric Siefer, Carrie Shea, & Seth Green, 2002

THE BROWN RECLUSE 5

Sixty feet right of Widow's Walk (approach from Bob's Delight) climb thinly iced rock (pins needed) to an overhang. A strenuous pull on thin ice with marginal protection clears the roof and gains a thin smear to the top. A bold lead.

Chris Rowins & Jim Surette, February, 1985

BOB'S DELIGHT 4

This is the farthest right of the amphitheater routes and is the obvious flow about 75' left of the north end of the railroad trestle. A sheltered, south-facing location makes this fine, one pitch route often the warmest in the area. The only drawback is that the ice tends to melt out from behind, creating hollow ice and potentially dangerous conditions. Nevertheless, it is very popular. Rappelling is usually the best descent option.

Most likely John Drew, Winter 1970-71

FRANKENSTEIN: The Trestle Cut/Practice Slab South

TRESTLE CUT FLOWS 2-4 M5

Just after the trestle the tracks enter a narrow corridor blasted out of the rock that offers several fun routes. The easiest way to climb the routes is to lead whichever one is in the best shape (usually the left-hand route) and then toprope the others. Alternately, you can climb up and around the left end (can be scary) or climb through the woods to the right of the Practice Slab South and then traverse the woods. There are usually three or four distinct lines here that vary from grade 3 to 4 along with some M4/5 topropes. The easiest descent is via rappel. It is an excellent, sheltered practice area. To the right of the trestle cut is a large, low-angled slab with several lines (grade 2-3-). It's higher than you think; either rappel with two ropes or descend off to the right. This area was much more exciting back in the late 70's and early 80's when the trains regularly came through!

FRANKENSTEIN: Lost in the Forest Area

There are several somewhat hidden ice flows in the woods just north of the Practice Slab South. Depending on the year and snow depth, a number of routes can be found here. For years these routes have had different, often contradictory route descriptions. These routes often provide a less crowded alternative to the more popular climbs nearby. An approach trail begins just beyond the Practice Slab South. The best descent for the next routes is to hike back down through the woods to the left of Lost in the Forest or rappel.

LOST IN THE FOREST 2-3

This is the left-hand flow, a wide rectangular ice bulge about 50 feet high. In the past this was often mistaken for A Walk in the Forest. A big snow year can virtually cover this climb. The right side offers a fun, steep toprope.

Most likely John Drew, Winter 1970-71

A DRIP IN THE WOODS 4+

About a hundred feet right of the former route a steep column sometimes seeps off a ledge below the top of a cliff band. Climb the column strenuously to the ledge; rappel from the obvious tree.

unknown

A WALK IN THE FOREST 3-4

About 150 feet right of Lost in the Woods is a big wide flow about 100 feet high that is bordered on the left by a broken right-facing corner and becomes increasingly steeper as you go to the right. There is room here for several parties. Many have thought they were on the (much harder) Mean Miss Treater when climbing this flow. Sorry folks.

Most likely John Drew, Winter 1970-71

MEAN MISS TREATER 4

This is the steep flow about 200 feet right of the former route and well left of A Case of the Willeys. It is not often in shape, but when it does come in offers a pitch of steep, thin ice.

Unknown

WPP 3+ M1 R

The right side of this section of cliff ends at an abrupt left-facing corner. This corner provides excellent, relatively easy, but scary mixed climbing. Bring rock gear.

Unknown

Beyond this route the cliff is broken by trees. The next cliff band to the right is the Case of the Willeys cliff and in a good year four thin lines are found here. The next route is the left-hand line, then there are two thin smears that have no recorded ascents (Brad White and Mike Grady scratched up something here in 1978); A Case of the Willeys is the far right-hand line.

THE HOWLING 4+ X

On the left side of the Case of the Willey's cliff-band and 40' right of Mean Miss Treater, climb thin ice up to a steep curtain then easier ice to the top. The climb was extremely thin on the first ascent and used "Spectres, tied off screws, and small trees" for protection.

Kurt Winkler & Richard Gunning , January 31, 1996

A CASE OF THE WILLEYS 3-4

This is the farthest climb to the right before Waterfall It is a full pitch high and has an obvious ledge at mid height with an oak tree on it. Begin in a small corner facing left and follow an often thin flow to the top and rappel.

FRA: Todd Swain & John Mauzey, February 22, 1983

Of historical interest is the origin of this famous saying, "a case of the Willeys." The Willey family were among the first setters of the area in the early 1800's. After several days of violent rain in August of 1826, a landslide swept down the east face of Mt. Willey. Hearing the roar of the slide and fearing their house would be demolished, the Willey family sprang from their dinner table and fled outside into the night. A search party would later find the bodies of Samuel Willey, Jr., his wife, two of their five children and two hired hands buried under the rubble. The other three children were never found. Incredibly, their home was virtually untouched, having been protected from the slide by a large boulder. And from inside the house came the howls of the only survivor, the family dog. Hence, "a case of the Willeys," a familiar phrase with a spine tingling origin.

FRANKENSTEIN: Standard Route Area

The next series of climbs are clustered near the huge blue cascade of Frankenstein's Standard Route and rivals the Amphitheater in terms of the number of high quality routes. Be very careful climbing here, especially below other parties. Although Standard Route is the big moderate attraction, if there are a lot of people around consider Standard Left or The Penguin as great alternatives to queuing up in the bowling alley. About ten minutes walk past the trestle look for a shadowed flow up in a hollow in the hillside. This first flow is:

WATERFALL 3

Located to the south of Standard Route in a very secluded recess, it is one of the easiest and most ascended climbs at Frankenstein Cliff. The falls are readily visible as a one pitch flow rising in a series of steps. Descend around the left side or rappel the route with two ropes.
Al Rubin & Oriel Sola-Costa, Winter 1970-71

STANDARD LEFT II 3

This excellent route climbs the independent flow that spills down the buttress just left of the left-hand cave. After two pitches, join the regular route on the right. Descend as for Standard Route.
Al Long & Al Rubin, Winter 1973-74

STANDARD ROUTE II 3+

November

April

The most popular moderate climb at Frankenstein and likely in all of New Hampshire. About ten minutes north of the train trestle this massive blue flow drops 300 feet and almost reaches the tracks. It comes in early, stays late and is often crowded. The normal ascent line (although there are variations) climbs up the center to a belay from bolts in the right-hand cave. The second pitch climbs the steep central wall to bulges. A third pitch wanders up and left to the trees or climbs a steep wall (4). Walk right (north) for about 500' and then down a snow gully north of Dracula.
Sam Streibert & Dennis Merritt, Winter 1970-71

Brad White up the pegboard on pitch two of Standard Route; get here early or get in line.
S. Peter Lewis

TANDARD

REA

Standard Left
Standard Route
Window Route variation
Standard Right variation
The Penguin

S. Peter Lewis

STANDARD RIGHT 3+/4-

To the right of the normal first pitch you can climb a steep curtain straight up to join The Window Route. Further right is a left-facing corner (3 M3) that can be climbed to join The Penguin.

unknown

THE WINDOW ROUTE 3

From the right-hand cave it is often possible to climb through a window in a hanging curtain to the right (if you're first you may have to hack the window yourself—way fun) and then up to a tree ledge. From here you can merge left onto Standard's regular finish, do that route's harder finish, or traverse right to The Penguin.

unknown

BREAKING GLASS 4

Climb straight up from the cave belay by stemming off the Window Route curtain and then climbing strenuously up through a notch. When the curtain forms well this is a cool little variation; when it forms poorly expect hard mixed moves.

unknown

ETAL CAVE 3+

About 75 feet right of the normal start for Standard below the right-hand cave climb up the buttress to a small cave (rock gear) then head left up steeper and fatter ice to a tree ledge. Continue on routes above or rappel.

FRA Richard Doucette, Tom Maguire & Ged Fay, February 16, 1997

HE PENGUIN II 4

An independent line between Standard and Dropline. Begin about one hundred feet right of Standard at a thin flow to the right of a buttress, up this on mixed ground to a tree below a bulge. The second pitch climbs the bulge and then continues up mixed ground aiming for a final column that is easily seen to the right of the top pitch of Standard. The last pitch takes the thin and steep column to the trees. (The final pitch can also be approached from the left after the second pitch of Standard.) Several alternate finishes of about the same difficulty on the right have been climbed by Brad White et al.

unknown; several parties may have done it in the late 1970's

SCRATCH AND SNIFF 4

This route climbs an independent line between The Penguin and Dropline.

Andy Orsini & George Hurley, December 1996

DROPLINE 5

Before Everest and IMAX Dave Breashears wa just a great climber. Note the 55 cm too leather boots, and um...sweater; Dropline, 198.
S. Peter Lew

This dramatic icicle saw several attempts, including a spectacular fall, before it was finally completed. The line couldn't be more obvious; the yellow icicle is up and to the right of Standard Route. Start on the left and work up steep slabs of ice, often very thin, below the main pillar and belay on the left in a small protected corner. The final exposed column, typically hollow at the start, is only a couple of feet thick and is vertical the entire way. Descend as for Standard Route.

Rainsford Rouner, Peter Cole, & Rick Wilcox, February, 1976

LAST EXIT 5

The improbable ice ribbon just to the right of Dropline. It has only been in shape on a couple of occasions, so has had few ascents. The seconds did not follow the leader on the first ascent.

Rainsford Rouner, Winter 1978

The ever-stylish Kurt Winkler toppir out on Welcome to the Machine grade 5 condition
Lee Steve!

WELCOME TO THE MACHINE 4/5

This ephemeral route drips down the wall to the right of Last Exit. The first tim it came in it was truly desperate and deserved the grade 5 rating. In the 2000 01 season it came in really fat and was climbed many times (including solos).

DROPLINE AREA

A. *Dropline*
B. *Last Exit*
C. *Welcome to the Machine*
D. *The Coffin*
E. *Dracula Right (around the corner)*

S. Peter Lewis

Although it still carried the grade 5 rating, in these conditions the difficulty was more like 4 (sorry folks). Under normal conditions expect long sections of vertical ice and an overhang. Climb the plumb line 40 feet right of Last Exit.

John Imbrie & Karen Messer, January, 1978

THE COFFIN 4+

An independent line that runs the height of the cliff between Welcome to the Machine and Dracula. There are two starts. To the right of the starts of Dropline and Welcome to the Machine is a small buttress; walk down and around the bottom of this to a shallow groove. Climb up the groove and over several steps to a belay on the highest ledge below the upper flow. Alternately, begin in the next groove to the right, about 40 feet left of Dracula and just right of an overhang just off the ground. Pitch two climbs the crux flow to the top of the cliff.

Todd Swain & Butch Constantine, February 11 (left), and 14 (right), 1983

DRACULA 4+

Hidden in an acute, right-facing corner to the right of the previously mentioned routes. If Standard is the classic moderate climb, then Dracula is the classic hard route and can be ascended in a number of ways. The climb features

John Tremblay ropeless in his office on Dracula in the mid-1980's.

S. Peter Lewis

three steep sections with resting ledges in between. Climb the first two steps in one long pitch, stemming on the second steep section to take some of the weight off your arms. Belay on a good ledge on the left with a pine tree (partially fixed anchor in the crack above; bring nuts). The short final pitch climbs columns to an awkward bulge and the trees. Overhanging icicles often make this the crux of the route. A rappel from the ledge at the top of the normal first pitch is possible but the tree is small and the fixed anchor is old and funky.

John Bragg & A.J. LaFleur, Winter 1973

DRACULA RIGHT SIDE 4/5

The right side of Dracula offers a much more strenuous alternative, with thin ice and poor protection at the start. After overcoming a prolonged vertical curtain 20 feet right of Dracula, a flared stemming corner offers some relief before the woods.

Dale Bard & partner, Winter 1977

BURIED ALIVE 4+

Twenty-five feet farther right of Dracula Right Side climb up corners and through inverted caves and connected hummocks to the woods. Early ascentionist Brad White likened the pitch to climbing up through a toilet seat—while it doesn't sound good the climbing is actually superb.

FRA Henry Barber & Ron Hauser, February 1989

FRANKENSTEIN: The Hanging Gardens

To the right of Dracula the cliff continues for a couple of hundred feet, curving uphill to form the left wall (going up) of the obvious low-angle snow gully that is the common descent for all climbs north of Waterfall. This is home to a number of short and sometimes desperate routes that are easily toproped. It is a good place to head if there is time left at the end of the day or you enjoy steep mixed climbs. The climbs range in difficulty from 4 to 5+ and M8 and include several overhanging routes.

CLAWSICLE 4/5

This climb forms a hundred feet or so right of Dracula. It consists of a short, steep pillar that flows down out of a shallow bowl. In some years it gets diverted to the left and drips down the wall over a small roof offering great mixed climbing (5+ M5). George Hurley also reportedly scratched his way up a line or two left of Clawsicle in the 1990's but as his habit, like a pine marten, he left little trace of his passing.

FRA: Kurt Winkler & George Hurley, Winter 1984/85

Ahead of his time, John Trembla cranks the FA of Without Reason
S. Peter Lewi

WITHOUT REASON 5+

This is one of the shortest routes of its grade in the area, and a testimony to the boldness of John Tremblay. Just as the cliff band begins to turn uphill to form the left wall of the descent gully, a large sloping ledge will be seen about fifteen feet above the ground with a large slanting overhang above it. Climb an ice smear on the right to reach the ledge, traverse left, and then swing onto the free-hanging icicle that drips down off the roof. Several pull-ups will get you high enough to tap your crampons into the bottom of the icicle, then climb strenuously to the top. Protection is sketchy, bring rock gear.

John Tremblay & Pat Hackett, January, 1986

WITHIN REASON 6

This is one of the hardest lines in the region. Start up the initial smear of the former route and then step onto a hanging dagger and climb it to a roof and exit to the right.

Joe Josephson & Maury McKinney, late 1990's

Jared Ogden on what some might consider unreasonable terrain on Within Reason at the Hanging Gardens.
Mark Synnott

197

SOMETHING ABOUT YOU MAKES ME WILD M8

This is a wild line going straight out the massive overhang/roof immediately to the right of Within Reason. Look for a 4 foot diameter "silver dollar" flake at the start of the route. This and the other routes nearby are some of the most difficult short pitches in New Hampshire.

Jared Ogden, Mark Synnott and Randy Rackliff in 2000. Synnott toproped the route and then Ogden led it placing all the gear, mostly small cams. At the time it was one of the hardest mixed pitches in New Hampshire.

SCRATCHING POST 4+

Far to the right of Something About You Makes Me Wild is a pillar. Stem off the rock (piton) to reach the freestanding column.

FRA: Kurt Winkler & Bruce Luetters, Winter 1983-84

Uphill from Scratching Post are a number of short routes that were all done in the late 1970's by Chris Hassig and friends. They range from 3-4 and are all easily toproped.

THE HOUSE OF BLUE 2-3

About 40 feet north of the descent gully is a big blue flow in the woods that is an excellent teaching/practice area.

BEGINNERS' SLAB NORTH 1-2

This is the final climb when walking north along the tracks. The slab is low-angled, providing good practice for leading or French technique.

unknown

FRANKENSTEIN: Lost Helmet Crag

This is the short crag located high on the east side of the road directly opposite Dracula. Park at a pullout where the road crosses the Saco River and bushwhack up through the woods for about a half hour to reach the crag. A sunny exposure means that the following routes stand a good chance of falling off on a warm day. Descend by rappel or walk off. Climbs will be described from left to right.

PIGLET 2-3

On the extreme left end of the cliff and 20 feet left of Snugcicle is a shallow corner.

Mike Arsenault & Anne Lepine, March 9, 1996

THE SNUGCICLE 2-3

On the left end of the crag is an ice flow capped by a squeeze chimney.

FRA: Todd Swain & Mike Hannon, February 15, 1983

ROBOT LOGIC 3+

To the right of The Snugcicle and just left of the center of the crag is a steep icicle.

Kurt Winkler & Joe Perez, Winter 1982

EXTENSOR 4+

Right again is a route characterized by serious mixed climbing to a crux squeeze chimney filled with ice. Pegs helpful.

Kurt Winkler with Joe Perez, Winter 1982

TAP TAP CRASH 3+

The farthest right route on the crag. Up a thin, detached curtain to thicker ice and the top.

Kurt Winkler and Joe Perez attempted the thin curtain in 1982 but "it fell down" (with the leader) so they started to the left (5.4); Todd Swain and Mike Hannon did the first direct ascent on February 15, 1982.

CRAWFORD NOTCH: MOUNT WEBSTER

Five miles north of Frankenstein Cliff in Crawford Notch is a trio of mountains whose faces are virtually covered with ice each winter: Mt. Webster, famous for its alpine gullies that offer some of the longest climbs in the region; Mt. Willey, home to perhaps the most often travelled route in the White Mountains, Willey's Slide ; and Mt. Willard, a complex face with classic climbs at every grade.

Mt. Webster's gullies, located on the face that rises above the east side of Route 302, while moderate in terms of sheer difficulty, involve an elevation gain of almost 2,500 feet, and therefore have an

WEBSTER, WILLEY, WILLARD AREA

A. Webster: Shoestring Gully
B. Webster: Horseshoe Gully
C. Webster: Central Gully
D. Willey: Willey's Slide
E. Willard: South Face
F. Willard: Upper East Face
G. Elephant Head

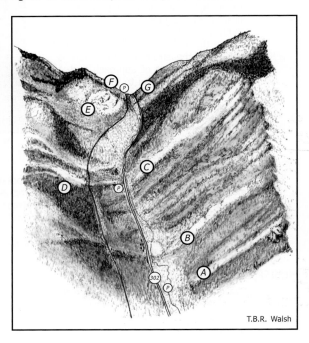

T.B.R. Walsh

additional degree of seriousness attached to any ascent. Do not neglect to take into consideration the tiring descent and possibility for rapid weather changes when planning your itinerary. Park on Route 302 as close to the base of your intended gully as possible, then head directly to it. The only obstacle in your way will be the Saco River. Fortunately, the river is only twenty feet wide at this point and fairly easy to cross.

For the descent, do not count on the Webster Cliff Trail, the safest way down, being packed out. The fastest way will probably be through the woods on either side of your gully and a swift glissade down the lower snow sections which will bring you back to the highway. A day on Mount Webster should be considered comparable to a trip up Huntington Ravine—just ask anyone who has come down the Webster Cliff Trail in the dark. Routes will be described from south to north.

SHOESTRING GULLY III 2 (5.5 3)

Not to be underestimated; the upper reaches of Shoestring Gully.
Brian Post

The southernmost ice gully on the massive west face of Mt. Webster. Park along the road below the climb if conditions allow or at the Ethan Pond Trail parking lot .3 miles south on Rt. 302. The lower section of the climb consists of low angle snow climbing, while the upper gully is considerably narrower, steeper, and usually full of ice, depending on how much snow has fallen. The normal finish is about six pitches long and takes an easy line on the left. This is an excellent climb well worth the effort. In total, there is roughly 2,500 feet of approach and climbing from the road to the ridge at the top. To descend, walk straight back into the woods from the top of the climb for just a few minutes until you intersect the Webster Cliff Trail (usually packed), turn right and follow it back to the road. You can also rappel the route via V-threads and trees (be careful of parties below).

There are two other finishes possible: The Chockstone Exit (5.5) leaves the main gully on the right two pitches from the top ascending an obvious gully/chimney system; The Direct Finish (grade 3 mixed) takes a direct line up the final rock wall one pitch above the previous finish. Highly recommended.

Original route—unknown; the Chockstone Exit—Kurt Winkler & John Colebaugh, February 2, 1986; the Direct Finish—FRA: Alain Comeau, January 1986

HORSESHOE GULLY III 1-2

The next gully to the north of Shoestring Gully, a few hundred feet to the left although nowhere near as prominent. Similar to its neighbor, but can be without any ice if there has been heavy snow.

unknown

LANDSLIDE GULLY III 1-2

The long gully directly opposite the parking lot at the Willey House site and south of Central Couiloir by a few hundred yards. Start from the pond and bushwhack to the base of this obvious snow climb. Descend as for Shoestring or back down the gully.

FRA: Todd Swain & Ned Getchel, 1978

CENTRAL COULOIR III 3+

This gully with its many offshoots at the top is located about halfway up the notch somewhat south of Willey's Slide. Head through the woods in as direct as possible a line to the base. Although it is a typical snow couloir at the start, the section leading to the upper headwall provides moderate ice climbing. At the headwall, there are three natural finishes to the climb. The original finish is farthest left up a squirmy chimney (3+) for two pitches. The central line climbs shattered, brushy steps at M1, and the third is described below as a much harder finish. To descend, again, aim straight back for the Webster Cliff Trail or descend the route—either option is long.

unknown

CENTRAL COULOIR VARIATION FINISH 4+ 5.8

The right-hand finish climbs very steeply for two pitches (4+ 5.8). Descend as for Central Couloir.

FRA Kurt Winkler & Doug Huntley, December 29, 1993; Gerry Handren may have climbed this route around the same time

For the next two routes and one variation start up Central Couloir until about 1.5 pitches below the upper headwall on that route. An obvious traverse on treed ledges leads to the base of these routes.

GREEN CHASM III 3 5.6

Traverser right 100 yards to a huge chasm. A pitch of snow leads up and over a chockstone. The next pitch (3-3+) is the crux and there is one more easier pitch to the top. Walk straight into the woods to the Webster Cliff Trail and descend as for Shoestring.

Kurt Winkler & Peter Gamache, March 17, 1989 (Jose Albeyta may have climbed the route earlier)

VO₂ GULLY 3+ R

The next gully right of Green Chasm is unclimbed. Further right but left of Heart Palace is the two-pronged VO_2 Gully. Climb the left-hand prong for one pitch.

VO₂ MAX 3

Climb the easier right-hand prong.

Kurt Winkler & Charles White climbed both variations to this climb in February 1998

HEART PALACE 4-

The farthest right ice flow, on the upper headwall, 100 yards right of the Green Chasm. Climb up to an interesting cave and then up a pillar out right to easier ground above. It is easy to rappel the pitch with two ropes.

Kurt Winkler, Sunil Davidson, Drubha Hein & Shraddha Howard, March 10, 1990

HALF BREED II 3 5.2

Can be climbed as a variation start to Central Couloir or as a route in itself. In the middle of the large slab left of Central Couloir is a long, thin runnel. Four pitches of thin ice, the first being mixed and the hardest, bring you to a point where it is possible to traverse right to Central Couloir and either continue up that route, or descend.

Jerry Handren & Sharon Hirsch, December 7, 1990

FOOLS PARADISE III 3

A long variation to Central Couloir that begins several pitches up that route and looks for excitement by breaking left aiming for a large flow up high. After four pitches of iced-up rock, climb the flow for a full pitch through the woods to an exit crack and a further pitch of ice to the top.

Tom Vinson & John Gospodarek, February 11, 1983

NORTH SLABS 1-2

On the northern end of the Webster Cliffs are several open, low-angled slabs which occasionally ice up enough to be worth a climb.

unknown

THE PILGRIMAGE II 3

The rock buttress at the extreme northern end of Webster Cliffs contains a narrow ice gully. What applies to other pilgrimages may apply here—the approach is the crux. Hike for about an hour up difficult scree to the base of the climb. After easy terrain at the start, climb a steeper ice gully over bulges to the top for a pitch or two. Descend through the woods to the left (bushwhacking) or rappel.

Mark Whiton, Winter 1978

CRAWFORD NOTCH: MOUNT WILLEY

November

April

Mount Willey is a huge bulk of a mountain that dominates the west side of Crawford Notch. Its claim to fame is that it is home to perhaps the best easy ice climb in the White Mountains, Willey's Slide. Willey's is one of the most visited ice climbing areas on the East Coast. It is located on the lower east face of Mount Willey and is easily seen from Route 302 about halfway up Crawford Notch. Just north of the Willey House historic site at the very bottom of the notch are two dirt pullouts, one on either side of the road. Look for a large boulder just in the woods on the west side of the road and you'll find the trailhead. Follow the beaten path up to the railroad tracks, turn right a few steps, then turn left and hike up to the slide. Since the slide is so heavily used, it should be obvious that safety precautions be observed; avoid climbing below other parties and always wear helmets. After a big snow Willey's can be very avalanche prone.

WILLEY'S SLIDE II 2

Four to six or more full pitches of mixed snow and ice climbing can be done up this low-angled flow of superb ice. There are a multitude of moderate ice bulges and occasionally an ice cave near the top. After taking a moment to enjoy the marvelous view from the top, simply work your way down through the woods on either side back to the base. There is an additional small flow of similar angle down right in the woods which is worth a visit.

unknown

CRAWFORD NOTCH: MOUNT WILLARD

The most extensive ice climbing locale in the north end of Crawford Notch is the south face of Mount Willard. In addition to the lower slabs, there are worthwhile short slabs and gullies to choose from on the upper face. One of the pleasant aspects of ice climbing here is, undoubtedly, the southern exposure which often makes for warm and comfortable climbing. But it can also be very windy.

Parking for Willard is best found at the top of the notch at a plowed pullout on the west. Walk south along the railroad tracks until beneath the lower slabs. If you intend to do a route on the Upper Wall only, approach via Hitchcock Gully (2-3), the lower continuation of a prominent chimney system quite visible from the railroad tracks, one of the short climbs to either side of it, or ascend a low-angle slab well to the north. To descend from the large tree covered terrace in the center of the face above all the lower routes, walk right until below the upper chimney of Hitchcock Gully. Two short rappels, the first from an obvious white birch tree, or one long rappel will get you into the lower snow-filled portion of Hitchcock Gully which is often an easy glissade to the tracks. If you complete a route all the way to the top of the face, bushwhack up towards the summit and you'll intercept a usually well-packed hiking trail which leads back to the head of the notch and the cars. Routes will be described from left to right.

MOUNT WILLARD: Willey Brook

STREAMLINE II 2

This route and its neighbors climbs out of the ravine of Willey Brook, about a half a mile north of Willey's Slide. Park as for Mt. Willard, and walk 300 yards south of Cinema Gully to a trestle. Walk up the right side of the stream for a quarter of a mile to a fork. Bear right and go 100 yards to a streambed on the left side of a rock slab. Follow this for many pitches.

Kurt Winkler & Phyllis Austin, January 15, 1983

FLAT FOOT FLOOGIE 2+

A two pitch route up the slab right of Streamline. Begin in an icy corner and climb a hundred feet to a horizontal crack. One more pitch and rappel.

Kurt Winkler & Phyllis Austin, February 8, 1986

CANDLEPIN 4

A perfect grade 4 pillar in a hidden gully right of Flat Foot Floogie.
Kurt Winkler & Phyllis Austin, February 8, 1986

MOUNT WILLARD: South Face

This is the big sweeping cliff on the south side of Mount Willard that dominates the view as you drive up the notch. The lower left part of the cliff is home to some of the finest steep routes in the area while the slabs to the right offer long, and often thin climbs. The upper cliff above the obvious tree ledge has just a couple of lines with many more found around to the north on the Upper East Face.

CORNIER DE LA MOUSE II 3+

Located in a hidden buttress around the corner to the left of Gully #1. Ascend a left-facing corner with mixed climbing, eventually exiting out right onto icy slabs. Two pitches.
Chester Drieman & Todd Swain, January, 1981

GULLY #1 II 4

The left-hand of three steep icefalls on the lower left side of the face. Approach via the snow gully below the right-hand gully (Great Madness) and traverse left along the cliff base to the start. The flow is somewhat narrow and can be done in one or two pitches. Descend left to the base or rappel.
A.J. LaFleur, John Bragg, & Peter Cole, January, 1974

Gully #1: DIRECT START 3-4

Below the approach snow gully is a slab that occasionally ices up to give a long, thin pitch as a direct start.
Kurt Winkler or Brad White, early 80's

GULLY #1 1/2 4+

This variation climbs a steep V groove to the right of Gully# 1, and is harder than the main flow.
Most likely Ken Andrasko circa 1977

GULLY# 2 II 3+ 5.7

Using the same approach as for Gully #1, you'll find the start of this route. Hanging icicles dripping down an overhanging rock band mark the start. Avoid the icicles by beginning on the right and angling back left to reach the upper ice flow. The rock is harder than the ice on this one. If you climb directly up the ice on the left, the grade is NEI 4-.
John Bragg & Peter Cole, February, 1974

GULLY #2 1/2 II 3

Ascends the ice between Gully #2 and Great Madness. Climb the long snow slope to the base of Great Madness. An easy pitch over ice bulges leads to a belay at a rock wall on the left. Move out left and climb through an awkward notch to easier ice slabs above.
Todd Swain, Dick Peterson & Brad White, December 7, 1980

WILLARD SOUTH FACE

A. Cornier de la Mouse	E. Great Madness	I. Rikki-Tikki-Tavi
B. Gully #1	E. Freeze Frame	J. Cauliflower Gully
C. Gully #2	G. Cinema Gully	K. tree covered ledge
D. Gully #2.5	H. Parallel Universe	L. Upper East Face

GREAT MADNESS AREA DETAIL

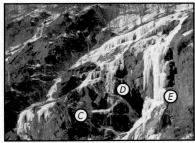

Brian Post

GREAT MADNESS II 5

The right most of the three ice flows is the most difficult. It is located about a hundred yards left of the base of Cinema Gully, the prominent central snow and ice gully. A short easy pitch leads to the base of a sustained vertical pillar, the crux. Climb strenuously to easier slabs and the tree-covered terrace.

Jim Dunn & Dale Wilson, January, 1982

FREEZE FRAME II 3 5.7 A0

A mixed route up the face just to the left of Cinema Gully. The best approach is to start up Cinema Gully then move off left beneath its first ice bulge along a set of sloping, snow-covered ramps. Follow an obvious sloping ledge up to its right end, then aid (A0) off a bolt to slabs and a tree belay. Climb through trees to another belay at the base of an ice flow in a right-facing dihedral. Follow this to the tree-covered ledge.

Todd Swain & Butch Constantine, January, 1982

CINEMA GULLY II 2

This highly recommended climb ascends the beautiful wide open snow and ice gully in the center of Mt. Willard's lower slab, and is so named for an early cinematography project. Several pitches of moderate climbing lead to the large tree-covered terrace in the center of the face. The start of the route, while quite easy, is often quite thinly iced, and setting up secure belays can be difficult until you reach thicker ice higher on the climb. Nonetheless, it is a fine route. Trending right high on the route will raise the grade to about 3. Once on the tree-covered ledge, there are several options: descend around left of Gully #1 (nasty bushwhack), walk right across the terrace and rappel down Hitchcock Gully (fairly straightforward; look for obvious white birch tree at the top of lower Hitchcock), or continue up any number of short climbs on the upper wall to the summit of Mt. Willard. The descent down Hitchcock Gully is the fastest and easiest option however difficult it may sound.

unknown

A sunny day at the Cinema—one of New Hampshire's all-time classic easy ice routes.
Brian Post (wildrays.com)

PARALLEL UNIVERSE
III M6 5 R/X

This is one of the longest winter routes on Mt. Willard with over 700 feet of climbing—much of it thin and scary. From the base of Cinema Gully head uphill to the right for several hundred feet, passing under an obvious big overlap a half-pitch up, to a shallow depression in the face (near the start of the summer route Star Trek). Climb straight up the slabs for two very thin pitches to a bolted belay on a ledge on the left near a clump of small trees (at the base of the Milky Way pitch on Across the Universe). Step left and climb the large, left-facing groove (as for Ursa Major) above to the tree-covered ledge. Thrash straight up the treed slope to the upper cliff and an obvious groove capped by an overhang. Climb the mixed groove, skirt the roof on the left, and then climb another thin ice pitch straight up (the groove heads left) to the very top of the cliff. Hike down the Mt. Willard trail back to the top of the notch.

FA Paul Cormier, Jim Shimberg & friend, 1998

RIKKI-TIKKI-TAVI II 5-

Verglas and poor protection make this an intimidating route which is not often in shape. Ascends the approximate line of the Ursa Major rock climb. Begin 200 feet right of Cinema Gully beneath the right end of a large iced overlap. With negligible protection, climb the ice smear up and over the overlap (the crux). Belay at an ice bulge on easy slabs. Continue up thin ice and snow to a belay bush on the right. Head straight up to a rock band after surmounting easy bulges. The last pitch moves right to a right-facing corner leading to the trees. Bring cams and small nuts in addition to short ice screws for protection.

Todd Swain, Dave Saball & Brad White, January, 1982

MOUNT WILLARD: Upper East Face

The following short routes are found on the upper east face of Mt. Willard. They are appropriate sequels to any of the previous climbs, or worthwhile done alone. To climb them on their own either climb the lower portion of Hitchcock Gully or one of its neighbors, or climb Willard Slab Right and traverse left. The only exception is Cauliflower

Gully which is best approached by climbing one of the routes on the South Face.

CAULIFLOWER GULLY 2-3

This is the gully that is clearly visible from the road, curving around the left side of the large upper cliff directly above Gully #1. A nice route that offers a logical finish to Cinema Gully or any route on the left side of the cliff. From the tree ledge above Cinema Gully traverse up and left for a couple of hundred yards through steep woods to reach the flow. Two pitches up the gully lead to the very summit of Mt. Willard. Descend down the Mt. Willard trail back to the parking lot at the top of the notch.

Todd Swain & George Hurley, February 13, 1983

EAST FACE SLAB 3

Climb the large obvious ice slab immediately left of the upper chimney of Hitchcock Gully. Similar in nature to Cinema Gully, it is another logical finish to that route.

unknown

REAR WINDOW II 4

This route description pieces several pitches into a nice independent line all the way up the cliff. When combined with the following route this makes for a grand adventure. Climb the Lower Hitchcock snow gully to the belay tree for its first technical pitch. The first pitch climbs out left onto a thin slab and then a second pitch climbs straight up to the tree-covered ledge below the East Face Slabs. Walk across the ledge to a narrow gully just left of Upper Hitchcock. Climb the shallow gully (3+) to the trees above and then walk straight uphill to the next cliff-band. The final pitch climbs a steep column on an 80⁰ wall. The easiest descent is to rappel down to the tree ledge, then down Lower Hitchcock.

Alain Comeau climbed the first two pitches with Paul Durand, Michael Medvin, and Mark Meche on January 21, 1996. The third pitch, the gully left of Upper Hitchcock, was probably climbed in the 1980's. The final steep pillar was climbed by Paul Cormier and Cindy Hargis in 1997. The editor of this guide, knowing about the route left of Upper Hitchcock and needing to name it something beside "unknown," called the route "Rear Window" before hearing the name from Comeau. It's a small world out there.

SURPRISE PARTY BUTTRESS 3+

Hike up through the woods to the left of the Lower Hitchcock snow gully for 500' or so until you come to an obvious buttress. This is at the very right end of the lower slabs on Mt. Willard and just around the corner to the left from Lower Hitchcock. The first pitch climbs very thin ice up the buttress. Pitch two climbs an ice curtain to trees, joining Rear Window after its first-pitch traverse.

Kurt Winkler & Marty Wolons, January 21, 1996. On the approach, Winkler and Wolons found tracks in the snow. At the base of the new route they found John Tremblay and Pat Hackett. Tremblay and Hackett decided not to do the route, graciously offered the route to Winkler and Wolons, and left to do a new grade 5 mixed route over near Elephant Head Gully. Winkler and Wolons climbed up two pitches and were surprised to see Comeau and company a hundred feet ahead of them, snagging the first ascent of Rear Window (what Winkler and Wolons had supposed were going to be the 3ʳᵈ and 4ᵗʰ pitches of their new route).

WILLARD UPPER EAST FACE

A. *East Face Slab*
B. *Rear Window*
C. *Upper Hitchcock Gully*
D. *East Face Slab Right*
E. *rappel to Lower Hitchcock*

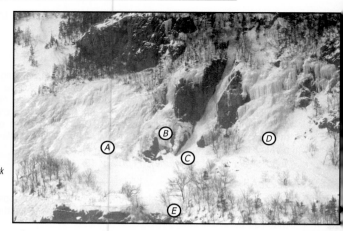

HITCHCOCK GULLY 3-

This is the most obvious, right diagonally running dike/gully ascending the entire height of the southeast face. Approach along the railroad tracks from the head of the notch until below the gully (about 500' before reaching Cinema Gully). Hike up the snow gully until it steepens and ends at a cliff band. Climb (often mixed) up the snowy rock right of a shallow cave to reach the tree-covered ledge above. The gully above is deeply recessed and looks like a tiny Pinnacle Gully and offers spectacular climbing of a moderate nature. The easiest descent is to rappel down the gully (trees and/or V-thread) to the terrace and then again down the lower gully. Descent by bushwhacking to the Mt. Willard trail (up and left from the top of the climb) is possible but not recommended in deep, unpacked snow.

unknown

LEFT HAND MONKEY WRENCH 3

From the base of the cliff band at the top of the snow gully on Lower Hitchcock head right into the woods for about 100' to a right-facing corner. Climb slabby ice to a bulge then stem the corner to the top. You can rappel the route with one 60m rope. A good alternative if Lower Hitchcock is jammed.

FRA Randy Noble & John Bussulak, February 1997

ZIG PIG M5 4

This and the following route climb up a buttress to the right of Lower Hitchcock Gully. Find a free-hanging curtain and dry tool up 30 feet of broken rock on its right side to gain the curtain which is followed to the trees. This is reported to be an excellent route.

Ben Gilmore & Kevin Mahoney, February, 1999

PEACE OF MIND M5 4

Mixed climb up to the left side of the hanging curtain.

Kevin Mahoney & Ben Gilmore, February, 1999

The next routes climb above the ledge at mid-height on the Upper East Face.

EAST FACE SLAB RIGHT 3/3+

The moderate water ice flow to the right of Hitchcock Gully. Very thick and reliable with several lines available. Rappel to the tree ledge and then down Lower Hitchcock.

unknown

THE CLEFT 2-3

To the right of the East Face Slab Right is another obvious deeply cut gully. It is somewhat easier than the upper portion of Hitchcock Gully.

Alain Comeau & Doug Madara, winter 1976-77

OUT OF TOUCH 5

This route is found inside The Cleft on the upper east face of Mount Willard. Climb any of the lower routes to reach the wide bench below the upper cliff band. About a hundred feet inside The Cleft there is a short, steep smear on the right wall that starts about 15-feet above the floor. Climb up and slightly left to gain a crack (some rock gear) then move up and right to reach the ice. Climb the thickening ice to the trees. The easiest descent is to rappel the route, descend The Cleft and then rappel into Lower Hitchcock. There is reportedly another route inside The Cleft of about the same difficulty.

Mike & Chris Dube, January 2, 1998

THINKING OF JANET 4+

After a thin, vertical curtain, climb a steep ice flow just right of The Cleft.

Franck Vernoy & friend, winter 1976-77

LONG DISTANCE LOVE 3

Climb the moderate pillar set back in a recess to the right of the former route.

Franck Vernoy & Alain Comeau, Winter 1976-77

DAMSEL IN DISTRESS 4 5.8

On the far right side of an amphitheater, mixed climbing gains a short cascade of water ice. Rappel to the trees and descend Lower Hitchcock..

FRA: Ed Webster, Susan Patenaude & Todd Swain, Winter 1980-81

READ BETWEEN THE LINES 4

On the far right side of the upper cliff, look for an ice-choked chimney reminiscent of Pinnacle Gully. Harder than it looks. Rappel and descend Lower Hitchcock.

Dougald McDonald & Chris Dube, January, 1987

WILLARD SLAB RIGHT 2

To the right of the former routes is a low-angled slab that drops down almost to the railroad tracks. Rappel from trees. This is a nice practice slab similar to (but a lot less crowded than) Willey's Slide.

unknown

THE CORKSCREW 5

Up and left of the former route is a short, steep cliff band. In a good year a thin, twisting, yellow dagger will drip down the right side of this outcropping. Climb through the woods on the left side of the slab and then trend left along the cliff band. A striking, fierce route that is seldom done.

FRA Tom Burt, Kevin Mahoney, Paul Cormier, & Ben Gilmore in 1998; Jon Sykes may have climbed the route around the same time

MOUNT WILLARD: Trestle Wall

This is the 75' high road-cut crag on the Willard side of the tracks that is passed on the approach to any of the south face climbs. Just opposite a small trestle is a steep, broken crag that has some interesting mixed terrain. In a good year the crag will be covered in icicles.

TRESTLE GULLY 3

This is the obvious, short, right diagonalling, square-cut gully on the extreme right end of the crag.

FRA: Todd Swain & Jim Frangos, February 23, 1983

UNKNOWN 3+

Just left of the former route climb a vertical bulge then left on a ramp, then right up another bulge.

unknown

OLD ANXIETY 5+ M3

Further left and right in the middle of the cliff is this thin line. Belay from the middle of the trestle and climb straight up on thin ice past a piton at 15' to a final hard pillar.

Paul Cormier, Maury McKinney, Karen Eisenberg, & friend, January 1, 1998

THE SNOT ROCKET 3-5 (M5)

At the left end of the crag is a short buttress that leads to an overhanging wall with an obvious drip. Climb either the left side of the buttress (3) or the right side via an inside corner and roof (4, M5 piton at 25') to a terrace and belay (the right-side variation is an excellent mixed pitch). The second pitch climbs the thin, free-standing pillar to the woods. The story goes that the leader placed and then removed screws on the upper pillar so he would have a place to put his mono points without kicking.

Henry Barber and Jay Reilly (Australia) did the first recorded ascent of the right-hand variation to the first pitch in January 1998; Paul Cormier and Greg Cloutier did the complete route later in the season

MOUNT WILLARD: Elephant Head

At the very top of the notch is a small cliff that forms a natural replica of an elephant's head when viewed from the north. There are a number of climbs on the south side of the notch in the vicinity of this unique landmark. (It could be argued that this is really part of Mount Webster and not Mount Willard, but since the parking is the same as Willard we have chosen to buck the geologic tide.) Routes will be described from north to south.

ELEPHANT HEAD GULLY 3+

In the road cut at the head of Crawford Notch, directly south of the elephant's trunk, lies a one pitch ice fall. You couldn't ask for a shorter or an easier approach. This is a great route if you find yourself with an extra hour at the end of the day. Most parties stay right although a left-hand finish is possible. Don't leave gear at the base and be careful not to knock ice into the road. Rappel from trees (once with 60m).

Unknown

In addition to Elephant Head Gully there are many other toprope problems in the vicinity. The wall to the right of the main gully typically has several thin drips. Paul Cormier, Pat hackett, and John Tremblay were active here climbing several grade 5 mixed pitches including an ice-choked chimney farther to the right. Left of the main gully are some shorter problems which can be toproped. On the Elephant Head itself a climb has been made right up the nose by Todd Swain at a grade of 5- on ice only a half inch thick. Though led on the first ascent, a toprope seems prudent unless you love to scare yourself. These climbs are so close to the road that knocking ice down can be extremely hazardous—please be extra careful when climbing here.

THE FLUME 1-2

Below the head of the notch by several hundred yards are two low-angled gullies just off the road. Both these frozen streams offer long practice climbs with varying difficulties. Descent is usually made in the woods to the south side of the gullies. The Flume is the upper and less dramatic flow

unknown

SILVER CASCADE 1-3

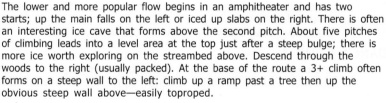

The lower and more popular flow begins in an amphitheater and has two starts; up the main falls on the left or iced up slabs on the right. There is often an interesting ice cave that forms above the second pitch. About five pitches of climbing leads into a level area at the top just after a steep bulge; there is more ice worth exploring on the streambed above. Descend through the woods to the right (usually packed). At the base of the route a 3+ climb often forms on a steep wall to the left: climb up a ramp past a tree then up the obvious steep wall above—easily toproped.

unknown

GOATBELL GULLY 3+

This hidden gully begins about 300 yards south of Silver Cascade. Turn into the woods opposite where the Saco River meets the road and follow a deepening gully until it forks and becomes very deep and distinct. The left-hand fork is the climb, two pitches of moderate ice with a 35 foot 80 degree column at the top. Descend through the woods on either side.

Todd Swain and Ed Keller, January 4, 1983; in all the years since this route was reported the authors know of no one who has found it, although one local climber recalls rappelling into it on a descent off Mount Webster (he was lost at the time).

CRAWFORD NOTCH: MOUNT AVALON

Although the approach is sizable, the east face of Mt. Avalon offers several ice slabs of moderate difficulty. The climbs vary in length from those which are of bouldering size to flows of over 120 feet. Rappelling off is the quickest means of descent. To approach the area, find the Mt. Willard Trail at the top of Crawford Notch and follow it for approximately one mile. Where the trail turns sharply left, one can get a clear view of the flows on Mt. Avalon. A relatively straightforward bushwhack (snowshoes may be helpful) takes you in from that point. The flows are also just visible from the site of the Old Crawford House. They will be described from left to right.

PEER PRESSURE 3

Trees divide the ice flows into three distinct sections. This route climbs the wide left-hand slab. The climbing is sustained.

Todd Swain, Brad White & Dave Saball, December 20, 1980

MELLOW YELLOW 3

The right section of the central ice flow is a yellow slab of moderate ice.

Todd Swain, Dave Saball & Brad White, December 20, 1980

TALLY HO II 2

An easy route ascending the ice to the left of The Battle of the Bulge.

Todd Swain, December 20, 1980

THE BATTLE OF THE BULGE 3

Located at the right end of the Mt. Avalon ice flows, this route has an obvious steep wall at its start.

Todd Swain, Dave Saball & Brad White, December 20, 1980

DANG'S GULLY 3-

To the right of all the other flows is this cool, short gully.

FRA Dave Adams & Ed Butler, March 14, 2002

CRAWFORD NOTCH: MOUNT TOM

This 4,000' mountain west of Mount Avalon requires a long and arduous approach. If you want to get away from the crowds, this is the place to go. Hike west on the Avalon Trail and then head right (north) to Mount Tom.

TOM'S DONUT 4+

Hike in from the top of Crawford Notch along the Avalon Trail then bear right on the A-Z Trail continuing until a spur trail leads north to the summit of Mt. Tom. Look for an ice filled corner that leads to the top of a rock buttress; rappel.

Bradley White & Jim Shimberg, Winter, 1986

T.B.R. Walsh

PRESIDENTIAL RANGE

The White Mountains' Presidential Range is the highest, most barren, string of mountains in the northeastern United States. Mount Washington (6,288 ft.), the highest peak in the range, truly dominates as a massive bulk of rock whose summit is nearly 4,000 feet higher than the Appalachian Mountain Club Visitor Center at the base. Mount Washington and the other peaks of the Presidential Range extend well above timberline. This region, covering several square miles, is rocky and windswept and has an ecosystem and weather comparable with arctic regions far to the north.

More than any other area covered in this book, the Presidential Range is the most dangerous. It is close to large population centers like Boston, New York, and Montreal, near substantial towns (N. Conway and Gorham), easy to get to (you can be at timberline in just a couple of hours), and famous enough to be on everyone's winter tic-list (Mount Washington is regarded as having the worst weather in the world and is home to the highest wind gust ever recorded on the surface of the earth, 231mph in April 1934). These factors have combined to create an unfortunate statistic: more people have died in this range from accidents and exposure than in any other mountain range in the United States. Almost every year, and sometimes several times in a year, tragedy strikes. In almost every instance a series of decisions were made that led inexorably to disaster, and which in hindsight appear very avoidable. Please don't add your name to the list of people who have died here; use common sense:

- be prepared, physically, technically, and emotionally for your climb
- check the weather and conditions and take the forecasts seriously
- sign in and sign out at Pinkham
- don't hesitate to turn back in the face of worsening weather, dwindling time, or poorer than expected performance (the mountain isn't going anywhere; you can always come back).

AREA HIGHLIGHTS

Location:	This mountain range is west of Rt. 16 and east of Rt. 302 about 20 miles north of N. Conway
Routes:	New Hampshire's alpine playground; long alpine gullies and ridges
Access:	Parking at trailheads, hiking several miles necessary for most routes
Descent:	Long, often exposed hikes; many routes end above timberline
Weather:	"Summit" (weather section), November through April
Equipment:	A standard ice rack plus a few rock pieces typical; consider two ropes
Superlatives:	Great early season ice in Tuckerman Ravine, classic Huntington Ravine Gullies (Pinnacle, Damnation); remote gullies in Great Gulf, Madison Gulf, and King Ravine
Amenities:	The AMC Pinkham Notch Camp has most everything, N. Conway, 20 miles south, and Gorham, 15 miles north, have everything
Warnings:	This range is home to the worst weather in the world; be prepared for arctic conditions; temperatures well below zero and high winds common; there are tragic accidents every year; sign in and out at AMC Pinkham Notch Camp

PRESIDENTIAL RANGE

A. Pinkham Notch
B. Tuckerman Ravine
C. Huntington Ravine
D. Great Gulf
E. Madison Gulf
F. King Ravine
G. Mount Washington summit
H. auto road (closed in winter)
I. Cog Railroad (closed in winter)

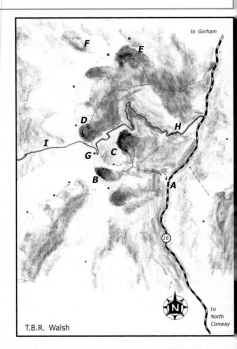

T.B.R. Walsh

PRESIDENTIAL RANGE: MOUNT WASHINGTON

Darby Field was the first white man to climb Crystal Hill, as Mount Washington was first called. He climbed the mountain, guided by two Indians, in 1642 hoping to find vast mineral resources. Though disappointing in terms of material riches, the history of Mount Washington is truly rich in terms of human triumph and adventure. From the 1920's the obvious challenge of the mountain's rugged terrain and harsh environment was a natural attraction. Throughout the generations, many people whose names are well recognized in the mountaineering world, Noel Odell, Robert Underhill, Bill House, Bradford Washburn, to mention a few, found adventure and inspiration on the flanks of Crystal Hill. Up until the 1960's, Huntington Ravine was THE place to ice climb in northern New England. Even today, the mountain's fearsome arctic environment and classic alpine ice routes have kept it as a prime training ground for those preparing to go to the world's highest, remotest, and coldest mountain ranges.

New England? Yup. We got real mountains. Climbers halfway up Mount Washignton's summit cone on a perfect day.
S. Peter Lewis

The launching spot for most technical climbs on Mt. Washington is the AMC Visitor Center at the top of Pinkham Notch about 20 miles north of North Conway village on Rt. 16. The village of Glen, five miles north of N. Conway, is the last place for getting supplies before you head up the notch (except for a couple of convenience stores). The AMC's Visitor Center consists of a large lodge and several bunkhouse and office buildings. Lodging and meals are available (call 603-466-2727 for reservations) and this is also the place to make camping reservations for the two areas open to winter camping high on the mountain: the Tuckerman Ravine shelters or the Harvard Cabin. The Visitor Center also provides up to the minute condition reports and weather forecasts for the Presidential Range. Even if you plan another approach to the routes on the mountain it is wise to stop in at Pinkham and get up-to-date reports. Winter climbers on Mount Washington and the other peaks in the range are also asked to sign in and out in the staging room located at the parking lot level in the Visitor Center. Winter rescues are, unfortunately, not uncommon and registering your itinerary at Pinkham can mean the difference between life and death.

MT WASHINGTON: Pinkham Notch

In the relative shelter to be found near the top of Pinkham Notch in the vicinity of the AMC Visitor Center are a number of short climbs that offer a more sensible alternative when the windchill is extreme on Mount Washington.

GLEN ELLIS FALLS 2+

Just before the height of land in Pinkham Notch, on the west side of the road, is a summer parking area for Glen Ellis Falls. The parking lot may or may not be plowed; park at your own risk. Across the road from the parking lot, follow a trail to the bottom of the obvious falls. A long period of cold weather is necessary for the falls to be climbed safely due to the tremendous volume of water that roars down behind the ice.

FRA: Todd Swain, Chris Taylor & Curt Robinson, 1979

ICEMEN DON'T EAT QUICHE 4-

Park at the AMC Pinkham Notch Visitor Center parking lot and head across the road onto the Lost Pond Trail. Take this trail across a marsh, stay right and continue along aiming for the yellow flows that are high and slightly south. You will cross Lost Pond on the approach. The first pitch is moderate and ends on a ledge at 60 feet. Pitch two climbs the obvious yellow column.

unknown

JACK FROST 2-3

Climb the first pitch of the previous route then follow a low-angled gully up and left to a steep bulge and the woods.

Todd Swain & John Mauzey, January 10, 1983

PASS THE QUICHE M7

From Icemen contour 75 yards north until you come to a north-facing overhang. Climb up to a hanging dagger via sustained dry-tooling past three pins and a couple of questionable fixed nuts.

Tim Martel & Justin Preisendorfer, January 2000

ICE-CENTRIFICLE FORCE 3+

Behind the Glen Ellis Falls parking lot, up and right, is a mixed route that wanders up the steep hillside. Up a verglased slab, left to a 25 foot pillar and then ferret out another 80 feet of mixed climbing to trees.

Butch Constantine, January 9, 1983, with a direct finish by Todd Swain & John Mauzey the following day

PINKHAM CASCADE 2

Just south of the AMC Visitor Center at the height of land in Pinkham Notch is an obvious, brushy, low-angled roadside flow that is good for practicing French technique.

unknown

MT WASHINGTON: Tuckerman Ravine

Tuckerman Ravine is one of three major glacial cirques on Mount Washington. Named for Prof. Edward Tuckerman, a noted botanist, Tuckerman Ravine is best known for its unparalleled spring skiing. However, in the early season the headwall of the ravine provides some marvelous alpine-style ice climbing. Get on these routes in November or early December before they are buried in snow and you'll be rewarded with some wonderful alpine climbing. Begin the approach at the AMC Visitor Center at the top of Pinkham Notch; follow the Tuckerman Ravine Trail for 2 1/2 miles past the AMC shelters and Forest Service cabin and up to the base of the ravine. Routes are described from left to right. Descend either down the summer trail which skirts the north side of the headwall, Hillman's Highway, the long snow gully on the south side, or down easy snow chutes to the sides of the routes.

Mount Washington's summit and most famous cirque, Tuckerman Ravine, in mid winter. Compare headwall conditions with the early season shot on the next page. (Sometimes there's 100 feet of snow in the ravine!)
S. Peter Lewis

TUCKERMAN RAVINE 1-4

DODGE'S DRIP 2+ M3

This route is not on the headwall itself. Left of the headwall is an obvious buttress then a diagonal snow ramp (Hillman's Highway). Farther left and high on the ridge are a series of short rock buttresses with steep gullies between them. The farthest left gully is called Dodge's Drop. After a nasty bushwhack and some snow climbing, climb the prominent rocky buttress right of Dodge's Drop via snow, rock, and the occasional ice patch. Descend by walking right from the top of the buttress and then down Hillman's Highway.

Unknown

LEFT OF LEFT 3

On the left side of the main headwall descends a long snow gully, Left Gully. This route climbs a short flow on the left side of the gully near the bottom. Rappel or thrash off right.

unknown

HEADWALL ROUTES II 1-4

Early in the season the headwall is covered with drips, ramps, corners and gullies and any number of variations are possible. The left side is about 3+, the middle has some steeper pillars up high, and the right side is about 3. This is a wonderful place to get a feel for ice climbing in an alpine environment without a huge commitment. Descend to the right (north) and down the line of least resistance on the right side of the headwall (following the summer trail) or hike south and then east and down Hillman's Highway. Avalanche danger can be high; check posting.

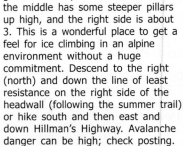
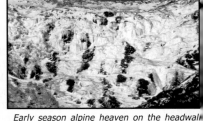

Early season alpine heaven on the headwall
Doug Millen

Although the steeper lines were undoubtedly first climbed in the late 1970's, probably by AMC folks, the first recorded technical foray on the headwall was by Herschel C. Parker and Dr. Ralph Larrabee on December 26, 1894 (no typo). Herschel returned the following February to make a complete ascent.

LEFT OF RIGHT 3+/4

On the right side of the headwall, above the summer trail and left of the prominent Right Gully, a short flow drops down a buttress.
unknown

MT WASHINGTON: Huntington Ravine

Huntington Ravine is the next cirque north of Tuckerman Ravine on the eastern flanks of Mount Washington. Up until the 1960's it was the focal point for almost all ice climbing activity in the region. With its 1,500 feet of elevation gain, exposed alpine setting, and objective dangers from cornices, windslab conditions, and extreme weather, the ravine is never to be taken lightly. Its record of accidents, some of which befell very experienced mountaineers, clearly illustrates the dangers. More climbing accidents have taken place here than at all the other ice climbing areas in this book combined. It is clearly to the benefit of the climbing community that the U.S. Forest Service has two full-time snow rangers who check both Huntington and Tuckerman Ravines daily for possible dangerous snow conditions. Should conditions warrant, especially after heavy snow falls, they may post a warning advising climbers not to use the ravines.

The Harvard Mountaineering Club maintains the Harvard Cabin during the winter as a convenient base for climbers using Huntington Ravine. It is located just southeast of the ravine on the fire road leading up from the Tuckerman Ravine trail to the cirque. A user fee/reservation system is in effect at the cabin and one should arrange the details at Pinkham prior to hiking up. Capacity is limited as the cabin is small, but a certain amount of tent space is allowed in the immediate vicinity.

HUNTINGTON RAVINE

A. *Escape Hatch*
B. *South Gully*
C. *Odell's Gully*
D. *Pinnacle Gully*
E. *Central Gully*
F. *Diagonal*
G. *Damnation Gully (top)*
H. *Lion Head*

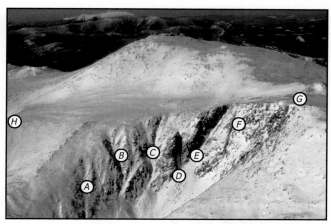

S. Peter Lewis

The approach to Huntington Ravine involves hiking up the first 1.7 miles of the Tuckerman Ravine Trail then turning right on an obvious fire road just a few hundred feet above the large bridge over the Cutler River. In a couple of hundred yards the Lion Head winter trail will be seen on the left. This is one of the standard descent trails from high on the mountain. A quarter of a mile from the junction with the Tuckerman Ravine Trail you will see the Harvard Cabin on your right. (Note: the Huntington Ravine summer trail leaves the Tuckerman Ravine trail on the right 1.3 miles from Pinkham; take it only if you are prepared to break trail as it is not maintained for winter travel.) After the Harvard Cabin, continue up the trail into the bowl at the base of the ravine. There is a litter and first aid cache here. Allow almost two hours to reach the first aid cache from Pinkham. Be conscientious and check weather and snow conditions before you leave the camp.

Several descents are possible once you've finished a route in Huntington and are standing on the Alpine Garden. By far the most aesthetic descent is to traverse the Garden to the south reaching the cairns which mark the Lions Head Trail which is followed down to its junction with the fire road just below the Harvard Cabin and then back down to Pinkham Notch. The assumption here is that the weather is fairly pleasant and there is no time pressure. However, if the weather is bad or rapidly deteriorating, you'll be looking for a quick way to drop down into the woods. Do so by hiking along the south rim of the ravine (if you've been climbing in Odell's, Pinnacle, or Central Gully) until you pass the top of South Gully and come upon the top of the Escape Hatch (marked by a cairn). This shallow snow gully allows a hasty descent back to the bottom of Huntington Ravine during inclement weather. Use good judgement here since this gully has at times avalanched, and at times has been hard ice. DO NOT use the Escape Hatch early in the season or in low snow

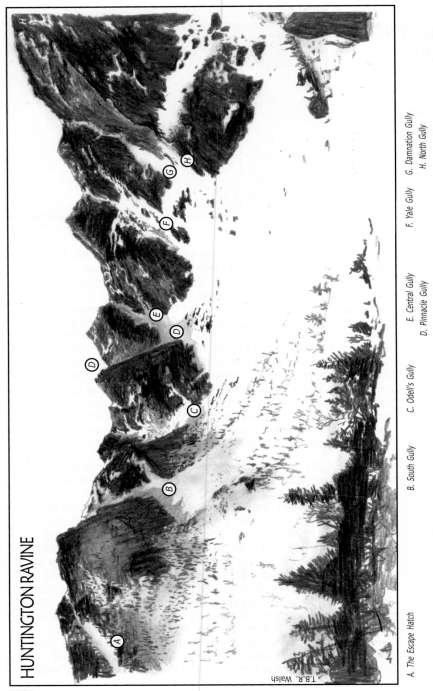

HUNTINGTON RAVINE

T.B.R. Walsh

A. The Escape Hatch

B. South Gully

C. Odell's Gully

D. Pinnacle Gully

E. Central Gully

F. Yale Gully

G. Damnation Gully

H. North Gully

years as it can be a horrendous thrash. Should you be climbing on the northern side of Huntington, walk right from the top of your gully until the rim begins to lose altitude, then scramble and bushwhack your way down easy terrain into the woods aiming for the first aid cache. Always carry a map of the region and a compass (and know how to use them).

Few parties who spend the day climbing in Huntington Ravine ever make it a point to press on to the summit of Mount Washington. There are absolutely no open facilities on the summit for shelter and the folks at the weather observatory don't like to be disturbed. A number of rescues have ensued as a result of "going for the summit" in bad conditions. In situations of poor visibility it is the better part of valor to head down. And remember, if the weather worsens, do not hesitate to rappel back down your climb—your life is worth more than any amount of climbing gear you may leave behind. Routes will be described from left to right (south to north).

THE ESCAPE HATCH 1

The shallow snow gully on the far south side of Huntington Ravine, commonly used as the quickest descent route from the Alpine Gardens.
unknown

SOUTH GULLY 1

The first major gully on the left-hand side of the Ravine. Several pitches of easy snow climbing with occasional ice make this a good, easy route.
unknown

ODELL'S GULLY II 2-3

Ascending the obvious and classic ice gully immediately left of Pinnacle Buttress, Odell's Gully is characterized by a large icefall which divides above into three separate flows. The middle is easiest (2/3), the left somewhat harder (3+), and the right is the most difficult (3+ to 4+). Left of all three variations, and beginning about halfway up, is a rock buttress with a good mixed route (M2). In bad weather, locate a ramp at the top of the left flow which descends to the bowl near the base of South Gully.
Noel E. Odell, Lincoln O'Brien, J.C. Hurd, & Robert L.M. Underhill, March 16, 1928

THE SHURUYEV-MIRKINA-DYNKIN ROUTE III 5.9 A2 3

This new mixed route breaks through the overhanging rock above Pinnacle Gully. After climbing the first pitch of that route the climb aids through an overhang on the left to a 70-degree face. Pitch three climbs through another overhang then a crack to yet a third overhang; belay here or continue climbing the crack all the way to the ridge and an intersection with the summer climb Pinnacle Direct which is followed up the aréte to the top of the buttress. The intricate, committing, mixed climbing combines bits of the summer routes Primal Scream and Pinnacle Buttress Direct and requires mastery of a variety of techniques.
Alexey Shuruyev & Olga Mirkina climbed partway up the second pitch on January 26, 2002, before retreating in the face of bad weather. Shuruyev returned on February 24, 2002, and completed the route with Boris Dynkin.

PINNACLE GULLY III 3

One of the most aesthetic ice gullies in New England, this is the narrow gully between Pinnacle Buttress and Central Buttress. The first pitch, the crux of the route, consists of sustained sixty degree ice. The remainder of the gully is somewhat easier, with several more pitches of moderate snow and ice. The right-hand wall of the gully occasionally ices up providing a mixed adventure that varies based on the courage and experience of the party. If continuing up to the Alpine Gardens and down either the Escape Hatch or Lion Head Trail is out of the question, you can descend the snow slope between the top of Pinnacle Buttress and Odell's (can be dangerous and difficult). Aim for Odell's midsection, cross over it on a ramp system, then over a block and connect to the ramp that leads to the bottom of South Gully.

Samuel A Scoville & Julian Whittlesey, February 8, 1930

Pinnacle Gully's six-hundred feet of alpine perfection on a great day.
S. Peter Lewis

CLOUDWALKER II 4 5.7

A mixed route following the summer line of a climb by the same name up the massive buttress left of Central Gully. Just above the start of Central, climb an iced crack on the left to a thin smear, and then more ice to a crack out left below a roof.

FRA Chris Dube & Bill Holland, January, 1989; Brad White about the same time

LEFT WALL OF CENTRAL GULLY 2+/3

This very short variation climbs the wall to the left of Central Gully a couple of hundred feet below the top of that route.

Alan Wilcox & Willlam P. House, March, 1934

CENTRAL GULLY II 1

Bordering the wall of the Central Buttress, this prominent snow laden gully was the first winter route in Huntington Ravine. It is one of the longest climbs in the ravine. Begin at the top of The Fan just to the right of the base of Pinnacle Gully. After one or two leads of low angle ice climbing, several more pitches of straight forward snow climbing lead to the Alpine Gardens. An immense cairn marks the top of the climb.

A.J. Holden & N.L Goodrich, February 23, 1927

DIAGONAL II 2

To the right of Central Gully, hidden behind a rock buttress, is a gully running diagonally left. The bottom ice slabs of Yale Gully must be ascended to reach this gully's base. Once there, an easy snow gully leads to the top.

unknown

HUNTINGTON SOUTH

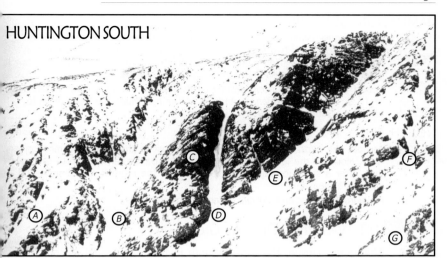

A.	ramp to South Gully
B.	Odell's Gully
C.	Pinnacle Buttress
D.	Pinnacle Gully

E.	Central Gully
F.	Diagonal
G.	Yale Gully (start)

HUNTINGTON NORTH

F. Diagonal
G. Yale Gully
H. Damnation Gully
I. North Gully

ALE GULLY II 2-3

After taking any of several routes up the lower ice slabs directly in the center of the ravine, Yale Gully follows a slightly right-leaning shallow gully to the lip. A long, varied and enjoyable route. The assorted variations at the start are all about the same difficulty.

unknown

AMNATION BUTTRESS II 3

The broken buttress to the right of Yale Gully is a good mixed route. Take a line directly up the middle of the buttress following the line of least resistance.

unknown

DAMNATION GULLY III 3

A classic gully climb, the left of two deeply cut gullies on the north side of Huntington Ravine. Two short ice bulges add spice to what is otherwise a predominantly snow-filled gully. Occasionally a cornice forms on the rim, but it is easily avoided. Damnation is the longest climb in the ravine.

Robert Underhill and Lincoln O'Brien climbed all but the crux bulge in late winter of 1929; William L. Putnam & Andrew J. Kaufman made the first complete ascent on January 31, 1943

NORTH GULLY II 3

Ascends the north most gully in the ravine, just to the right of Damnation Gully. Move up the lower snow gully to where Damnation and North Gullies fork. After a steep ice bulge, the remainder of the route is mixed snow and ice and quite pleasant.

Maynard M. Miller and William Latady, December, 1942

MT. WASHINGTON: The Great Gulf

This grand cirque, the most remote in the Presidential Range, rises well over 1,000 feet from tiny Spaulding Lake at its base. Darby Field described the cirque in 1642 although the name may have originated by a remark made by Ethan Allen Crawfrod who became lost in the clouds in 1823 and came to the "edge of a great gulf." The quickest approach (though all are long) is via the Great Gulf Trail which leaves the west side of Rt. 16 about two miles north from the base of the Mount Washington Auto Road (The Glen House). The distance to Spaulding Lake is 6.5 miles, which will take 3-4 hours on a packed trail and who knows how long in a foot of new snow. The Gulf can also be approached by climbing up the Tuckerman Ravine Trail and then dropping down the other side, but this makes for very demanding day, in essence climbing Mount Washington twice. However you get there, climbs in the Great Gulf, even though of only moderate difficulty, are very serious given the long delay in getting rescuers to the scene of any accident. Bivouac equipment and self-rescue capabilities are essential.

GREAT GULF HEADWALL III 1-2

Ascends the headwall of the large cirque, the Great Gulf, on the north side of Mt. Washington. In lean snow years a considerable amount of water ice will be found on the flanks of this 1,000 foot headwall. A long approach, no matter which route you choose.

unknown

WAIT UNTIL DARK GULLY III 3

Not visible from Spaulding Lake, Wait Until Dark Gully is the most prominent fault line up the right side of the Great Gulf. It ends just beneath the summit of Mt. Clay. At the start, stay to the left up a series of ice bulges. Above, follow a moderate snow and ice gully, with some danger from snow slides, to its top. Hike up to the Cog Railway, the summit, and then return down the Auto Road

Kurt Winkler & Jim Tierney, February, 1981; climbed during a lean snow year, the round trip took fourteen hours car to car.

PRESIDENTIAL RANGE: MADISON GULF

April

The following selection of routes is located in the peaceful setting of Madison Gulf, situated between the east face of Mt. Adams and the south ridge (the Osgood Ridge) of Madison. Six or more flows grace the Madison Gulf Headwall in winter and offer a secluded alternative to the often crowded atmosphere of Huntington Ravine. Approach from the Glen House via the Osgood Trail. Follow the Madison Gulf Cutoff to the Madison Gulf Trail and the bottom of the gulf. When you start to see ice, break left and up around the left side of the gulf. A flat snow shelf leads along the base of the routes—but don't try to go straight up to the routes unless you like to crawl through snowy brush. The hike is roughly four miles long and has been described as anywhere from casual to horrendous. The approach is best early in the season or during lean snow years. As with routes in the Great Gulf, climbing in this area should be approached with an extra meas-ure of caution since rescue is potentially many hours away. Routes will be described as you approach them from left to right. The climbs are 1-3 pitches long—a 60m rope will make descending easier.

MADISON GULF

A. *Pointillism*
B. *Point of No Return*
C. *Exclamation Point*
D. *Pointless*
E. *Point*
E. *Counterpoint*
F. *Point Du Pinceau*

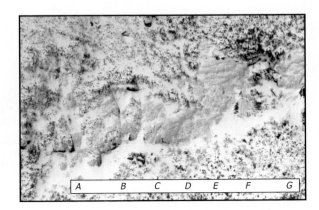

POINTILLISM 2-3

This is the left-hand climb. Low-angled slabs lead to a steep little column and the woods. Descend left.

Todd Swain, solo, December 21, 1982

POINT OF NO RETURN 4

The next obvious flow to the right. Climb moderate ice for two pitches to two prominent vertical columns; climb one of the two to the top—reminiscent of Pegasus at Frankenstein.

Todd Swain, solo, December 21, 1982

Walk four hours for this? Sure. Brad White on the first ascent of Exclamation Point in Madison Gulf.

Ken Grinnell

EXCLAMATION POINT 3+/4

To the right of the previous route is a wide flow with a cave at its base. This route climbs the steep flow left of the cave. A variation climbs even steeper ice to the right of the cave.

Brad White & Ken Grinnell, 2002

POINTLESS 3+

Climbs the right side of the flow via a slab capped with a 15 foot 80 degree column. Descend by rappel or bushwhack around left (north).

Todd Swain, solo, December 21, 1982

POINT II 3+

The massive central ice flow just left of a rock rib which splits the ice. Two leads up moderate ice lead to the crux third pitch, which boasts a short, vertical headwall. One final lead gets you up to the top. Descend on rappel from tree anchors on the climb's left side.

Matt Peer & Alec Behr, February 4, 1980

COUNTERPOINT II 4

The right side of the large ice flow is considerably harder. After one lead of moderate ice, climb two more pitches with some vertical ice. Descend as for the previous climb.

Matt Peer and Alec Behr, February 4, 1980

POINT DU PINCEAU 4

This fine route climbs the right-most flow for two pitches.

Kurt Winkler & Doug Huntley climbed the first ascent on the last day of their tour-de-force, Link'em Up (see next)

LINK'EM UP (Unrated)

This is just one example of what New England climbers can do if they put their minds to it and is described here not so much as a specific route description, but rather as inspiration. Day 1: Hike up the Tuckerman Ravine trail to the base of Pinnacle Gully, stash climbing gear and camp at the Harvard Cabin. Day 2: climb Pinnacle Gully, traverse over the summit cone of Mount Washington to the top of the Great Gulf and stash camping gear. Rappel the Wait Until Dark Gully, climb back up gully, pick up gear and hike to bivy in snow cave at Sphinx Col. Day 3: leave snow cave just before collapse, hike (in the rain) over the exposed ridge for several miles to Grey Knob and beg caretaker to put another log on the fire (this is sort of a rest day). Day 4: hike back up over Mount Adams and bushwhack down to bivy at the base of Madison Gulf. Day 5: Climb a new two-pitch grade 4 ice route in Madison Gulf (see above) carrying all your gear, then head down the Valley Way Trail to a "huge dinner in Gorham."

Kurt Winkler & Doug Huntley, March 8-12, 1994, preparing for bigger things

PRESIDENTIAL RANGE: KING RAVINE

King Ravine is located on the northern side of Mt. Adams. As for this and other cirques in the Presidential Range, it takes a fairly light snow year for any of the underlying ice to be exposed on the routes. During normal to heavy snow winters, don't expect much ice. However, you will be guaranteed a long walk in, especially if the trails aren't tracked. Start the approach at the Ravine House Site parking lot (the sign may say Appalachia) on Route 2 in Randolph approximately six miles from Gorham, NH. Begin the hike on the Airline Trail, to the Short Line, joining the Randolph Path for a mile or so, and then continuing on the Short Line Trail to the bottom of the Ravine (not as complicated as it sounds). This is yet another isolated area to climb in, although, unlike the Great Gulf and the Madison Gulf, help in an emergency is readily at hand at Grey Knob, a Randolph Mountaineering Club cabin at timberline near the western rim of King Ravine. It is staffed all winter and is reached by the Randolph Path from the base of the ravine. Avalanche danger can be high in King Ravine and slides are common. There has been at least one serious accident in recent years. Unlike the ravines on the East side of the Presidential Range, avalanche conditions are not monitored by the Forest Service so no hazard reports or forecasts are given. Climbers venturing here should review recent weather history, carry transceivers (and know how to use them), and use good judgment.

KING RAVINE HEADWALL III 1-2

Most winter ascents follow the summer trail up The Headwall. Once you emerge from The Gateway, probably the best descent will be to cross over to Madison Springs Hut and return to the road by the Valley Way Trail.

unknown

GREAT GULLY III 1-2

On the right-hand side of the King Ravine Headwall lies the Great Gully. This long snow and ice gully reaches the lip of the King Ravine headwall just below Thunderstorm Junction. Descend via the trail to Crag Camp, and then the Spur Link to the Randolph Path. Beware of avalanches on this wide open gully.

unknown

P.F. FLYER II 3-4

To the right of Great Gully lies another gully that is hard to see and even harder to approach but is well worth the effort. Four pitches of moderate climbing lead to an easier escape left or a harder mixed finish straight up.

Paul Flannegan, George & Peter Wallace, winter 1976-77

EVANS NOTCH

Evans Notch is a beautiful, isolated spot straddling the Maine and New Hampshire border several miles east of Mount Washington. It is reached via Route 2 and 113 from the north and via Route 113 from Fryeburg, Maine, from the south.

Truly "off the beaten path," the history of climbing in the notch is a bit sketchy. In the mid 1970's Tom Lyman climbed in the area, but his routes were not recorded. In 1976 Doug Burnell saw the cliffs while on a snowmobile trip with his father and began to explore the area, doing a number of routes, primarily with Doug Tescher. In the early 1980's Kurt Winkler made several trips with various partners cleaning up some new routes. In the late 1980's and into the 1990's Bob Parrot and Rob Adair, Rich Page, and Bob Baribeau have made forays and ferreted out most of the remaining lines. The area is isolated and hard to get to but the few parties that go in here each winter are rewarded with quiet, beautiful and rewarding adventures. The trip, either on skis or snowshoes, and the quiet, uncrowded atmosphere make it a worthwhile destination. Unlike many areas in this book, Evans Notch does not lend itself to easy-to-follow route descriptions as the hillsides and flows are complicated, often discontinuous, and spread out. If you plan to climb here, consider the following descriptions to be starting points; be prepared to make some discoveries on your own.

The road through the notch is closed during the winter so the approach calls for an uphill ski or snowshoe of about 3 miles in either direction. Heading north, the main flows are seen on the left along the east face of East Royce Mountain.

AREA HIGHLIGHTS	
Location:	Rt. 113, the southern end (usual approach) is 45 minutes from N. Conway; the northern end is 20 minutes from Gorham
Routes:	backcountry areas and routes, many moderate climbs
Access:	Park at either the south or north end of the notch; hike, ski or snowmobile for several miles into the climbs; some areas much nearer the road
Descent:	The best option is usually to rappel; consider 2 ropes
Weather:	"Notch" (weather section), December through March
Equipment:	A standard ice rack plus a few rock pieces typical; consider two ropes in case of emergency
Superlatives:	Great short routes at *Shell Pond* and near *The Basin*, longer routes on *East Royce Mt.*
Amenities:	N. Conway and Gorham have everything
Warnings:	This is backcountry climbing with little traffic; let people know your itinerary and be prepared for self rescue

They are surrounded by trees and vegetation, but are generally steep and between 1 and 3 pitches in length. The routes in Evans Notch will be described from south to north beginning at Shell Pond and continuing to the main area on East Royce Mountain.

To get to Evans Notch from the south find your way to the village of Fryeburg, Maine, which is about eight miles from N. Conway, NH on Rt. 302. At the west end of the village take Rt. 113 north west back into New Hampshire and follow it north through the villages of N. Fryeburg and Stow for about twenty miles to where the plowed road ends near The Basin, a pond at the southern end of the notch. Fryeburg is the last place to get supplies. From the end of the road continue on snowshoes, skis, on foot, or on a snowmobile for an additional three or four miles. The main areas will be obvious across the notch on the west side.

To get here from the north, find your way to the town of Gorham Maine and head east on Rt 2 for about 12 miles to the junction with Rt. 113 in the town of Gilead. Head south on 113 until the plowed road ends and then follow the road south via whatever means at your disposal until you see the ice. Gorham is the last place to get supplies. This is a longer approach, involving at least five miles of travel once you leave your car. Day trips here are hard unless you use a snowmobile or are fast on your skis.

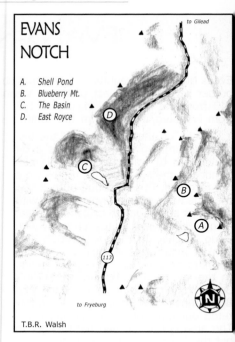

EVANS NOTCH

A. Shell Pond
B. Blueberry Mt.
C. The Basin
D. East Royce

to Gilead

113

to Fryeburg

T.B.R. Walsh

EVANS NOTCH: SHELL POND

Described (with hyperbole) as a "mini-Frankenstein," Shell Pond is an excellent area with many possibilities and is sure to be far from the crowds. It is reached via a dirt road, Shell Pond Rd., that heads east 0.7 miles north of the AMC's Cold River Camp on Rt. 113 (about a mile south of The Basin). How far you will be able to drive on Shell Pond Rd. is dependent on road conditions. The road is on private property and every courtesy should be given to the landowners. If the road is plowed, drive 1.1 miles to a gate just a few hundred yards before a stone house. Please avoid walking through the yard by using fields to the south.

Just past the house a snowmobile trail will lead east in the direction of the obvious cliffs. In just a couple of minutes a bridge will be crossed and soon you will reach the cliffs. This is a complex area and a little exploring will reveal a multitude of routes. A favorite 'secret' area for years, accurate first ascent information is hard to confirm, although Bob Parrott, Jeff Butterfield, Randy Rackliff, Steve Damboise and others have been responsible for most of the development here.

SHELL POND ROUTES 3-5

The first cliff reached will be a 40 foot vertical wall on the left that is about a hundred feet long and has many toprope problems in the grade 4-5 range. Farther east and uphill is a larger cliff. On the left end of this cliff is an easy slab that is climbed for a pitch and then finishes up a short, steep, grade 3 step. To the right and around a buttress is a beautiful 60 foot grade 4 column in a corner. Rock pro will be helpful for this one.

Continuing on the snowmobile trail a 70 foot wall will be found to the south with an obvious 5.4 chimney on its left side. The main wall is grade 4. This cliff is easily seen from the end of the dirt road.

Farther along the trail, climb over a shoulder to reach more climbs in the woods. From left to right find a 100 foot grade 4-, a 50 foot grade 4, a full pitch grade 3 and a short, 40 foot, grade 5 pillar. In addition to these areas there is a huge cliff up and right of the rest that is reported to be home to a very spectacular route that has yet to come into shape. This and many other possibilities abound for those willing to explore.

EVANS NOTCH: BLUEBERRY MOUNTAIN

Just before reaching the stone house on the Shell Pond Rd. you will see two trails leaving to the north, the White Cairn Blueberry Ridge Trail, and the Stone House Trail; both lead to the summit of Blueberry Mt. Below the summit on the south side is a 180 foot ledge with at least two flows on it, a thick grade 3 on the left, and a grade 3-4 chimney on the right. The approach takes about an hour when packed.

EVANS NOTCH: THE BASIN

The Basin is the home of beautiful Basin Pond in a mountain cirque at the southern end of Evans Notch. The surrounding hills are home to several interesting winter climbs.

MICA MINE 2-4

Before The Basin there is an old mica mine up on Deer Hill with some toproping on its left side. This is a very minor area but may be worth exploring.

unknown

BUBBLE GULLY II 3+

Just after the official entrance to Evans Notch, turn west at signs for The Basin. Park in a parking lot and walk across the frozen lake to a cliff on the right. At the crag's left end, and hidden around a corner, is a narrow 150 ft. gully. Climb the gully in two leads. The second lead is steep and short.

Kurt Winkler & Joe Perez, February 17, 1980

BLOWING BUBBLES II 3

This is the obvious diagonalling gully visible from The Basin. It is several hundred yards left of Bubble Gully. The flow is characterized by two obvious tiers, the first being the hardest.

FRA: Bob Parrott & Barry Rugo, January, 1992

COLLARBONE GULLY 3

A short distance north of the entrance to The Basin is an obvious red brick house just off the road on the right. Behind the house and slightly north is a small crag on the east side of the road. Collarbone Gully follows a narrow slot on the cliff's right side with an overhanging wall above. The route has been described as a "mini-Pinnacle Gully" by the first ascentionists.

Bob Parrott & Dave Lattimer, early 1980's

BICKFORD BROOK 3

Just south of the brick house mentioned above follow the streambed of Bickford Brook to a cliff that you can see from the main road. Climb the big streak up the slab. According to local activist Bob Parrott this brook gives over two miles of really cool ice bouldering and is a tremendous adventure.

EVANS NOTCH: EAST ROYCE MOUNTAIN

This is the major climbing area in Evans Notch. Route 113 runs through the notch but is not plowed in the winter. Park either at The Basin (on the south) or at the junction with Route 2 (on the north). The approach from either end is about three miles long and is easily skied. The climbs are all found on the east face of East Royce mountain amidst a jumble of cliff bands and tree ledges and can be identified from the road. Descents can be difficult; be prepared to rappel or bushwhack. The isolated here means rescue will be delayed, so bring extra equipment and food and tell someone your itinerary.

RIGHTS OF SPRING II 4 5.6

This route ascends the left side of the lower Main Face. The major feature is a large right facing corner near the top, with a curtain of ice to its right. The first pitch climbs an ice flow below the corner to a tree belay on the left. Move out right from here to the first major ice flow. A huge icicle will be seen in the major dihedral above. The third pitch starts with thirty feet of mixed climbing to reach solid ice. A steep column on the final wall leads to the finish. To descend, first hike up and left to a mineral boulder, then down and left through a valley until you reach the Laughing Lion Trail. Follow this to a beaver pond, then crash through the brush to the road. An alternate descent traverses right to a snow slope where a series of low-angled rappels will bring you to the bottom in the vicinity of Exit Stage Left.

Kurt Winkler & Joe Perez, February 21, 1980

CALIFORNIA KID 4-

After an initial vertical section of 15 ft., the flow eases to a series of steep steps with a few thin spots. Belay at trees above and rappel.

Bill Kane, John Bragg & Rick Hatch, December 30, 1981

WHEN FRIGHT MEETS MIGHT 4+

A logical finish to California Kid climbing the central pillar on the curtained wall above (just right of the last pitch of Rights of Spring). Two pitches, the first with poor protection, the second traversing left under an overhang to steep ice, get you to the top. Descend as for Rights of Spring.

Todd Swain, Kurt Winkler & George Hurley, January 7, 1983

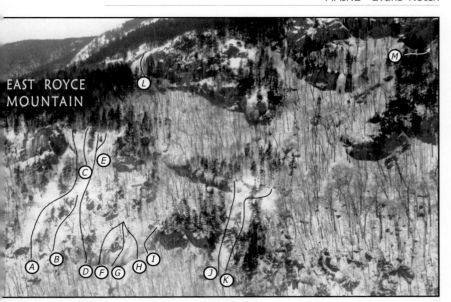

EAST ROYCE MOUNTAIN

A.	Rights of Spring	F.	Exit Stage Left	K.	Pilgrim's Progress
B.	California Kid	G.	Curtain Call	L.	French Canadian Reality
C.	When Fright Meets Might	H.	Exit Stage Right	M.	to Pitchfork Face and Love Diet
D.	Opening Night Jitters	I.	Prompter's Box		
E.	Balcony Seat	J.	Three's Company		

OPENING NIGHT JITTERS 4

A three pitch route that begins right of California Kid climbing a steep curtain and then lower-angled ice to trees. Rappel. This was the original line on this part of the face and went all the way up. Head right and rappel.

Brad White, Doug Burnell & Mike Brady, Winter, 1978

BALCONY SEAT II 4

This route continues the line of Opening Night Jitters all the way to the top of the cliff and finishes up a steep flow just to the right of When Fright Meets Might. Descend right and rappel.

George Hurley & Marc Chauvin, about 1983

EXIT STAGE LEFT 4+

To the right of Opening Night Jitters is a steep runnel which leads to lower angled slabs above. This and the following three routes are easy to rappel.

Kurt Winkler, February 10, 1982

CURTAIN CALL 4

An excellent column to the right of Exit Stage Left, complete with a steep column and layback moves. The crux is getting established on the icicles at the start.

Kurt Winkler & Jim Tierny, February 10, 1980

EXIT STAGE RIGHT 3

The slightly easier curtain just right of Curtain Call.

Kurt Winkler, Todd Swain & George Hurley, January 7, 1983

PROMPTER'S BOX 2

Climb the hidden gully 100 feet right of Curtain Call. A curtain leads to a ramp and the top.

George Hurley, Todd Swain & Kurt Winkler, January 7, 1983

THREE'S COMPANY II 4

The route climbs the left side of the Pilgrim's Progress trio of ice flows. Stay generally left the entire way. After a pitch up steep bulges to a tree belay, climb mixed snow and more ice bulges to another tree. Pitch three is the crux: ascend a thinly iced slab to an alcove below an ice curtain barrier. Finish up the second set of icicles from the left.

Kurt Winkler on the entrance moves of Exit Stage Right on the first ascent.
Todd Swain

Kurt Winkler, Joe Perez, & Phil Ostrosky February 24, 1980

FRENCH CANADIAN REALITY 5

Climb one of the lower routes and continue thrashing up through the woods until you come to the 90-foot cliff above. A distinct pillar awaits you. Some very serious mixed routes have been climbed left of the pillar.

Bob Baribeau, January 1995

LOVE DIET 5+

To the right of French Canadian Reality on the Laughing Lion Cliff (a k a Pitchfork Face) lies a prominent right-facing dihedral. Climb this corner with difficulty to a belay at 140'. Climb thin ice to overhanging icicles staying right for the honest (hardest) line.

Bob Baribeau, January 1995

Love Diet climbs hanging daggers way up on the Pitchfork Face.
Bob Baribeau

LOVE DIET VARIATION START 5

Twenty feet left of the dihedral climb a thin pillar that dribbles from a V-slot. Climb to the slot and then angle back to the tree belay as for Love Diet.

Bob Baribeau & Landon Fake, December 1990

PILGRIM'S PROGRESS III 4

The route is a long collection of pitches and flows. Attention to directions here will make locating the route easier. Looking at the main cliff from the road, there is an intrusion of light-colored rock shaped like a pitchfork in the topmost sheer cliff. Under this, rising from the ground, is a heart-shaped series of ice falls that are joined at their base and top. At the start of the flows is a hidden flow that branches off right. This is Pilgrim's Progress. Climb two bulges and belay after a full pitch. Another long pitch follows easy ice up and left to more bulges and a tree belay on the right. Walk up and right into the woods about 200 yards to a large rock overhang. Bypass this by walking further right up to and around a distinctive prow of rock to another ice fall. (This is easily visible from the road as the upper ice flow below and to the right of the pitchfork face.) Climb a short pitch up bulges to the right of a vertical icicle to a flat area and belay. The crux climbs the long ice flow above to the trees. Descend by going left at the top of the climb and through trees, down ramps and hills, to the tree buttress that forms the right edge of Pilgrim's Progress, walk down this to the base. The first ascent took five hours car to car.

Kurt Winkler and Joe Perez, February 9, 1980. On the first ascent, the two climbed the ice flow coming down off the rock overhang for 50 feet

BASHO III 4 5.6

A thinly iced mixed climb on the far right end of the cliff band. At a series of rock overhangs, this flow ends distinctly 30 feet below a roof at an oak tree. The last pitch awaits completion. Cross the stream and walk directly up to a rock band below ice. Climb up snowy rocks to a 3 foot notched overhang, through this and left to a short rock step and trees

Crack climber Jim Shimberg on the first ascent of Fracture Point.
Rich Page

above, then climb right to a two piton belay below the ice (5.6). The crux climbs the thinly iced rock above for 30 feet. Traverse left then up and exit right to a tree belay (long pitch, bring rock gear and short screws). Climb thickening bulges above to an oak tree. Rappel down trees to the right of the climb.

Ken Andrasko & Kurt Winkler, December 21, 1980. The first ascent took 5 hours and ended under a full moon

FRACTURE POINT 3/4

This climb and its neighbors are on West Royce Mt. Follow the Laughing Lion Trail south of East Royce until you see ice on the right. A short hike (snowshoes helpful) leads to the ice. This is the left-hand line.

Jim Shimberg & Rich Page, 1990

HAGAN'S HIGHWAY 2/3

The next climb to the right. An easier line lies farther right.

Jim Shimberg & Rich Page, 1990

BEYOND THE NOTCHES

This land beyond the notches abounds with ice. Spread out over a large geographic area are many climbing areas and individual routes that would shine bright if clustered down south. But lost in the north they have taken on an air of shrouded mystery, full of rumors and clues. It is probably safe to say that there are more routes still to be found than have been documented in this vast area. But then the lure of the north has always been rooted in the desire to explore.

Our research has turned up the following information. This is not an attempt to document every worthwhile route in The North Country. Rather we hope to remove some of the mystery, provide some basic information, and perhaps stimulate climbers to head north and see what they can find. Areas will be described approximately from west to east.

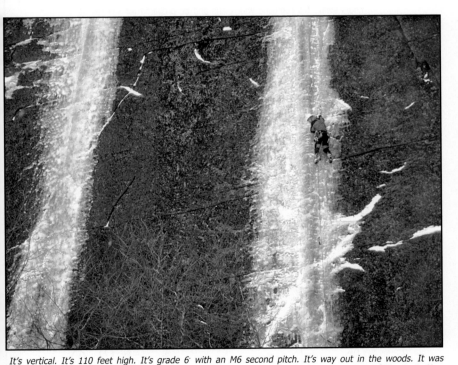

It's vertical. It's 110 feet high. It's grade 6 with an M6 second pitch. It's way out in the woods. It was discovered only in 1999. And it's only the beginning. The backcountry areas of Vermont, New Hampshire and Maine are home to a motherlode of amazing ice and mixed routes that haven't felt a pick yet. You just have to get out there and look. (Jon Sykes at Goback Mountain, 2001).
Jamie Cunningham

AREA HIGHLIGHTS

Location: Many areas spread out over northern New Hampshire and Western Maine

Routes: Climbs of all grades; roadside to backcountry

Access: Park below the crag or at trailhead, hikes from 5 minutes to an hour or longer

Descent: Typically hike down but rappel descents common

Weather: "Valley" to "Notch" (weather section), most areas December through March

Equipment: A standard ice rack plus a few rock pieces typical; consider two ropes in case of emergency

Superlatives: Hard ice and mixed routes way out in the backcountry; great practice ice at *Mt. Winthrop*; lots of ice near road at *Reflection Crag*; backcountry adventure at *Larry Flume* and *Red Rock Mt.*; quiet climbing in *Grafton Notch* (*Amphitheater, Tremblay-Hackett, The Sty*); cool climb at Squaredock (*Big Science*); all-time Northeast classic at Mt. Kineo (*Maine Line*); lots of places to explore

Amenities: Small towns throughout the region; hit or miss

Warnings: These areas see far less traffic than the other areas in the book; help is likely many hours away; tell someone your plans and be prepared for self rescue

BEYOND THE NOTCHES AREAS

A. Goback Mountain
B. Beaver Brook Falls
C. Mount Forest
D. Mount Winthrop
E. Larry Flume
F. Gentian Swamp
G. Reflection Crag
H. Tumbledown Dick
I. Pine Mountain
J. Red Rock Mountain
K. Dixville Notch
L. Grafton Notch
M. Mount Dimmock
N. Squaredock Mountain
O. Bear Mountain
P. Knight's Hill Crag
Q. Needle's Eye
R. Angel Falls
S. Worthley Pond
T. to Mount Kineo

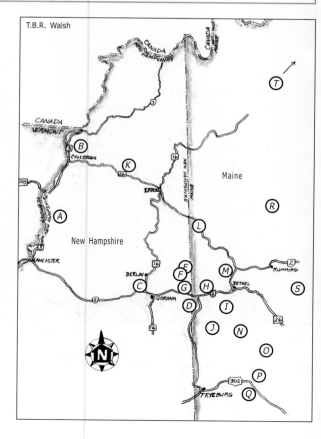

BEYOND THE NOTCHES: GOBACK MOUNTAIN

This remote 3,485′ peak in the town of Stratford in northern New Hampshire is home to one of the most spectacular ice climbs in the Northeast. Nowhere will a plumb-line be found to rival Valhalla—a thin yellow drip dropping straight down a vertical wall. The cliff on Goback faces northeast and isn't visible from any main roads. The Nature Conservancy (603-356-8833) owns the land at Goback as a nature preserve. **There is no rock climbing on Goback cliffs in any season, including a ban on bolting, fixed gear, cleaning routes, and removing any vegetation from the cliff. Slings on trees should be camouflaged as best as possible.** The Goback cliffs have been identified as a potential Peregrine nesting site, so **no ice climbing after March 30th.** Please keep this area open by complying with these simple rules. Getting to the cliff requires driving on rough back roads and hoofing it for several miles on snowshoes or skis along a logging road that is also used as a snowmobile trail. This road also crosses some private land before reaching The Nature Conservancy's property. This place is way out there! Be prepared for a long day in the woods (let someone know where you're going, bring extra gear & clothing, a headlamp, food and water, a

PUBLISHER'S NOTICE: *The authors and publisher of this guidebook take the responsibility of gathering and reporting information about climbing very seriously. It is our intent to accurately inform climbers about great places to climb in northern New England while at the same time honoring the rights and wishes of the landowners on whose property climbing exists. Just prior to going to press we consulted with The Nature Conservancy about ice climbing access at Goback Mountain. They own the land and are obligated to balance the protection of biological diversity with other uses of their property. Although recreational use is permitted under the terms of the conservation easement held by the state of New Hampshire, it must be consistent with The Nature Conservancy's conservation goals for the property, and sometimes it is necessary to prohibit certain uses. We support the efforts of The Nature Conservancy and strongly desire to help them in being good land stewards. Although climbers as a whole are typically a responsible and conscientious user-group, climbing is becoming more and more popular and sensitive areas, such as Goback Mountain, are being put at risk. After talking to The Nature Conservancy, we have chosen not to give specific directions to Goback or include a photo of the cliff so we can assist them in protecting the resource. It must be stressed that although ice climbing here was not prohibited under the terms of the conservation easement at the time of printing in January of 2003, climbing access at Goback is not guaranteed in the future. Failure to comply with the rules could result in the unfortunate closure of a great climbing resource.*

map & compass, etc.) and don't plan on help arriving quickly if there is a problem (it would probably take Mountain Rescue at least five hours to respond). Routes will be described from left to right and the easiest descent for all routes is via rappel from trees (two ropes needed).

VALHALLA 6- M6

This is without a doubt one of the most dramatic lines in all of northern New England and a testimony to both the vastness of our resource and the cunning explorative spirit of our climbers. We wonder how many more Valhallas are out there, dripping off unknown cliffs in our hills, waiting to feel our picks. Follow the dead-plumb, vertical, right-hand streak (4" to 18" thick in the FA) up the left wall to a belay where the ice ends. Pitch two is very short and very hard mixed climbing up a corner.

This route deserves to have its history told in full. A chance sighting from one of the nearby Percy Peaks by Mike Lee in the mid 1990's led to a long bushwhack by Lee, Chris Marks and Jon Sykes in 1999. They got close on a maze of logging roads but the cliff's magic routes eluded them. In December 2000 Lee and Eric Pospesil made a second

John Sykes carefully tapping his way up one of the greatest discoveries in recent years, Valhalla.
Jamie Cunningham

attempt to reach the cliff and "hit pay dirt." In March 2001 Pospesil, Sykes and Shad Lawton returned to find "the steepest ribbon of ice" any of them had ever seen in the Northeast. However, the day was bitterly cold and despite Sykes starting up, Valhalla would have to wait. They did the first ascents of The Oath and The Secret that day, wonderful routes in their own right. For two weeks the climbers thought of little else. They set out on March 18 with five friends and some of their spouses "to create a piece of New England climbing history." Pospesil warmed things up by leading the first ascent of Goback Gully, a 170' 4+ mixed route that would shine anywhere else. Then Sykes got on Valhalla and carefully picked his way up. It was 110 feet high, the climbable ice was only shoulder wide, and it varied from 4 to 18 inches thick. Nick Farley, Pospesil and Lawton followed. They all thought it was grade 6. Three days later Sykes returned with Vermont climber Will Mayo who confirmed the grade and added a hard (M6), 30 foot mixed finish that was followed by Chris Marks and Larry Boehmler. Rich Gottlieb, owner of Rock and Snow in New Paltz, NY made a subsequent ascent of the route and emailed Sykes the following testimony: "This is gem of such purity and rarity that it transcends the whole process. I have been hard at it for almost 25 years...this climb is a vein of pure gold that has risen to the surface revealing the stripped-down essence and nature of climbing."

GOBACK GULLY 4+ M4

Twenty feet to the right of Valhalla the cliff forms a distinct corner. Just right of the corner is a deep groove/gully with a chimney on the right and a tight right-facing corner on the left. Climb the corner on mixed ground to a platform, step across to the right side of the gully on a frozen tree-bridge to reach a Repentence-like flow in the back of the gully. Climb up this to the top.

Eric Pospesil, Shad Lawton, Larry Boehmler & Jamie Cunningham, March 18, 2001

Eric Pospesil on the FA of the scratchy Goback Gully. The upper tube of Valhalla is just visible at top left.
Jon Sykes

THE SECRET 4+

Forty feet right of Goback Gully is a series of ice tiers that drip down the wall. Follow the line of least resistance up the 190' long flow.

Eric Pospesil, Shad Lawton & Jon Sykes, March 3, 2001

THE OATH 4+

The first route at Goback. Fifty feet right of The Secret another set of yellow pillars and curtains drips down the wall. Start on the right, climb to a snow ledge at 1/3 height, and then climb the steep pillars above. The members of the first ascent party took an oath to keep the crag secret until they had climbed all the routes.

Jon Sykes, Eric Pospesil & Shad Lawton, March 3, 2001

BEYOND THE NOTCHES: BEAVER BROOK FALLS

BEAVER BROOK FALLS 1-3

About three miles northeast of Colebrook NH., on Rt. 3 is Beaver Brook Falls. A unique climb that is typically heavily mushroomed. Several variations are possible; descend off to the right.

FRA: Todd Swain & Matt Peer, solo, January 14, 1982

BEYOND THE NOTCHS: MOUNT FOREST

NORTH SLABS 3-4

This huge slab, crisscrossed by tree ledges, lies just south of the city of Berlin in northern New Hampshire. From the middle of town take side streets through neighborhoods until you are below the cliff (this is obvious). Follow splotches and sheets of ice up the slabs for several pitches.

probably John Tremblay & Pat Hackett in the late 1980's

BEYOND THE NOTCHES: MOUNT WINTHROP

MOSES SLAB 2-4

On Route 2, five miles east of its intersection with Route 16 in Gorham NH, is an excellent practice area on the north side of Mt. Winthrop. Located directly opposite a public rest area, parking and access couldn't be more straightforward. The main feature is a 200 foot slab that is situated just off the highway, providing two pitches of low-angled ice. Descend to the left or rappel from trees. There are also some short, steeper flows (4) to the right.

unknown

BEYOND THE NOTCHES: LARRY FLUME

LARRY FLUME 3-5

This is a wild chasm on the slopes between Mt. Ingalls and North Bald Cap, just north of the village of Shelburne, NH. Just east of Mt. Winthrop take North Rd. (note: North Rd. intersects Rt. 2 about three miles east of Gorham and then again about five miles east; this is the eastern intersection) north, cross the Androscoggin, bear left and then take an almost immediate right onto Mill Brook Rd. Stay left and drive to the end and the Austin Brook Trailhead, about 2.5 miles from Rt. 2. Follow the Austin Brook Trail for about a half mile, pass the Dryad Falls Trail on the left and continue another half mile or so to an obvious swamp. Go right and follow the drainage that fills the swamp (keep to the right side) until you enter the obvious narrow chasm of Larry Flume. There are a number of climbs here, all on the right wall starting with a grade 3, then a grade 4, then a stunning grade 5 pillar.

unknown

BEYOND THE NOTCHES: GENTIAN SWAMP

GENTIAN SWAMP WALL 3-4

Continue on the Austin Brook Trail across the swamp and when the trail starts sharply uphill head up and right into the woods aiming for the obvious ice flows. There are a number of excellent climbs here about 200' high in the 3-4 range.

unknown, although Paul Cormier has poked around in here since the 1980's

BEYOND THE NOTCHES: REFLECTION CRAG

REFLECTION CRAG 2-4

This broad cliff is about three miles east of Gorham, NH on the north side of Rt. 2 in Shelburne, and can be seen easily across from "Reflection Pond" as a "sea of blue" on the hillside. This is a really nice area with at least a dozen possible grade 2-4 routes from 20 feet to 180 feet high. To get there turn onto North Rd. just east of Reflection Pond and take it north across the Androscoggin River to a left turn onto Hogan Road. Park near the Centenial Trail trailhead (how far you can drive depends on plowing). Continue hiking along the Hogan Rd. until you can turn right and head up to the ice. All routes can easily be rappelled or you can thrash down through the woods. This has been a popular North Country area for years and the following reported routes are just a sampling of what the intrepid climber will find. Climbs will be described beginning with the short stuff on the right and heading left (longer routes will be found further left but no details are currently available).

TWIZZLER 3

Climb a narrow flow with a tree in the middle of it. The first ten feet are vertical and then the climb lies back.

FRA Joe & Judy Perez, January 1996

SPINDRIP 3/4

This is the next wide flow to the left. In a good year the route will tend to be harder.

FRA Joe & Judy Perez, February, 1995

FIFTH COLUMN 4

This climb is a few hundred feet left of Spindrip and consists of a group of vertical columns.

FRA Joe & Judy Perez, January 1995

Some years the dirt road that goes past the Centennial hiking trail is plowed for two or three miles. Approximately two miles down this road there is a small parking area that is not far from the base of a cliff. This cliff may be Steven's Point on the AMC map. A wide flow of ice can be seen on the lower right side of the cliff. The approach takes about fifteen minutes and routes are described from right to left.

BRIDGEWORK 2

A forty-foot flow up a 70-degree wall to a low-angled slab.

FRA Joe & Judy Perez, January 1995

ICICLE OVERBITE 4

A twenty foot vertical column on the left side of the flow.

FRA Joe & Judy Perez, January 1996

BEYOND THE NOTCHES: TUMBLEDOWN DICK

TUMBLEDOWN DICK MOUNTAIN 2-4

Continue east on Route 2 past the junction with Route 113 (turning south leads to Evans Notch). Take the next road on the north and cross the Androscoggin River. Bear right and go a couple of miles to a pullout under an obvious crag. This is the south side of Tumbledown Dick Mt., a popular rock climbing area for North Country residents, which has some interesting ice as well. Though there is no center-stage route here, pitches of up to grade 4 can be ferreted out of the crag if you don't mind doing a little exploring.

BEYOND THE NOTCHES: PINE MOUNTAIN

PINE MOUNTAIN 3-4+

This is a great, sunny crag with at least a dozen different possible lines. From the junction of Rt. 2 and Rt. 5 in Bethel head west on Rt. 2 toward Gorham, NH. After a bit over three miles you will come to the tiny hamlet of West Bethel. Turn south on the Flat Rd. and drive 1.4 miles—the cliff will be obvious to the west on a hillside (shown as Pickett-Henry Mt. on some maps). Access is a problem here. There is a farm in front of the cliff and it may or may not be possible to

Pine Mountain in a lean year; in a good year the ice is end to end.
S. Peter Lewis

get permission to cross private land. Just west of the intersection of Rt. 2 and Flat Rd. is right-of-way owned by Portland Pipeline which used to provide a nice ski approach, however, recent development in the area makes this access uncertain. However you choose to approach, please respect private property. Left of the main cliff is a 4+ pillar first reported by Aaron Cormier and Litty Parker in 2000. A four pitch route up the center was reportedly climbed at about grade 4 by Arne Klepinger in January 1992. On the right side of the main wall is a 2-3 pitch grade 4 and even further right are a series of one pitch routes in the grade 4 range.

BEYOND THE NOTCHES: RED ROCK MOUNTAIN

Located several miles east of Evans Notch, Red Rock Mountain has several flows that will be of interest, especially for those with a flair for adventure considering that the approach may be the crux. There are two approaches, each of which will involve a four mile trip on skis or snowshoes. From the south take Route 5 north from Fryeburg, Maine, for about 12 miles passing through the small village of Lovell, and then continuing to the even smaller village of North Lovell. Turn left on West Lovell Road which leads around the northern tip of Kezar Lake. Go 1.8 miles then turn right on Hut Rd., just before the bridge over Great Brook. Continue for 1.5 miles to the trailhead for the Great Brook Trail. Follow that trail northwest for about 1.5 miles, passing the junction with the Miles Notch Trail. Shortly you will cross Great Brook. About a half a mile farther the trail crosses the brook again and a smaller brook comes in from the right at a culvert. This is Red Rock Brook which is now followed north, keeping to the left at any forks, for another 1.5 miles to an amphitheater on the south slopes of Red Rock Mt. The flows will be obvious. From the north, follow the road, locally called Flat Road, which breaks south from Route 2 in West Bethel, Maine, opposite the West Bethel Post Office to a crossroads at 3.1 miles; take the road that runs west (right) continuing straight ahead at another junction just past a small cemetery. How far you may be able to drive on these roads in the winter is entirely dependent on conditions. The Miles Notch Trail leaves at the end of the road and is followed for 2.4 miles to the

Rob Adair enjoying the fruits of a long walk on the first ascent of Hot Lava.
Bob Parrott

junction with the Red Rock Trail which is followed an additional mile or so until near the summit of Red Rock Mt. The cliff at this point can best be accessed from the right (looking down) and may involve a rappel.

HOT LAVA II 4

Hot Lava is the most obvious of three or four flows on the face, the spectacular icefall reminiscent of Gully # 1 on Mt. Willard. The others have been climbed as well and are somewhat easier. There is also a 50 foot vertical curtain that will be passed on the southerly approach.

Bob Parrott & Rob Adair, Winter, 1986

GREAT BROOK II 2-3

Follow the southern approach to Red Rock Mountain and follow Great Brook for several miles of great ice wandering and bouldering up the flanks of Durgin Mountain.

FRA Bob Parrott

BEYOND THE NOTCHES: DIXVILLE NOTCH

PARASOL GULLY II 2+

A beautiful route in a beautiful setting. Dixville Notch is located in northern NH northwest of the town of Errol on Route 26. At the very top of the notch on the south side is a very obvious 400 foot snow and ice gully. Strong updrafts in the notch often cause running water in the gully to freeze in horizontal sheets with thin fingers of ice at the edges. These "parasols," give the route its name.

Jeff Pheasant, Steve Schneider & Tad Pfeffer, Winter 1976

BEYOND THE NOTCHES: GRAFTON NOTCH

About 1.5 hours from North Conway, N.H., Grafton Notch contains a number of quality ice routes. From North Conway take Rt. 16 north through Pinkham Notch to Gorham, turn right onto Rt. 2 and follow it for about 15 minutes to Bethel, Maine. From Bethel go north about six miles on Route 2 to the junction with Route 26 and take this northwest for about ten miles to reach the notch. Most of the climbing is on the south side of the notch in the vicinity of the Appalachian Trail parking lot. Short flows with a wide range of difficulties and easy approaches make the area attractive.

Grafton Notch has been a favorite destination for climbers in southern and western Maine for decades and many have learned the basics playing on its friendly flows. Unfortunately the history of the region is sketchy, and accurate first ascent information is almost impossible to verify.

HACKETT-TREMBLAY ROUTE II 5

This is one of the longest, steepest routes that you will see in the notch. It's on the north side of the road about 1/2 mile southeast of the Appalachian Trail parking lot. Two pitches of icicles and hanging columns call for a level head.

Pat Hackett & John Tremblay, Winter 1986/87

The steep dripfest of the Hackett-Tremblay Route.
Bob Baribeau

PRACTICE AREAS 2-4

A few hundred yards south of where the Appalachian Trail crosses the road is an excellent practice area on the southwest side of the road. Slabs, bulges and a short, steep section all are easily toproped. For some added adventure a stream bed can be followed which offers many pitches of very easy snow and ice climbing. Higher up, the stream enters a cleft with moderate climbing and there are some pillars on the left which are about 40 feet high. In the woods farther left are additional bulges and short steep flows. The main stream bed can be followed for a considerable distance in this fashion, alternately walking and then scrambling, and parties have explored all the way up to Old Speck Mountain. There are also some huge slabs on Old Speck that have climbing similar to Willey's Slide and have been climbed for decades.

unknown

Grafton's version of Willey's Slide on the west side south of the Appalachian Trail.
S. Peter Lewis

North of the practice areas and hanging over the parking lot for the Appalachian Trail is The Eyebrow, the biggest cliff in the notch. Several obvious lines typically drip down this wall. Approach the base of the wall by starting up the Old Speck Trail for several hundred yards and then bushwhacking.

STASH 2+

The far left end of the cliff is blocky and lower-angled. This is the left-most flow. This and the next route only form after a rain/freeze cycle.
FRA: Matt Peer & Tim Retelle, late 1970's

YELLOW MUSTARD CUSTARD 3+

Climbs the obvious yellow flow to the right of the former route.
FRA: Matt Peer & Tim Retelle, late 1970's

THE STY 5

Black streaks and birch trees mark this route which climbs the unbroken section of The Eyebrow cliff. Climb a steep, thin slab (mental crux) to birch trees on a shelf then move left and climb a 90 foot pillar. A rare visitor that took many attempts.
Bob Baribeau, January 1995

The Sty climbs the big icicle on the right.
Bob Baribeau

THE AMPHITHEATER 3-4

Farther north, about a half mile past the Appalachian Trail, you will see ice up in the woods on the southwest side of the highway. This small amphitheater is a fine toproping area with many climbs in the grade 3-4 range. Park at the first logging road on the southwest side of the road and follow this into the woods for about fifty yards. (Do not block the logging road with your car.) The amphitheater trail now leaves the logging road on the left. The approach takes about a half hour. There are many short climbs here spread out in a semicircle. A major feature is a strange twisting notch on the left side with a large icicle hanging down above. All routes are easily toproped.
unknown

BEYOND THE NOTCHES: MOUNT DIMMOCK

This small area is located in the village of Hanover, Maine, about 12 miles northeast of Bethel on Route 2. A road leads northwest from the center of town and very soon reaches Howard Pond. Before the pond, on the right side of the road, are two very obvious flows up in the woods on the south slope of Mount Dimmock. Both are about two pitches long and in the grade 3 range with good, consistently thick ice.
unknown

MEAT PUPPET 5

Head north on Rt. 5 past Howard Pond and a crag on your left (west) occasionally drips with ice. Hike west through "Goon Hollow" on an old road and two short but steep ice routes await you. The right hand line offers a hundred feet of steep ground.

Bob Baribeau with assistance from M. Annat, January 1995

CHAPTER SEVEN 5

The sister climb to Meat Puppet ascends a steep corner to the left and gains a 50 foot pillar.

Bob Baribeau, January 1995

BEYOND THE NOTCHES: SQUAREDOCK MT.

Squaredock Mountain sits on the west side of Rt. 5 about three miles north of the junction with Rt. 35 in Lynchville (just north of Lovell) in western Maine. It is a big, rambling cliff with good rock climbing and one famous ice route. If coming from the south, pick up Rt. 5 in Fryeburg go north about 20 miles to the junction with Rt. 35 (there will be a famous signpost with a dozen or more foreign-sounding town names on it), then turn north and continue on Rt. 5 for three more miles. At three miles you will cross the Crooked River for the second time; park in the vicinity of a side road to the east. Just before reaching this point you should have been able to see the cliff way off in the woods to the west. Walk back toward Lynchville over the Crooked River and in just a hundred feet or so take a snowmobile trail on the west. At this point things can become somewhat confusing as a hill in front of you will block the view of Squaredock. The trail will fork at the base of this little hill and either way will get you there, although the left-hand fork will be faster. Whichever direction you choose (trail conditions may dictate), make your way around the hill until you reach a drainage. The cliff will be obvious now. Head up the drainage until you can break up through talus near the center of the cliff.

The scrappy mixed ground on the approach to the crux hanging pillar on Big Science.
Jim Shimberg

The approach sounds complicated but really isn't and the reward is worth it. Allow about 45 minutes (much longer if the trails are not packed). Just left of the cliff's center is a striking chimney system choked with ice. This is:

BIG SCIENCE II 5

This has become a backcountry classic with tough mixed climbing low down and a free-standing column above and has been compared to the much more urban Repentence. Low-angled but often very thin climbing leads up into the chimney and the thicker, hanging ice above. After the pillar, an easier second pitch leads to the top of the cliff. While you may descend around either end of the cliff, the going is tough and a rappel descent may be much easier.

Paul Boissonneault & Felix Modugno, Winter 1988 (Bob Parrott and Jeff Butterfield had made an nearly successful attempt several years before)

SANCTUM OF PRIVILEDGE II 5 5.8

Seventy five left of Big Science is a rounded arete. Climb a shallow trough of black rock to the left of this aréte gaining thicker ice and a bulge. Two pitches of "pretty tough sleddin'."

Bob Baribeau, rope solo, February, 1992

About halfway between Squaredock and the junction with Rt. 35 (where the famous sign is) there is another cliff band off to the west that is visible behind an old gravel pit. Several parties have hiked in to this cliff and found climbs on its right side including a number of short steep columns.

BEYOND THE NOTCHES: BEAR MOUNTAIN

BEAR MOUNTAIN 2-4+

On Route 35 between Harrison and Waterford, next to the road and opposite Bear Pond, is a large broken cliff with a three pitch grade 3 chimney on the right as well as some great practice flows to the left of the cliff. At the practice area is a grade 4 hanging column that leads to a slab. In 1992 Bob Parrott attempted another hanging icicle on the main cliff to the right of the practice area but well left of the chimney. He climbed a 5.7 mixed pitch up a left facing corner to a ledge. On the next pitch he climbed a dagger hanging off the lip of a roof. According to Parrott the dagger was swinging back and forth as he climbed it. At the very top Parrott found only snow over granite so one move from the end he quietly downclimbed the dagger and retreated. "It's as close as you can possibly come to a first ascent and not get it" Parrott said.

The other routes here have remained unrecorded

BEYOND THE NOTCHES: KNIGHTS HILL

KNIGHTS HILL CRAG 3-4

This diminutive crag is home to a number of good practice flows. From the town of Bridgton head west toward Fryeburg on Rt. 302. Across from the Shawnee Peak ski area turn right (north) onto Knights Hill Rd. Follow the road several miles to an obvious power line cut that crosses it. Follow the power line to the right to a small crag that is graced with several short flows from grade 3-4. This area needs a cold snap to form.

unknown, although Bob Parrott has poked around this area for years

BEYOND THE NOTCHES: NEEDLE'S EYE

FLUME ROUTES 3-5 (mixed)

This little flume on the east side of Pleasant Mountain contains lots of toprope climbs of all grades including some very difficult mixed routes. At the Shawnee Peak ski area as described for the Knight's Hill Crag, turn south onto the Mountain Rd., pass the ski area and a condo development and shortly you will come to the East Peak hiking trail on the right. Hike the trail for about a half mile to a side trail on the left leading to the Needle's Eye (sign). Easier climbs exist spread out along the hillside farther south.

unknown; probably Bob Parrott in the 1980's

BEYOND THE NOTCHES: BRIMSTONE CLIFF

ANGEL FALLS 3-

This laid back backcountry gem is located northwest of Mexico, Maine, and is reported to be the highest waterfall in the state. Take Rt. 17 north from Mexico for approximately 16-18 miles to a dirt road on the left called the Bemis Track (at Houghton Station, about four miles north of the village of Byron). Ski or snowshoe in the Bemis Track northwest along Berdeen Stream for about 3.5 miles (Brimstone Mountain will be on your right) to the point where Mountain Brook comes in from the left. Follow Mountain Brook another short mile to the falls. There is a bolt at the top of the route that helps with the rappel.

unknown

Maine's tallest; the backcountry gem, Angel Falls.
Bob Baribeau

BEYOND THE NOTCHES: WORTHLEY POND

NATIVE TONGUE 5

This is a hard, steep climb that is well off the beaten track and is testifies to the pioneering spirit of Greg Bourassé, a Maine local who put up a number of hard routes in the 1980's. The route is located near Worthley Pond in Peru, Maine, about nine or ten miles south of Mexico on Rt. 108. Turn south on the Worthley Pond Rd., then right again on Greenwood Rd. and follow the west shore of the pond to its end. From there bushwhack northwest and then southwest along the flank of Tumbledown Dick Mountain until above Mud Pond. The climb will eventually become obvious.

Greg Bourassé, 1980's

Another great reason to go out in the Maine woods; Bourassé's 1980's classic Native Tongue.
Bob Baribeau

BEYOND THE NOTCHES: MOUNT KINEO

Mount Kineo is a huge cliff that stands out on a promontory in the middle of Moosehead Lake in north central Maine about 50 miles (as the crow flies) from Millinocket. It is about five hours north of Portland, Maine, and about 6.5 hours from N. Conway, New Hampshire. Road conditions can be treacherous as the last three hours or so are really in the outback—self sufficiency is the name of the game. Take Rt. 95 north from the Portland, Maine, area to exit 36 at Waterville then follow Rt. 201 north to Skowhegan. In Skowhegan take Rt. 150 north to the small village of Guilford then turn onto Rt. 15/6/16 and continue on through Monson and finally to Greenville at the southern tip of Moosehead Lake (your last chance for real supplies). Continue north on Rt. 15/6 along the western shore of the lake for about 15 miles to the village of Rockwood. Moosehead Lake is very narrow at this point and Mt. Kineo and its most famous route, Mainline, can clearly be seen across the lake to the north, about a mile away.

MAINE LINE III 5+

This is surely one of New England's most spectacular ice climbs, a thin, mushroomed ribbon that looks like it would be more at home in the Canadian Rockies. Because of the roadtrip approach it may also be one of the hardest climbs just to get to. The climb is usually done in three pitches, the second

253

being the crux, nearly a full pitch column of candled, mushroomed ice. It is possible in good conditions to avoid the very hardest section, but the climb will still be grade 5. Because the climb faces south, a prolonged cold spell is needed for it to form well, and even then the sun can do weird things to the ice. Descend way around to the left (west).

FRA Clint Cummins & John Imbrie, December 29, 1977 (Note: Research has determined that the route was actually done in 1975 or 1976 by a party who were more interested in adventure than fame and thus chose to leave this route, one of the most spectacular in the Northeast, unreported. Bravo!)

Well worth driving many hours for, Maine Line is simply one of the biggest, meanest chunks of frozen water in all of New England. Seen here in fat conditions, the route gets baked by the sun so is not always well bonded—it is advised that you climb the route on a cold day. Les Enfant Blue De Kineo climbs the discontinuous drips to the left.

Joe Terravecchia

LES ENFANT BLUE DE KINEO III 5+/6- M5

A hundred feet to the left of Maine Line lies the start of this amazing route. Three pitches of unconsolidated daggers, hanging icicles and sustained mixed sequences characterize this route. A rare visitor to Kineo. This route is indicative of the potential of northern New England climbing; hard-core climbers getting on and then getting up stuff that a decade ago would be considered simply unthinkable.

Bob Baribeau, rope solo, January 1998; Jim Ewing and Will Mayo climbed the route entirely free in January 2000

Bob Baribeau reports that another, even more desperate climb exist to the right of Maine Line. He climbed most of what he describes as possibly "one of the largest vertical icicles in New England" in 1990. Jim Ewing and Will Mayo have also been on this route. The climb awaits a complete ascent.

Jim Ewing starting the first free ascent of one of the Northeast's toughest, Les Enfant Blue De Kineo.
Will Mayo

LAURA & GUY'S GREAT ADVENTURE III 4 5.6

Several hundred yards right of Maine Line, on the east face of the cliff is another obvious route. This is a long mixed route.

FA: A bit sketchy, but Guy & Laura Waterman and Geoff Childs were known to have explored in the area (Guy broke his ankle high on the route at one point and had to be rescued by Laura); the first recorded ascent was by Kurt Winkler and Paul Boissonneault, Winter 1986

WHITELINE FEVER IV 5R

Just left of the former route a ribbon of ice sometimes forms giving an independent line the height of the cliff. Two pitches of poorly protected thin columns lead to a fat grade 4 finish. This is one of the longest grade 5 routes in the Northeast with almost 700 feet of stout climbing.

Jon Sykes & John Mallory, January 12, 2001

atahdin, Maine's big mountain and the most rugged piece of granite east of the Rockies, is home to the longest, most serious alpine rock and ice climbs in the Northeast. In this view of the summit of Pamola Peak the first technical winter route on the mountain, the Chimney, is prominent. Chimney Pond, the launching spot for all Katahdin routes is at lower left. Expect long, cold, windy—and fulfilling days here.

Brian Post (wildrays.com)

KATAHDIN

No mountain, no, not even Mount Washington, is as dramatic and obviously alpine as Maine's crown jewel, Katahdin. The name, given by the Indians of the region, means "the Greatest Mountain," and thus need not be preceded by "Mount." And somehow it's fitting. A huge bulk of granite such as this needs no clarification; it's clearly a mountain. Though Katahdin is 1,000 feet lower than Mount Washington, in many ways it is a more majestic mountain. It is far out in the wilderness, rises abruptly out of the relatively flat north woods, has few nearby rivals, has a lower timberline level, is less weathered, and has more dramatic cirques than Mount Washington, and is home to the East's only "knife-edge."

The first known winter ascent of Katahdin by a non-Indian was during the 1880's. It was a nontechnical climb which followed various ridges to the top. In 1923, an AMC party climbed The Chimney, and qualified for the first technical winter ascent of Katahdin (and one of the earliest in New England). Also of note is the fact that part of that team succeeded in doing the first all-female ascent. Despite this early activity, it wasn't until the 1970's that serious attempts on the big East Face of the mountain took place.

In February of 1971, George L. Smith led an impressive eleven-member party in a Himalayan-style attempt on the East Face. Unfortunately, they failed when typically harsh winter conditions set in. A year later, John Porter's party succeeded in scaling the East Face. Although Porter modestly explained, "Our route is undoubtedly one of the easier possibilities," the Gallery Route was a major breakthrough and is only occasionally repeated.

During the winter of 1972-73, Bob Proudman and his friends from the Pinkham Notch crew visited Katahdin twice. On the latter of the two trips, in March, they did seven routes, four of which were first winter ascents. Among these were The Diamond and Waterfall Gully, both technically and psychologically demanding. Though their success was partly assured due to mild March weather, it was nonetheless a very impressive tally.

The harsh winter of 1973-74 brought cold, high winds and little snowfall. Misha Kirk's party, whose members had just met for the first time for the climb, managed four winter ascents. With winds over 60 m.p.h. and temperatures dipping to -20°F at base camp, this was quite a feat considering that two of the party members had learned to climb just that summer. A month later, Bob Proudman returned, but this time disaster struck and Katahdin claimed its first winter climber. This accident is well documented in *Appalachia* and will always stand as a reminder of the seriousness of any Katahdin expedition.

In 1974-75, Rick Wilcox and John Bouchard visited the South Basin with a group of Chamonix guides. This group knocked off a few routes as part of their New England tour. Throughout the rest of the 1970's and into the early 1980's other significant routes were completed by various well-known New England climbers including such pioneers as John Imbrie (Frost Street) and Clint Cummins (Walk on the Wild Side) as well as Karen Messer, Dennis Drayna, and Michael Lehner.

The 1980's and 1990's brought more climbers and more radical changes to Katahdin. Fast, alpine ascents became

AREA HIGHLIGHTS

Location:	Central Maine 20 miles north of Millinocket; 5 hours drive from Portland
Routes:	The longest, most exposed, most extreme, most remote alpine climbs in the Northeast; classic alpine gullies and ridges
Access:	Park at Togue Pond, hike or ski nine miles to Roaring Brook then another 3 miles to Chimney Pond; approaches to routes vary from 30 min. to 1.5 hours
Descent:	Long, exposed, above timberline; be prepared to rappel in an emergency
Weather:	"Summit" (weather section), November through April
Equipment:	Large standard ice rack, rock gear, two ropes, camping gear suitable for arctic conditions
Superlatives:	This is simply the greatest alpine playground in the Northeast: short, hard ice climbs (*Pamola Ice Cliffs*), long easy alpine climbs (*Chimney, Elbow Gully*), great long harder alpine and ice routes (*Waterfall, Chauvin-Cole, Cilley-Barber*), remote alpine routes on the big wall in North Basin (*Black Fly*), amazing mixed routes (*Hanta Yo*)
Amenities:	Bangor (70 miles south) last big city; Millinocket has just about everything
Warnings:	The most serious climbing in New England: a remote location, long routes, a harsh environment; there are lots of regulations; read regs section carefully and contact Baxter State Park at least a month before your trip

he standard. Geoff Heath's five hour olo ascent (from Chimney Pond and ●ack) of the Cilley-Barber Route is an npressive example, as are explorations by climbers like Dave Getchell, ●r., Landon Fake, Kevin Slater, Kurt ●/inkler, Bob Baribeau, P. Marten, Jon ●ierney, and others.

Overshadowed by the larger ●eaks of New Hampshire's Presidential Range, Katahdin is easily under ●stimated. Katahdin is much more rug●ed than the Presidentials and its ●arsh weather is notorious. Geologic●lly younger, the mountain has sharper ●idges, more jagged buttresses, and ●rger glacial cirques. In addition to its ●errain, Katahdin's remote location and ●ery limited facilities make rescues ●uch more difficult. Self-sufficiency ●n't just a good idea here, it is man●ated, and all climbers must go ●hrough a complex registration pro●edure (see regulations sidebar).

Perhaps more than any other al●ine area in New England, slab ava●anches are common on Katahdin. ●here have been several serious acci●ents, and knowledge in assessing ●valanche danger is highly recom●nended. Routes to be particularly cau●ious of include: The Chimney, Wa●erfall Gully, the Cilley-Barber Route, ●he Funnel, The Diamond, and The ●lack Gullies.

Every leader has the responsibil●ty of assuring him or herself that the ●eam is fit and properly experienced ●nd has prepared for the intended ●enture. Bear in mind the variable ●veather and snow conditions. What ●night be a steep ice climb one year ●vhen snow is scarce, could be filled ●vith snow to the point of being a fine ●ki run (or an avalanche chute) the ●1ext season.

Katahdin and the surrounding ●nountains are part of Baxter State ●ark. Because of its remote and al●ine environment, the park has more ●ules than any other area covered by

KATAHDIN REGULATIONS...

(Note: The following information was gathered from baxterstateparkauthority.com in October, 2002 and is for reference only. Do not rely on these regulations without obtaining updates from the park at the time of your trip (www.baxterstateparkauthority.com).

DAY-USE:

No special permission is required for one-day trips below treeline. Visitors should check in and out at the self-registration boxes, or at Park Headquarters (by phone, if more convenient).

Special permission is required for all day-use climbs above treeline. Winter camping, snowshoeing and backcountry skiing; winter mountain hiking and climbing; and ski-mountaineering or snowboarding (that is, any winter overnight use, or any winter above-treeline travel) require a permit and is subject to these administrative policies and procedures.

PARTY SIZE:

A minimum party size of four (which may consist of separate teams of two) is required for winter mountain hiking and climbing or ski-mountaineering or snowboarding above treeline.

A minimum party size of three is required for overnight activities below treeline at roadside campgrounds and campsites.

A minimum size of four is required for camping at Chimney Pond or Russell Pond. The maximum winter party size is ten.

Joining or Leaving a Party—A member may join a party already in the Park if: **1)** An application has been submitted and approved three business days before the first scheduled day of the trip. **2)** The party inside the Park already meets minimum size requirements and does not exceed ten persons.

continued

this book. Each party should contact the Park well in advance for current regulations and information: Baxter State Park, 64 Balsam Drive, Millinocket, ME 04462, (207) 723-5149, baxterstateparkauthority.com. No overnight activity is allowed in the Park without a special winter use permit and you must get this permit in at least two weeks in advance of your trip. While there is some hoop-jumping and paperwork involved with climbing at Katahdin, it is well worth the effort, and the regulations go a long way in preventing accidents.

Getting to Katahdin isn't easy. The driving time from southern Maine and New Hampshire is upwards of six hours—and that only gets you to the end of the plowed road. Since virtually all Katahdin climbers will be coming from the south we will give directions starting from Portland, Maine. Get on I-95 and follow it north through southern Maine to Bangor. About an hour north of Bangor get off on Exit 56 at Medway and take Rt. 157/11 to the mill town of Millinocket. This is your last stop for supplies. From Millinocket follow the winter road (marked) for another 20 miles or so to the entrance to Baxter State Park on the Golden Road at Abol Bridge. From there it is a 12 mile ski to the campground at Roaring Brook. You need to check in before your climb and can do that at either the park headquarters in Millinocket or at Roaring Brook. You will also go through an equipment check at Roaring Brook. The next day you will schlepp the remaining 3.5 miles to Chimney Pond. There is a bunkhouse at Chimney Pond which can accommodate 12 people and there is additional tent camping nearby. Additionally, the latest condition reports and route updates are also available here—check with the ranger.

From the bunkhouse at Chimney Pond, one has a commanding view of

MORE REGULATIONS

3) For parties at Chimney Pond, two or more members meet the new arrival at Roaring Brook.

Two or more members may leave a party already in the Park if:
1) The remaining party size does not drop below minimum size requirements.
2) An early departure time (6:00AM) is observed, so that departing members are outside the Park before nightfall.
3) The ranger is notified of the departure or, if no ranger is available, the departing members sign out on appropriate registers.

OTHER RULES:
For administrative purposes, winter party applications will need one designated leader and two designated assistant leaders.

Camping is permitted only by reservation in authorized sites.

Parties must register with the ranger at Chimney Pond, or self-register at unstaffed ranger stations or ranger stations, upon arrival at any campsite.

Winter parties going to Chimney Pond by way of Roaring Brook must stay at Roaring Brook the first night.

Winter parties must have confirmed camping reservations (including all paperwork and full payment submitted) at least seven (7) days prior to the actual start of the trip.

REQUIRED EQUIPMENT:
Because of the likelihood of extreme weather conditions in Baxter State Park in winter, and because rescue of injured persons may be delayed for hours or days, the following equipment is required as part of every winter visitor's basic kit.

continued again

THE LAST OF THE REGULATIONS

Winter camping gear (personal):
- Showshoes or skis, with repair materials
- Insulated pacs or mountain boots
- Sleeping bag rated for winter conditions
- Sunglasses or snow goggles
- Pack
- Matches or other fire-starting device
- Food (with two-day reserve)
- Warm clothing
- Topographic map and compass
- Flashlight or headlamp

Winter camping gear (group):
- First aid kit
- Axe and camp saw
- Outdoor thermometer and wind-chill chart
- Snow shovel

Winter mountain hiking or climbing or ski-mountaineering or snowboarding gear (in addition to winter camping gear):
- Ice axe
- Crampons
- Helmet (required for technical climbs)
- Climbing rope (one per party of two)
- Sleeping bag or bivi sack (one per party of two)
- Climbing equipment appropriate to terrain
- Baxter State Park highly recommends that you bring appropriate avalanche assessment and safety equipment, along with a competent working knowledge of how to use it.

whew!

Focus, focus; remember why you're wading through these regs: the biggest, baddest alpine routes east of the Rockies
Brian Post

the East Face, with the Pamola Ice Cliffs on the left. The climbs on the main East Face can be reached by crossing the pond and continuing up the valley.

The climbs on the Pamola side involve short scrambles through deep drifts and prickly brush. Descents off the main part of the East Face are made down the Cathedral Trail (avalanche prone at timberline), the Dudley Trail or the Saddle Trail depending on your top-out point. The upper part of the Dudley Trail, the Knife Edge, is extremely exposed and is considered technical terrain in winter, while the Saddle Trail offers perhaps the least tiring descent. Descents from the top of the Pamola Ice Cliffs can be made from either end (left easier), or in the middle where there is a gap between the Lower and Upper Ice Cliffs.

This beautiful area of New England offers some of the hardest, longest, and in particular, the most remote climbs to be found in the Northeast. We hope you get the chance to climb in this wonderful place.

The authors would like to extend special thanks to Bob Baribeau for working with us to organize this chapter. Bob's three dozen trips to Katahdin (climbing every established route along the way) made him the perfect person to edit this section and he went out of his way to help including donating lots of photographs and making several trips down to meet with us.

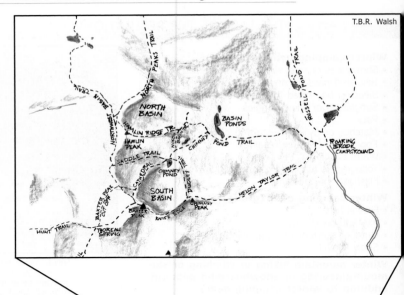

T.B.R. Walsh

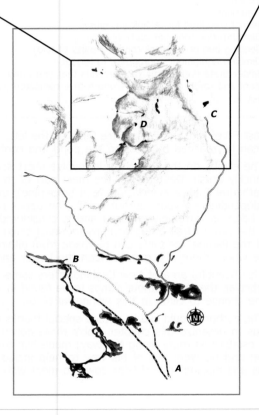

BAXTER
STATE PARK
OVERVIEW

A. road from Millinocket
B. Abol Bridge entrance
C. Roaring Brook
D. Chimney Pond

KATAHDIN: PAMOLA ICE CLIFFS

These dramatic ice cliffs, clearly seen across Chimney Pond on the southeast side of the South Basin, are home to Katahdin's steepest ice climbs. The climbs here are shorter than the big gully climbs, but make up for their small stature with unrelenting verticality. There are two parts to this section: an upper on the right (toward the Furies) and a lower one on the left (toward the Dudley Trail). The upper ice wall is broken up into four distinct routes, though many variations exist. The lower ice wall starts with Mini-Pinnacle #3 on the extreme left, and continues right ending at Wicked Right.

MINI-PINNACLE #3 2

This is a short gully found at the extreme left end of the rock band above Chimney Pond. One pitch up this fairly low angle gully. Descend off to the left.

unknown

MINI-PINNACLE #2 II 2

Found on the lower Pamola Ice Cliffs, this is the slightly larger gully and the second couloir in from the left. The first pitch is a moderate angled slab trending from left to right with a probable belay under the rock wall where the gully steepens. Move out left and up the bulge until the angle eases back. Descend off to the left, passing Mini-Pinnacle #3.

unknown

ZORRO II 4

Counting from the extreme left end, this will be the third climb to the right on the lower Pamola Ice Cliffs. It takes a meandering line up through the center of the cliff. Work up through zigzags of mixed snow and ice to any one of a number of potential belays. Continue up the gully climbing a steep bulge along the way. You can descend left or right.

A.J LaFleur, Peter Cole & John Bragg, mid 1970's

Although known for its long and serious alpine routes, Katahdin is also home to some short, interesting climbs like Mini Pinnacle #2 that make a great alternative on a nasty day.
Brian Post

STRANGE BREW II 3

Start just left of the Hands Across the Water in a right-facing dihedral. Work your way to the base of the ice by traversing in on rock ledges from the left. One very long pitch or two short ones will get you to the top. The crux is the first steep bulge before the dihedral.

unknown

PAMOLA
ICE CLIFFS

A. Frost Street
B. Stairway to Heaven
C. Walk on the Wild Side
D. South of the Border
E. Wicked Right

Brian Post

HANDS ACROSS THE WATER II 4

Found at the right end of the lower section of the Pamola Ice Cliffs, or what would appear to be the closest ice flow to the pond. Climb one or two pitches up the fairly steep and wide flow until it is possible to move off to the right and descend below the upper ice wall.

John Bouchard, Rick Wilcox & Jean-Claude Druyer, January, 1975

WICKED LEFT 3

One hundred feet left of Frost Street a slab of ice steepens and hugs rock on the left for one pitch.

Jim Morrissey, Bob Baribeau & M. Annat, March, 1993

FROST STREET II 5

This route is the farthest left of the major flows on the upper ice wall. A difficult route with scary climbing up a forty foot vertical crux section.

John Imbrie & Dennis Drayna, December, 1979

STAIRWAY TO HEAVEN II 4

Up a series of columns from ledge to ledge. It's easier than it looks.

Bob Proudman & Paul DiBello, January, 1974

WHERE DO THE CHILDREN PLAY II 4+

Between Stairway to Heaven and Walk on the Wild Side begin at a narrow and thin flow and then shallow gully to belay in semi-shattered alcove below a short, steeper bulge. The second pitch climbs the bulge to easy ground and the top.

FRA: Jim Ewing & Rich Baker, January, 1984

WALK ON THE WILD SIDE II 5

This classic route ascends the big, thick flow right of the previous route for two pitches. Slightly easier variations will be found on either side of the central line.

Clint Cummins and Mike Lehner, February, 1975; interesting historically is the ascent of a mixed route in the area in 1969 by Paul Ledoux and Al Rubin—this was most likely the first time that curved tools were used on Katahdin.

initial steep ice. The first ascent party bypassed some steep ice by rock climbing a chimney on the left which had a big rotten chockstone in the way. Near the top of the climb, the main gully fans out into three separate couloirs, each of which offer similar difficulties. Good rock belays will be found throughout the length of the route.

Paul DiBello & Dana Jones, March, 1973

WATERFALL GULLY IV 4

Characterized by two impressive ice pillars at the beginning of the gully, this climb can be found several hundred yards left of the Cilley-Barber Route. From the base of the lower snow bowl, work your way left up to the base of the ice flows. Two pitches, the first one moderately steep and the second one an even more spectacular ribbon of ice, constitute the crux. The remainder

Waterfall Gully's start is certainly obvious enough. Above, the route dog-legs right.
Lauren Head

of the gully is predominantly a snow climb as the route slowly turns a dog-leg right and joins the remaining ridge just east of The Cilley-Barber Route. You can also exit right (with one short rappel) after the first two pitches if you want a short climb or need to retreat. This route was reportedly climbed leashless by the first ascent party! (Just imagine the gear they had.)

Mark Lawrence & Bob Proudman, March, 1973

WATERFALL LEFT IV 4

On the second pitch of Waterfall Gully, climb thin ice slabs on the left to a short pillar. Continue up and right joining the normal route.

Landon Fake with assistance from Kevin Slater, March, 1987

WATERFALL GULLY EAST IV 4

Climb the first two pitches of The Waterfall. Take the first snow gully to the east, then 750 feet of mostly snow will take you to the Knife Edge. This is a long and committing route with some danger from avalanche.

Jorge Urioste, Mike Gilbert, Misha Kirk & Joanne Selle, January 1974

TOWER RIDGE IV 4 5.5

Climb the first two pitches of The Waterfall and continue up the snow gully trending right. A rock buttress on your left dominates the left skyline. Several scrappy leads take you to the base of this buttress which was first ascended in 1928 by an AMC party. A fissure splits the buttress and leads to the Knife Edge. Climb the fissure.

FWA Bob Baribeau & Landon Fake, March 4 1994

WEXLER ROUTE IV 3 5.6

Arnold Wexler pioneered a summer rock climb in 1946 that ascends the rock wall on the right. Tough mixed climbing.

FWA unknown

The west side of the large rock buttress that separates The Waterfall from The Cilley-Barber Route is home to several routes that in winter contain much scrambling, with mostly fourth class climbing with the odd fifth class move.

WATERFALL
BUTTRESS III 3+ 5.5

After the initial pitches of ice of the Cilley-Barber head left aiming for a shallow depression that occasionally contains ice and always sports interesting mixed climbing. Six long leads will take you to the summit ridge.

Landon Fake & Christine Baker, February 1989

CILLEY-BARBER IV 4

An outstanding line that lures many who venture to Chimney Pond in winter. The initial two pitches climb an obvious icy break that gives access to the upper snow gully. Alternating snow and moderate bulges of ice lead to a right facing corner. Climb the ice in the corner and continue left or straight ahead. Finish on the summit ridge. Expect 600 meters of Katahdin's finest. Note: The crux ice lead doesn't always form but

Katahdin's most famous hard ice climb, the Cilley-Barber takes a striking line up a weakness in a steep wall—alpine climbing at its best. Waterfall Buttress heads left after the lower snowfield and climbs the obvious icy trough up the buttress.
Brian Post

don't let that deter you—it's a fine mixed pitch.

Henry Barber & Dave Cilley, February 1973; the crux was first climbed as a mixed pitch by Jim Morrissey & Bob Baribeau, March 2 1994

RHYTHM AND BLUES PILLAR 4+

This is the rarely formed, free standing pillar about 75 feet to the right of the normal Cilley-Barber start.

Kurt Winkler & Bob Baribeau, February 1988

HEATH'S FINISH II 4 5.6

The crux flow at the top of the Cilley-Barber has been turned on the right by hard mixed climbing.

Geoff Heath & partner, March, 1983

A depression immediately left of the Armadillo consists of bulging slabs and short headwalls. After a winter rain and hard freeze, verglas covers this deviously technical ground.

THE PRIMITIVES IV 4-

This is the dramatic snake of ice that wiggles up the depression left of the Armadillo. Begin up the Cilley-Barber and head right and up after the lower snowfield on easy ground. Just left of the Armadillo Buttress, start thinly and carry on for a full 600 feet of poorly protected ice to snow and a final steep headwall at the top. Catching this fine route in shape is a rare treat.

Bob Baribeau & Ray Geiger, March 3 1997

DILLO DIRECT IV 4

Longtime Katahdin devotee Peter Cole climbed this long (and better protected) companion to The Primitives with Eric Scranton. They started up the thin ice of The Pimitives and then moved right up a blocky snow gully for several pitches before heading back left to the final steep headwall. Cole said that he had been eyeing the line for many years, waiting for conditions to be just right for the ascent. It is reported to be an outstanding adventure (and way less scary than the former route).

Peter Cole & Eric Scranton, March 13 1996

ARMADILLO IV 3+ 5.7

This soaring triangular buttress with its detached flake and upper jam crack make for a very challenging route in winter. Only a handful of winter ascents are known. Approach as for the Cilley-Barber. After the initial two pitches head (right) toward The Black Gullies. Traverse left on a ramp to climb the right side of the detached flake. The left side of this flake is a serious off-width (5.8). Climb the jamcrack above and follow the arête for several more pitches to the summit ridge.

FWA Mike Hartrich & Tad Pheffer, January 1975

To the right of the Armadillo is an amphitheater which offers several separate ice and snow finishes as well as an excellent mixed route. Four of these climbs have been documented though others have undoubtedly been climbed. Approach by climbing the low-angle initial pitches of the Cilley-Barber Route and then bear right into this recess. The obvious triangular buttress of the Flatiron forms the far right margin of this enclosure.

BLACK GULLY EAST III 3

The left-hand line.

unknown

BLACK GULLY WEST III 3

The next obvious line to the right.

unknown

AMBEJEJUS BOOM HOUSE BUTTRESS III M4 3

"Ambejejus" is Ponobscot for "water that divides an island." Approach as for the previous two routes and head for the pyramid of rock that dominates the Black Gully amphitheater. Ascend a hairline crack to a perch (150 feet) or trend right then back left on face and crack moves to the same stance. Beautiful mixed climbing leads to within one pitch of the summit ridge. Stroll (or crawl) to Baxter Peak.

Bob Baribeau & Landon Fake, March 8 2000

HEADBANGER III 3 5.4

This is the farthest right route. Climb to the left side of the Flatiron and make a rising traverse that moves left for one pitch, then trends back right to reach the crest of the Flatiron. Follow this ridge to the top.

Bob Baribeau & Landon Fake, March 4 1993

The approach for the following four routes can be via The Cilley-Barber start or skirt the lower cliff band moving right taking mostly snow slopes and moderate rock until bearing back left. This should place you to the right of the Flatiron and under your chosen objective.

THE DIAMOND IV 3+

Climbs the first gully to the right of The Flatiron. Mixed ice and rock gains a snowfield that resembles a Diamond. An exit gully right leads to the summit cairn.

Bob Proudman & Paul DiBello, March 1973

GALLERY ROUTE III 3+ 5.6

This is the second gully to the right of The Flatiron. Hike up towards the left end of the lower cliffs; a hidden, slanting couloir runs directly up the left edge of the pyramid-shaped buttress which dominates the middle of the East Face. (An alternate start for this route and The Diamond begins up iced slabs right of the Cilley-Barber Route, the most obvious break in the lower cliff band, and traverses right to a short, steep trough and continue past The Flatiron.) This brings you to a large snowfield above the lower cliffs. Continue up, traversing slightly right, until you are in the second gully to the right of The Flatiron. Continue up this gully for two pitches of sparsely protected 5.6 climbing (under normal winter conditions). Here, the angle eases back and the route continues up right in a slanting chimney to the final upper snow fields. Proceed five pitches up the couloir to the summit plateau. One rope-length south brings you to the Baxter summit.

John Porter, Geoff Wood, David Isles & Larry Nolin, February 1972; this was the first route on Katahdin to climb all the way up the South Basin Headwall; Isles had been on the Everest International Expedition the year before and Porter had climbed extensively in the Himalaya.

RUDE LITTLE MAN IV 4- 5.5

Enter the second gully right of the Flatiron but trend right to distinct twin ice runnels. Climb these to easy slabs then a gully on the right, then easy terrain leads to the Tableland, the flat plateau that lies west and east of the summit.

Bob Baribeau & Landon Fake, March 3 1994

CHAUVIN-COLE ROUTE III 3+

This route climbs the East Face of the South Basin Headwall to within 200 feet of the summit. Trend right once past Chimney Pond and climb low angle ice and snow (the so-called Shelf Route that runs below Chauvin-Cole, The Funnel, Piggy-Wiggy and Dougal's Delight) several hundred yards right of the Cilley-Barber Route. A pyramid shaped buttress looms ahead. Ascend to the right of the central slabs and couloir up snow slopes then move back left to gain the icy groove. An excellent route.

Marc Chauvin & Peter Cole, 1982

CHAUVIN-COLE VARIATION START II 3+ 5.6

Climbs the icy slabs of the buttress directly from the snowfield, joining the upper trough after several mixed pitches.

Bob Baribeau & John O'Brien, February, 1984

PIGGY-WIGGY II 3

Farther right, this route was named for a stuffed animal which was the group's mascot. The first ascent party climbed

Looking like it would be more at home in Alaska, the Chauvin-Cole Route provides a surprisingly modest trip up one of Katahdin's big buttresses. The normal start is on the right and the harder variation start is to the left.

Brian Post

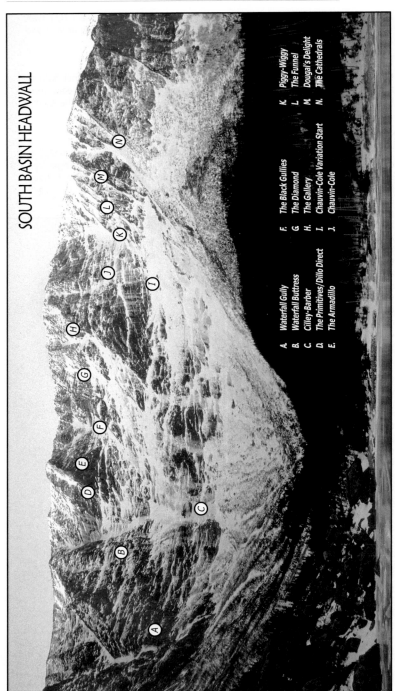

SOUTH BASIN HEADWALL

A. **Waterfall Gully**
B. **Waterfall Buttress**
C. **Cilley-Barber**
D. **The Primitives/Dillo Direct**
E. **The Armadillo**

F. **The Black Gullies**
G. **The Diamond**
H. **The Gallery**
I. **Chauvin-Cole Variation Start**
J. **Chauvin-Cole**

K. **Piggy-Wiggy**
L. **The Funnel**
M. **Dougal's Delight**
N. **The Cathedrals**

Katahdin's South Basin Headwall is the most impressive alpine setting east of the Rocky Mountains. Rising over 2000 feet from Chimney Pond to the summit of Baxter Peak it offers the greatest technical vertical-gain in the Northeast and has been a training ground for the region's best climbers for generations.

Brian Post

two ice pitches up the lower slabs. After a precarious snowfield, which later avalanched, they came across a steep ice wall. Three more pitches of ice will bring one to the upper snow. Escape right toward The Funnel or, as they did on the first ascent, at the top of the second snow bowl bear left for two pitches of mixed climbing, and gain the ridge approximately 400 feet north of the summit.

Misha Kirk, Jorge Urioste, Joanna Selle & Mike Gilbert, January 1974; Uriosite and Selle have been climbing legends in the desert Southwest including being credited with the major early exploration of Red Rock outside Las Vegas.

THE FUNNEL II 2+

The start and most of the route is the same as Piggy-Wiggy, except that you exit right and then up an easy snow slope.

unknown

DOUGAL'S DELIGHT II 2+

A tribute to the great Scottish ice climber. This climb starts on the shelf, just left of a bivy cave formed by a large rock. Start up the side ice flow and continue up for two pitches. The third pitch angles left onto a ridge. Some mixed climbing may be encountered here.

Misha Kirk & Mike Gilbert, December 1973

GULLY #3 II 2

Between the Upper Cathedral Saddle and The Funnel, there are three gullies. Gully #3 is the one closest to the Upper Cathedral Saddle. During most winters this is an easy snow climb of several pitches. Head up toward the Upper Cathedral Saddle and angle left as the gully is entered.

unknown

UPPER CATHEDRAL SADDLE (CATHEDRAL GULLY #2) II 1

In most winters this is an easy snow climb. A gully leads up to the Upper Cathedral Saddle.

unknown

CATHEDRAL GULLY #1 II 1

Climb up the obvious line between the two rock cathedrals. Mixed climbing and deep snow conditions may exist on the route.

Robert & Miriam Underhill, March, 1923

Note: these last three routes all can be used to descend toward Chimney Pond if weather conditions demand a fast descent.

The awesome North Basin at Katahdin features the biggest alpine wall in the Northeast. Remote and barren, it offers the ultimate backcountry alpine experience. Kurt Winkler ponders new ground
Bob Baribeau

KATAHDIN: NORTH BASIN

Katahdin's North Basin is considered by many to be the most dramatic alpine setting in the eastern United States. Barren and wild, it isn't hard to imagine that you're in the Wind Rivers rather than northern Maine. While many of the routes here are very long they are typically not as difficult as those found on the South Basin Headwall. But what the North Basin lacks in arm-pumping difficulty it more than makes up for in solitude and beauty and the pleasure that comes from covering a lot of ground. And a lot of ground you will cover; getting into the basin from Chimney Pond, up a route, and back down to the pond again is a huge day. Get an early start and keep moving.

The climbing history of The North Basin has always been a little sketchy. Though Elbow Gully may have been climbed in the 1800's, most of the gullies were explored in the 1970's and 1980's. In recent years the usual suspects have been back in here ferreting out new lines on the buttresses between the snow gullies.

From Chimney Pond, hike, ski, or snowshoe two tenths of a mile toward Basin Pond. Head north on the N. Basin trail passing the Hamlin Ridge Trail and proceed to Blueberry Knoll. Take the summer trail to Blueberry Knoll. Just before reaching the knoll, take a left and bushwhack into The North Basin to the base of your intended route. Descents are made either by going left to the summit of Hamlin Peak then making a short hike to the Saddle Trail which then leads back to Chimney Pond (best option), or by heading right passing Elbow Gully to the next gully north which can be downclimbed (or glissaded in good conditions) for 2,000 feet back to the base. Routes will be described from east to west—right to left. The climbs closest to Blueberry Knoll will be described first.

PAULA'S LAMENT II 3+

Icy slabs at the easterly (right) end of the basin occasionally ice up to give two pitches of fun climbing. NOTE: also called North Basin Slabs by Rob Ronan and Wendy Northfield, January 1983. It's quite possibly the same route although these slabs could provide more than one line.

Bob Baribeau, Kurt Winkler & Dennis Tefft, February 1988

POLITICS AND RELIGION 3+

West of the previous slabs a gully with twin ice bulges flank a trough. Don't argue over what line to climb.

Kurt Winkler & Bob Baribeau February 1988

ELBOW GULLY III 1-2

Right of Black Fly and bordering the right edge of the large face is an obvious wandering gully that is narrow at the start and finishes up a wide basin. At the bottom of the gully is an obvious steep column. This is Tut's Thumb. Scramble around this to the right to reach the start of the easy upper gully. Many pitches of mostly snow climbing, with a dog-leg left, lead to the top.

unknown

Yes, there are some very steep pitches at Katahdin. The vertical start to Tut's Thumb is about a day and a half from the nearest hospital.
Bob Baribeau

TUT'S THUMB 4+

Climbs very difficult ice as a direct start to the left of the normal Elbow Gully start. Above, easier climbing leads back to Elbow Gully.

FRA: Andy Tuthill, Bob Parrott & Rob Adair, February 1986

RESOLUTION M4+

This summer rock climb just left of Tut's Thumb contains some difficult entry moves before entering an icy crack.

Bob Baribeau & P. Marten, March 2002

HANTA YO IV 4- 5.7

This impressive mixed route ascends the rouge colored right flank of the Taber Wall (see the following route). Begin at the base of Elbow Gully and climb a short mixed pitch heading for an obvious ramp. In a couple of pitches this ramp will take you to Elbow Gully but not before passing below a red crack/chimney system on the left. Climb up this for 4-5 pitches of 5.4-5.6 rock and then one pitch of steep, thin ice (if you don't see the runnel, expect a real battle). A final pitch of rock (5.7) goes up and right to a headwall and the top.

FWA Landon Fake & Kevin Slater, February 1987

BLACK FLY IV 4+

In a depression left of Elbow Gully is a huge, 1000 ft. cliff, the Taber Wall. This classic route starts up the largest ice flow just left of a nose-like buttress on the left side of the cliff. Four hundred feet of sustained grade 4 ice, often thin, gain a snowy shelf. The original route traversed left for one rope length and then up three pitches of mixed ice and rock.

Dave Getchel, Jr. & Doug Carver, early 1980's

BARIBEAU DIRECT
IV 4 5.6

Climb Black Fly to the snow shelf. Directly above the shelf a blocky groove gives three pitches of mixed climbing. Finish at a cairn on the North Peaks Trail.

Kurt Winkler & Bob Baribeau, February 1988

FIN AND FEATHER
FINISH IV 4

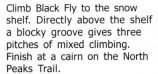

A cave with a rock groove on the left marks this alternate finish to Black Fly. A dribble of ice choking the crack assists the ascent. Several pitches of ice and snow then lead to the ridge.

Bob Baribeau & P. Marten, March 2002

Want to climb thousands, wait, make that tens-of-thousands of feet of stuff like this? Katahdin is the place. Bob Baribeau on the FA of the Baribeau Direct finish to Black Fly.
Kurt Winkler

Descent from the top of Hanta Yo, Black Fly, Elbow Gully, and other routes in the immediate vicinity is best accomplished by heading west (left) for the summit of Hamlin Peak. A short hike to The Saddle Trail and thence to Chimney Pond offers a speedy descent. Several moderate ice climbs exist to the west (left) of Black Fly. Most if not all have been climbed, although first ascent information is murky. Several of these lines can be ascended and linked to form an interesting traverse. Seven hundred feet west of Black Fly a longer line forms and leads to the ridge. This is The Elderly Gentleman.

THE ELDERLY GENTLEMAN III 3

A low angle slab of ice bordered on the left by a short left-facing corner marks the start of this route which lies left of Black Fly. Climb the corner (mixed); pull the overhang to reach an 8-inch crack. Up this to a belay on your left. Two additional pitches climb bulges of ice. The route meanders up a snow gully bordered by rock on the right to reach the cairned ridge. Descend Taber Gully or head for Hamlin Peak and the Saddle Trail.

Bob Baribeau & Andy Robidoux, March 1998

At the western edge of the North Basin and bordered on the left by Hamlin Ridge lies a rock wall. Several winter routes exist here. Katahdin veterans Landon Fake and John O'Brien have been active in this area and report mixed stuff up to three pitches long (with the occasional old piton found along the way).

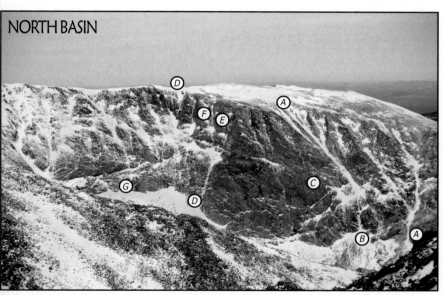

Brian Post

A.	Elbow Gully	E.	Baribeau Direct
B.	Tut's Thumb	F.	Fin and Feather
C.	Hanta Yo	G.	The Elderly Gentleman
D.	Black Fly		

CAMDEN

Though the mid-coast of Maine isn't on anyone's list of ice climbing hot spots there is a surprising amount of fun and exciting climbing here. With milder weather the routes do not form as consistently as the inland areas in the region but when conditions are right routes can come in fast and the climbing can be wonderful. Camden routes aren't overly steep, or long, but many consist of sustained calf-burners on thin, low-angle ice—often above highly stimulating runouts. Ice climbers should be prepared for sketchy climbing and would be wise to bring a selection of rock gear to supplement their ice racks.

The nearby ocean makes Camden winters somewhat erratic, though the long, cold nights of late December and January usually breed good ice. The thickest buildups occur after wet snowstorms followed by a couple of cold days. Since the cliffs face southwest, the sunny spells of February tend to wipe out the better routes. On the other hand, these sunny crags can be quite comfortable on those wicked days when it's 30 below and blowing 100 up on Mt. Washington. And should you arrive to find the cliffs washed out by a dreary, cold rain...well, Camden also hosts several great restaurants and pubs.

AREA HIGHLIGHTS	
Location:	Coastal Maine about 2 hours northeast of Portland
Routes:	Lots of short moderate routes on several crags
Access:	Park below the crags and hike for 10-20 minutes
Descent:	Hike off or rappel from trees or fixed anchors
Weather:	"Valley" (weather section) January & February
Equipment:	Standard ice rack and rock gear is essential (see route descriptions)
Superlatives:	Great moderate routes on Barrett's Cove Cliff (*Heathrow, Pharaoh's Beard, Continental Ice Sheet*) and at the Maiden Cliff (*Blue Vein*); great practice routes at *The Cataracts*
Amenities:	Camden, just two miles away, is a wonderful coastal town with all amenities

From southern and western Maine the best (and most scenic) approach is to drive north on U.S. Route 1 from Portland, Maine, for about 1 1/2 hours to a left turn onto Route 90 in Warren, then another left (north) onto Rt. 1 again at Rockport and follow that for another two miles to Camden. Follow Rt. 1 through Camden, and bear left onto Route 52 (a k a Mountain Street) just north of the village center. After about 2 miles, you'll crest a big hill and see the first of two major ice areas. The Maine Bureau of Parks and Lands manages most of the land here as a state park and have worked with the Access Fund and locals on a climbing management plan. The only restrictions are that power drills and chipping or gluing holds are prohibited. The boundaries between the Camden Hills State Park and the surrounding private land are not always obvious and climbers are urged to act respectfully and responsibly when climbing here. Historical information is sketchy for this area and not all routes will have first ascent information. Additionally, mixed route ratings have been reported using both traditional rock grades (e.g., 5.8) and the newer mixed system (e.g., M4).

CAMDEN: BARRETT'S COVE CLIFF

This 250 foot cliff, Camden's main crag, lies back at an angle of about 70-degrees and has often been compared to Cathedral Ledge's Thin Air Face. Park on Rt. 52 just south of the road to the town beach at Barrett's Cove. Bushwhack 200 yards straight up to the base, or follow the faint summer climbers' trail just left of the talus.

Most routes involve two or three pitches, often with significant sections of mixed terrain. Start climbs here early; it's not unusual for certain routes to be in fine shape in the morning and gone by mid-afternoon. The moderate climbs follow lower-angle chimneys and flows where protection is generally adequate with screws (bring some short ones) and rock gear. The harder lines launch out onto alarmingly thin smears up 70-degree faces with spotty or nonexistent pro; bring sharp hooking tools, swing 'em gently, and don't look down! Bolts and fixed gear are rare, though tied-off screws, Spectres, TCUs, tiny cams and small wires help lend some security.

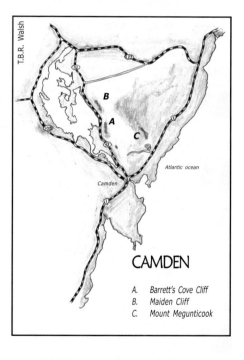

CAMDEN

A. Barrett's Cove Cliff
B. Maiden Cliff
C. Mount Megunticook

There are several descent options from the top of the cliff. Sketchy trails can be followed down either side, to the north dropping into a creek bed that leads back to the base, or to the (south) angling away from the cliff into open woods that will lead back to the road. (Don't cut back toward the base until you are almost to the road, unless you enjoy downclimbing vertical moss .) The other option is to rappel the cliff with two ropes from fixed anchors at the top of the cliff near Charlotte's Crack to a bolted anchor on the big Broadway ledge, and then again to the ground. Route descriptions run left to right.

Our special thanks to Ben Townsend for graciously allowing us to use his book, Rock and Ice Climbs in the Camden Hills, as the basis for this chapter—it sure helped us get things straightened out.

ARIZONA HIGHWAYS 3+/4

Start near the cliff's far left margin at a thin smear leading to a gully. The obvious hanging columns above (4) can be bypassed up ramps to the right. An alternate start begins to the right and follows a narrow chimney left to join the route near the top of the first pitch.

Geoff Heath & Pete McCartney, 1977

SOLSTICE WALL M4

A steely line tiptoeing up a rarely-formed smear above the right end of a long, low roof. Cruise the moderate gully, pass the left end of Broadway ledge, and belay in a chimney about 30' higher. Take a deep breath, traverse a brushy crack left (last pro), and finesse up the thinly iced face above. Rock gear is crucial, as is an early start. A variation on pitch two continues straight up the chimney (3+ 5.5) and usually offers thicker ice and better protection. A second variation takes the chimney to a chockstone then steps right to a handcrack and big block which lead to an alcove with trees. Rappel from trees (two long ropes), do a scrambly pitch out of the alcove, or dry-tool left past a bolt and join the top ice of Solstice (M4).

Geoff Heath & Dave Getchell, Sr., Winter Solstice, 1981

CHARLOTTE'S CRACK 5.7

This is the summer route up a diagonal crack above Big Chimney. It rarely ices up but is a useful winter rappel route: rappel 100+ feet from a 3-bolt anchor just east of the trees at the top to the Broadway ledge and another 3-bolt anchor, and then do another 100+ rappel to the base (60m ropes just make it).

PHARAOH'S BEARD 3+

A fine, fun line on the upper wall. From Broadway, above Skye Crack, follow the distinctive triangular flow marked by a pine jutting horizontally at the top. Usually thick enough to take ice screws though rock gear is needed at the top. Rappel 80' from two bolts to Broadway.

Dave Getchell, Sr., Geoff Heath & Pete McCartney, 1977

BIG CHIMNEY 2-3

Just right of a huge block at the base, this deep, vegetated cleft has not iced up enough to climb in the past 20 years. It is listed here as a geographic reference point.

George Smith, 1960s

CACHONGAS (unrated)

This route climbs up and right out of the Big Chimney and is reported to be the hardest route in Camden (with surprisingly good rock protection). A little mystery once in a while is a good thing.

Geoff Heath, early 80's

It may not be steep but Geoff Heath finds the Pharoah's Beard plenty thin. Note the1980's outfit and hardware
Dave Getchell, Sr

BARRETT'S COVE CLIFF

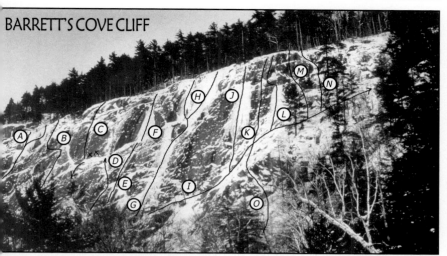

.	Arizona Highways	E.	Skye Crack	I.	Joe's Route	M.	Tritium Witch
.	Solstice Wall	F.	Pharoah's Beard	J.	Continental Ice Sheet	N.	Joe's Route finish
.	Charlotte's Crack (rappell)	G.	Heathrow	K.	Tangled Up in Blue	O.	Tangled up in Blue Direct
.	Big Chimney	H.	Clothesline	L.	Big City Woman		

KYE CRACK 3+ 5.4

About 30' left of the main Heathrow gully, an ice ribbon leads up to a juniper and (you hope) an ice-choked offwidth crack, then up mixed ground to trees on Broadway (160 feet). Typically the first protection comes 50-60 feet up; after that, use rock gear to 3".

Dave Getchell, Sr. & Geoff Heath, 1978

HOLLYWOOD WALTZ 4+ 5.4

An independent line between Skye Crack and Heathrow. Typically thin and poorly protected. Bring a selection of cams. There is a 2-bolt anchor on Broadway and it's 165 feet to the ground.

Geoff Heath, early 1980's

HEATHROW II 3+

The huge central gully offers the cliff's most reliable ice. The first pitch is low-angled and climbs either either unprotected terrain on the left (easier) or harder, slightly better protected terrain on the right. The two options merge about 60' up at an alcove (pin). From the alcove, climb slightly right up a short bulge (good wires) to a gully and make a hard rock traverse left at its top and then climb up to Broadway (165 feet, can be split). From Broadway, bash up blue ice straight to the trees; going right and up the gully leads to shaky mixed ground. A fine narrow flow sometimes forms left of a notch at the top.

Ken Clark, early 70s

PIDER LINE 3+

Occasionally an ice flow forms left of Clothesline with poor protection until the crux exit moves.

Jerry Cinnamon, 1994

CLOTHESLINE 3-4

An ice-hose leads up a squeeze chimney just left of Heathrow's top pitch. It's nice when thick, but very scary when thin. Take screws, small wires, and midsize camming units.

Dave Getchell, Jr. & Pete McCartney, 1977

DESPERADO 4+ 5.4

This outlandish smear clings occasionally to the steep slab right of Heathrow. Rarely more than an inch or two thick, the ribbon ends in a corner 100' up at bolts; don't count on any pro before that. Belay there, calm down, then finish straight up the corner and easy rock on the right (5.4).

Geoff Heath & Michael Opuda, 1982

Barrett's classic Clothesline with Dave Getchel, J. near the top climbing the crux groove
Dave Getchel, S

JOE'S ROUTE 2

An enjoyable, non-demanding mixed climb. Follow the line of least resistance for 2-3 pitches up the gully right of Heathrow, then up low-angle ramps leading right to a huge pine. Finish up the obvious gully above, heading either left or right at the overhangs as conditions dictate. To the right of the upper part of this route is a slabby wall with up to a half dozen short, typically thin moderate routes that sometimes come in when conditions are just right.

Pete McCartney & Dave Getchell, Sr., 1977

CONTINENTAL ICE SHEET II 3+ 5.6

High on the right wall, a big cascade marks the airiest, most sustained line on the cliff—and it even has pro if the ice is good. Start up Joe's Route and belay in one of two left-facing corners below the main flow. Launch up the columns onto the exposed ice sheet above (optional belay in a cleft), then scramble up left on mixed ground (165 feet).

Geoff Heath, Pete McCartney & Dave Getchell, Sr., 1979

TANGLED UP IN BLUE II 3+/4 5.7

A committing last pitch, but worth the wait. Start on the cliff's lower tier below Joe's Route, up the middle flow to a big pine. Ramps and a chimney lead to a belay ledge. The rarely formed crux pitch goes between Continental and Big City Woman, up thin cracks and dicey ice. Bring small wires and big confidence

Dave Getchell, Jr. & Geoff Heath, 1983

BIG CITY WOMAN 3 5.7

This obvious ice tongue right of Continental Ice Sheet stops short of the top. Start up Joe's Route and connect to the obvious steep flow that suddenly ends; step left and climb thin ice (or 5.5 rock) to the base of a flared chimney

(may require an aid move). Wild, but reasonably well protected.
Geoff Heath & Dave Getchell, Jr., 1982

TRITIUM WITCH 3-4

The right-most flow on the main wall, to the right of the Big City Woman chimney. Start up as for Big City Woman and continue straight up a narrow flow to the top. Rock gear possible.
Dave Getchell, Jr. & Geoff Heath, 1979

To the right and down from Heathrow and below Joe's Route, a broken-up area hosts several nice toprope flows (scramble off right) and direct starts to Joe's Route and Tangled up in Blue. Routes will be described from left to right.

WATERFALL 3

A wide, bulgy flow on the left that rarely forms.
unknown

TANGLED UP IN BLUE DIRECT START 3+

Up steeper stuff in the middle for two pitches. Climb straight up thinly to a small tree on a ledge and exit right to a large pine. Go left up a ramp and chimney to connect to Tangled up in Blue.
Geoff Heath & Dave Getchell, 1983

JOE'S DIRECT 2+

Go up a short bulge and snow ramp on the right to an alcove, then a pitch up the left-facing corner/gully to join Joe's Route at its final pitch.

Up and right of the main cliff is the diminutive Skyline Crag. Routes are described from left to right.

FAT BOY 2+

Climb thick ice near the left side of the crag.
Jerry Cinnamon & Ben Townsend, mid 1990's

LITTLE SISTER 4

Just right of the previous route climb extremely thin ice on an outside corner; poorly protected at the start.
Jerry Cinnamon & Ben Townsend, mid 1990's

TWISTER 3+

Climb the obvious chimney in the center of the cliff.
Jerry Cinnamon & Ben Townsend, mid 1990's

There is a hidden canyon situated up and behind Barrett's Cove Cliff called the Lost Valley. Left of Barrett's follow a streambed up and eventually right. Routes are described from right to left.

KING OF SWING 4+ 5.8

About 100' right of the next route, near the head of the canyon, steep ice leads to a traverse left and an exit up an overhanging corner (or continue scratching left).

Jerry Cinnamon & Dave Getchell Jr., about 1994

LOST VALLEY CATARACT 1-2

This is the obvious low-angled flow left of the head of the canyon. A right-hand variation at the top, Half Pipe, offers a harder finish.

Dave Getchell Jr. & Jerry Cinnamon, about 1994

CAMDEN: MAIDEN CLIFF

High on the western flank of Mt. Megunticook, a mile or so past Barrett's Cove Cliff, a tall white cross marks where a little girl fell to her death in the 1880s. Below the memorial, deep gullies hide several fine ice lines. The routes are hard to see from Route 52 but show up better from out on the frozen lake. Park where the talus comes close to the road, just before a group of cottages along the lake shore. There is usually a plowed turnout on the cliff side of Route 52. Bushwhack for two hundred yards straight up through the talus. The cliffs here are fairly broken up, with lots of trees, but you can find a number of 2-3 pitch routes in a good year. The flows are steeper than Barrett's, more on the order of Frankenstein-style pillars and gullies. Descend by rappel from trees, or scramble down a narrow gully off left. Routes are described from left to right.

FLYING SQUIRRELS 3 5.7

A rarely formed route about 100' left of Double Clutch. A column leads to a thinly iced slab that goes up and right to a thin runnel in a corner that leads up to and over a roof. Protection is sparse. Trivia: the original name of the route was *Flying Squirrels Under the Moon of Discrimination*. To date no guidebook author has had the nerve to use the entire name; even when dared to.

Justin Preisendorfer, rope solo, February 1998

DOUBLE CLUTCH 4

This is the left-hand ice tower just right of the descent gully, with an overhanging curtain at half height. An undercling past the curtain explains the name. A much easier pitch leads up and left to the descent gully.

Dave Getchell, Jr. & Pete McCartney, 1982

KISS OF THE SPIDER WOMAN 3 5.8 (A1)

Just right of Double Clutch a rarely-formed pillar leads to an overhang. Climb

the overhang either free or on aid and continue the line up thinly iced slabs to a belay. A steep gully above leads up to the exit on Pete's Puzzle.
Jerry Cinnamon & Ed Raiola, 1985

PETE'S PUZZLE 3 5.7

Right of Spider Woman, follow thin ice and mixed ground into a narrow alcove; puzzle out of the slot (fixed peg) and onto a verglased slab. Finish at will up gullies and flows above (300 feet). In Ben Townsend's rock and ice guide to this area Ben says, "Friends can often be placed to protect the start, although the fact that rock gear can be placed through the ice at the crux should give you some insight into the nature of this climb." Hmm.
Dave Getchell, Sr. & Pete McCartney, 1980

The next two routes are located about a hundred yards south along the road at the top of a steep gully. They can be seen from out on the lake. Rappel (one rope okay) on the left to get down.

VARICOSE VEIN 3+ 5.4

Climb a thinly iced ramp on the left heading up and right on a steep bulge.

BLUE VEIN   M5

A tight chimney on the right provides what some call Camden's finest ice climb. Technical groveling to reach a cool ice hose deep in the crack usually forms the crux; thinly iced overhangs above cap off the experience. Bring a bunch of rock gear in addition to ice gear for this classic route.
Geoff Heath & Dave Getchell, Sr., 1980

MAIDEN CLIFF

A. Double Clutch
B. Kiss of the Spider Woman
C. Pete's Puzzle
D. descent starts here

CAMDEN: MOUNT MEGUNTICOOK

South and east of the Barrett's Cove Cliff and Maiden Cliff the long ridge of Mount Megunticook runs toward the ocean. Along this ridge lie several small crags that are home to a number of short, interesting routes. As with the other areas here, it takes a good winter for routes to form and stick around for any length of time.

MEGUNTICOOK: The Middle Cliffs

This cliff is set well back from the road between Barrett's Cove Cliff and The Cataracts. It can be glimpsed from Rt. 52 just south of the big road cut at the crest of the hill south of Barrett's Cove. Find an old road north of the road cut and follow it along a streambed then turn left up an obvious drainage starting at a big boulder field about a half mile from the road. Follow the drainage uphill to an open area below a blocky amphitheater. You can also reach this area by a long traverse from the top of The Cataracts—this can be difficult in deep snow. Routes will be described from left to right.

THE SMEAR 2

A thinly iced slab at the bottom of an avalanche scar on the left.
Jerry Cinnamon & Ben Townsend, January, (both solo) January, 1992

UPRISING 3+

Behind a big tree at the left side of the amphitheater is this steep, left-trending flow.
Jerry Cinnamon & Ben Townsend, January, 1992

I HAD A DREAM M5

This route takes the steep, verglased wall right of Uprising then follows a corner to an overhang. Blind tool placements above the overhang lead to a crack on the left. Protection is reasonable.
Jerry Cinnamon & Ben Townsend, January, 1992

A couple of short, thick climbs will be found on the left side of the amphitheater and are approached by traversing right toward the base of The Stream.

THE STREAM 3

Climb the obvious flow at the head of the amphitheater.
unknown

STAIRMASTER M5

A rock buttress forms the right-hand margin of The Stream and is home to a series of short, stacked rock bulges. With rock gear for protection, delicately use the ice runnels and thin cracks to reach the top.
Justin Preisendorfer with Andrew Davenport, February 2000

AXE BUSTER 3+

Farther right is a short, steep wall with a thin runnel of ice.
unknown

MEGUNTICOOK: The Cataracts

This is a great practice area south of Barrett's Cove Cliff and about a mile north of the village of Camden on Rt. 52. Park near a steeply angled road marked by signs for the "Old Carriage Road" trail. Follow this road left (ignore a right-hand turn toward Mt. Battie) until it turns right after crossing a stream. Head left here to the Left Cataract (going straight leads to the Right Cataract). Routes are described from left to right. Descent for all routes is via easy scrambling.

The first area to be described is the Left Cataract area.

EVERDRIP 3+

Around the corner to the left of Left Cataract climb easily up into an alcove then climb a steep ramp on the left. Often thin; rock gear helpful. Sometimes there is a direct variation up a column to the right (4).

unknown

NEVERDRIP M5- 3+

Down and right from Everdrip is a left-facing corner with a roof and obvious horizontal crack on the right. Rock climb up to the roof and pull over onto hanging columns. Finish straight up on easier ground or on a bulge to the right. Bring small cams. There is another, more obvious and more frequently iced-up corner left of Neverdrip (4+).

Tim Martel & Justin Preisendorfer, January 1999

LEFT CATARACT 2+

This prominent route climbs an easy 300-foot waterfall and is a great practice area for beginners. There are numerous variations.

unknown

The next area is the Right Cataract. Instead of bearing left on the approach to the Left Cataract area, continue straight to this area just above the Old Carriage Road. The climbing here is not as extensive as the Left Cataract area and may not be worth it when the snow is deep.

RIGHT CATARACT 1-2

A collection of easy flows just above the carriage road. A good practice area.

unknown

BIXLER'S WAY (unrated)

Just right of Right Cataract and about halfway up the hillside is a steep right-leaning corner. When fat the crux moves at the top of the corner are not difficult; in thin conditions things are, well...much harder. Bring cams. Occasionally a direct finish is possible up a column on the left. In even better conditions a steep smear drips down the wall to the left (5).

unknown

DRAGON'S TEETH 4+

If you continue to the right along the cliff you will pass numerous rock climbs on a section of cliff referred to as The Ramparts. At the far right end of this cliff band is a vertical 50' icicle that occasionally touches the ground.

Geoff Heath, 1970's

To reach this next area, the Hot Spot, approach up the Carriage Road as fo
the Cataracts but don't turn off. Continue up the road for a long way to a
climbers' trail on the left (this may or may not be obvious depending on snov
conditions).

BEN AND JERRY'S ICE CLIMB 2+

This route climbs a wide indistinct gully. There are several variations and an
even easier flow lies just to the right. In a good year there are some steep,
40' columns to the left.

Jim Ewing, 1982 or so

MEGUNTICOOK: The Ocean Lookout

Farther east of the Cataracts and much farther from the road, lies
the Ocean Lookout. Follow the Carriage Road as for the Cataracts
but follow it all the way to its top and then turn left on the Table-
lands Trail and then left again on the Jack Williams Trail just under the
cliffs (2 miles). A popular winter solo outing is to continue up the
stream above the Left Cataract until you reach the Jack Williams Trail,
then head a bit right until under Scottish Gully. Ice climbing here ove
the years has been limited to the easier routes (probably because of
the long approach) although there is reportedly much potential in
the area. The only route mentioned here is at the center of the crag
(far to the left of the clean rock).

SCOTTISH GULLY (unrated)

This is the obvious, very short, moderate mixed climb well left of the clean rock
lines that characterize the right side of the crag.

unknown

MEGUNTICOOK: Mount Battie

Mount Battie is the southernmost peak along the Mount
Megunticook ridge. The south side of the mountain, just above Rt.
52 as it leaves Camden, contains a couple of ice climbs.

TOWER GULLY 1+

Just south of the water tower is this long easy route. It is long, easy, but
usually very thin. After any real snow it disappears.

unknown

GHOUL STREET 4+

This rare visitor climbs an icicle that drips down the right side of a huge roof
high above the cemetery at the corner of Rt. 52 and Gould St. Stay well clear
of the homes along Rt. 52 below the climb.

Steve Durgo & Ben Townsend, February, 1987

unknown

ACADIA NATIONAL PARK

to Ellsworth

T.B.R. Walsh

Atlantic ocean

ACADIA NATIONAL PARK

A. park loop road
B. Jordan Pond
C. Otter Cliff
D. The Precipice
E. Bar Harbor

AREA HIGHLIGHTS	
Location:	On Mount Desert Island about three hours northeast of Portland, ME
Routes:	Several fickle moderate ice and mixed routes; great alpine adventures after a big winter storm
Access:	Park below the crags and hike for 10-20 minutes
Descent:	Hike off or rappel
Weather:	"Valley" (weather section), January & February
Equipment:	Standard ice rack, rock gear helpful
Superlatives:	The gullies at Jordan Pond come in each season; great mixed climbing possibilities on The Precipice, especially after a winter Nor'easter
Amenities:	Nearby Bar Harbor has just about everything although it is a very quiet town in the winter; Ellsworth, 15 miles north, has more

Famous for its clean granite rock climbing and unique seaside setting, Acadia is also home to some ice climbing. Typically mild winters make things a little hit-or-miss but in a normal winter several routes usually come into shape. Another forty-five minutes or so up the coast on Route 1 from Camden turn south on Rt. 3 in Ellsworth and drive about 20 miles to the Park. Most of the Park Loop Road is open in the winter and camping is available at Blackwoods Campground. While this place truly bustles in the summer, the winters are very quiet—just enough motels and restaurants stay open to make it look like a real town.

ACADIA: JORDAN POND

The routes at Jordan Pond are the only ones in Acadia that can truly be called dependable. By that we mean there will usually be a few weeks each season when these routes are in climbable shape. From Bar Harbor follow Rt. 3 south to the Sieur de Monts entrance to Acadia National Park. Turn right then right again at the stop sign, onto the Park Loop Road. Follow the Loop Road south to Seal Harbo and then back north to the first big pond on the left. The following two-pitch climbs are obvious on the far side of the pond and can be approached across the ice if it is thick enough. If not, walk around the south end of the pond to reach the climbs.

CEDAR CHEST 3

This is the easier route.

unknown

JORDAN CLIFF DIRECT 4

This is the harder route.

unknown

ACADIA: OTTER CLIFF

OTTER CLIFF 4+

Renowned as a rock climbing area for its seacliff atmosphere, Otter Cliff occasionally sports a unique ice climb as well. To the left of the prominent Sea Stack (looking out to sea) by a couple of hundred feet or so, an ice curtain sometimes forms giving fifty feet of vertical climbing on frozen sea-spray. Usually top-roped—what a surprise.

Unknown

ACADIA: THE PRECIPICE

PRECIPICE MIXED STUFF (mixed)

The Precipice, or South Wall of Mount Champlain, is home to Acadia's longest and most well known rock climbs. Under the right conditions the broken cliff to the north of the big summer climbing area takes on a decidedly Scottish appearance. If a big storm whips the Maine coast out of the northeast and sends snow, ice pellets, sleet, and freezing rain slamming against Champlain, grab your tools and head on up. But be quick; the great climbing conditions may only last a few hours to a day or two. Take the Park Loop Road south as for Jordan Pond and drive two miles to the Precipice parking lot on the right. Directly above the parking lot is a big broken wall. The Precipice Trail ascends this semi-technical wall in the summer. If winter conditions are good, the wall will look terrible. Pick your line and scratch, grovel and scrape your way up for 4-5 pitches. There are no grades for such things. These routes are reported to be really fun.

unknown; this has been great sport for the (few) winter locals for years

In addition to these areas, other short climbs will be found along Sargen Drive next to Somes Sound, at the Hull's Cove quarry, at Enoch Cirque (north of the Beehive), and along the loop road on the south face of Champlain.

Index

A

ACADIA NATIONAL PARK
Jordan Pond
CEDAR CHEST 3 292
JORDAN CLIFF DIRECT 4 292
Otter Cliff
OTTER CLIFF .... 4+ 292
The Precipice
PRECIPICE ALPINE STUFF .... (MIXED) 292

B

BAKER RIVER VALLEY
Newfound Lake 126
BLOODLINE 3 127
DUOFOLD .... 3+/4- 127
GOOD KARMA ARETE .... 3+/4 MIXED 127
PIKE LINE 4 127
PILLAGE PILLAR 5 127
RED HEADWALL 5 127
SLIM JIM .... 3+/4 5.6 127
Rumney
ARTIFICIAL INTELLIGENCE 5 M5 130
BARBADOS 5 129
CENTERFOLD .... 3+ 128
DANDRUFF 4- 130
DUSTBOWL .... 3+ 5.6 133
FANGMANSHIP 5 131
FRANKY LEE .... 4+ 129
G3 GULLY 3 128
GALAPAGOS 5 129
ICE-OLATOR 4 132
JAWS PILLAR 5 129
JOHN'S PILLAR 5- 132
K-9 .... 4 131
LEARNING DISABILITIES 4 129
LOG JAM 3 131
LONG BOARD .... 4+5.7 131
MANDIBLE .... 3+ 129
MOLAR 4 131
PARALLEL GULLY 3 129
PRESTOR JOHN 4 132
PRESTOR PILLAR 5- 132
PRIVATE EYE .... 4+ 129
PSORIASIS 5 131
REASONS TO BE CHEERFUL .... 5+ 131
SASQUATCH 5- 133
SCOTTISH GULLY 3 128
SELSUN BLUE 4 130
SHAELYN'S WAY 5 128
SOFFIT BREATH 4 133
THE CAVE ROUTE 3 130
THE DAGGER .... 4+ 132
THE GEOGRAPHIC FACTOR 5 132

THE MEADOW FLOWS 2-4 128
TWIT .... 5+ 131
VENEER 4 130
VERY NICE ICE 4 M5 133

BEYOND THE NOTCHES

Bear Mountain
BEAR MOUNTAIN .... 2-4+ 251

Beaver Brook Falls
BEAVER BROOK FALLS 1-3 243

Brimstone Cliff
ANGEL FALLS 3- 252

Dixville Notch
PARASOL GULLY .... II 2+ 247

Gentian Swamp Wall
GENTIAN SWAMP WALL 3-4 244

Goback Mountain
GOBACK GULLY .... M4 4+ 243
THE OATH .... 4+ 243
THE SECRET .... 4+ 243
VALHALLA 6 M6 242

Grafton Notch
HACKETT-TREMBLAY ROUTE .... II 5 248
PRACTICE AREAS 2-4 248
STASH .... 2+ 249
THE AMPHITHEATER 3-4 249
THE STY 5 249
YELLOW MUSTARD CUSTARD .... 3+ 249

Knights Hill Crag
KNIGHTS HILL CRAG 3-4 251

Larry Flume
LARRY FLUME 3-5 244

Mount Dimmock
CHAPTER SEVEN 5 250
MEAT PUPPET 5 249

Mount Forest
NORTH SLABS 3-4 243

Mount Kineo
LAURA & GUY'S GREAT ADVENTURE .... III 4 5.6 255
LES ENFANT BLUE DE KINEO .... III 5+/6- M5 254
MAINE LINE III .... 5+ 253
WHITELINE FEVER .... IV 5R 255

Mount Winthrop
MOSES SLAB 2-4 244

Needle's Eye
FLUME ROUTES .... 3-5 MIXED 252

Pine Mountain
PINE MOUNTAIN .... 3-4+ 246

Red Rock Mountain
GREAT BROOK 2-3 247
HOT LAVA .... II 4 247

Reflection Crag
BRIDGEWORK 2 245
FIFTH COLUMN 4 245
ICICLE OVERBITE 4 245
REFLECTION CRAG 2-4 244
SPINDRIP 3/4 245
TWIZZLER 3 245

Squaredock Mountain
BIG SCIENCE II 5 251
SANCTUM OF PRIVILEDGE .... II 5 5.8 251

Tumbledown Dick
TUMBLEDOWN DICK MOUNTAIN 2-4 245

Worthley Pond
NATIVE TONGUE 5 253

C

CAMDEN
Barrett's Cove Cliff
ARIZONA HIGHWAYS .... 3+/4 282
BIG CHIMNEY 2-3 282
CACHONGAS .... UNRATED 282
CHARLOTTE'S CRACK 5.7 282
CLOTHESLINE 3-4 284
CONTINENTAL ICE SHEET .... II 3+5.6 284
DESPERADO .... 4+ 5.4 284
HEATHROW .... II 3+ 283
HOLLYWOOD WALTZ .... 4+ 5.4 283
JOE'S DIRECT .... 2+ 285
JOE'S ROUTE 2 284
KING OF SWING .... 4+ 5.8 286
LITTLE SISTER 4 285
LOST VALLEY CATARACT 1-2 286
PHARAOH'S BEARD .... 3+ 282
SOLSTICE WALL M4 282
SPIDER LINE .... 3+ 283
TANGLED UP IN BLUE DIRECT START .... 3+ 285
TANGLED UP IN BLUE .... II 3+/4 5.7 284
TRITIUM WITCH 3-4 285
TWISTER .... 3+ 285
WATERFALL 3 285

Mount Megunticook
AXE BUSTER .... 3+ 288
BIXLER'S WAY .... UNRATED 289
DRAGON'S TEETH .... 4+ 289
EVERDRIP .... 3+ 289
GHOUL STREET .... 4+ 290
I HAD A DREAM M5 288
LEFT CATARACT .... 2+ 289
NEVERDRIP .... M5- 3+ 289
RIGHT CATARACT 1-2 289
SCOTTISH GULLY .... UNRATED 290
STAIRMASTER M5 288
THE SMEAR 2 288
THE STREAM 3 288
TOWER GULLY .... 1+ 290
UPRISING .... 3+ 288

The Maiden Cliff
BIG CITY WOMAN 3 5.7 284
BLUE VEIN M5 287
DOUBLE CLUTCH 4 286
FLYING SQUIRRELS 3 5.7 286
KISS OF THE SPIDER WOMAN 3 5.8 (A1) 286
PETE'S PUZZLE 3 5.7 287
VARICOSE VEIN .... 3+ 5.4 287

CENTRAL NEW HAMPSHIRE NOTCHES

Kinsman Notch

BEAVER SCAT 4 123
BLARNEY STONE 3 123
COMPOSURE MAINTENANCE .... 4+/5- 122
HANGING BY A MOMENT 4 M6 121
HOLEY HELL .... 4 - 123
HOLEY HELL 4- 123
KILARNEY .... 2+ 121
LEPRECHAUN'S LAMENT .... 2+/3 122
POT '0 GOLD 4 121
RAMP ROUTE 3 122
SHAMROCK .... 3+/4- 121
STORE CRAZY .... II 4 5.7 123
THE BEAST .... 4+ 122
WINDOW ROUTE .... 4+ 122

Olivarian Notch

SNAKE ATTACK .... III 4 120
THE FEAR OF LIVING DANGEROUSLY .... II 4+ 120

Waterville Valley

DIXIE CHICKEN 3 123
FELINE FLOW 2-3 123
FLETCHER CASCADE .... 2+ 123

CRAWFORD NOTCH

Frankenstein Cliff

A CASE OF THE WILLEYS 3-4 191
A DRIP IN THE WOODS .... 4+ 191
A WALK IN THE FOREST 3-4 191
ANGEL CAKE 5- 188
BANSHEE .... 3+ 185
BEGINNERS' SLAB NORTH 1-2 198
BOB'S DELIGHT 4 190
BOW SAW BUTTRESS 3-4 186
BRAGG-PHEASANT .... II 5 182
BREAKING GLASS 4 193
BROCKEN SPECTRE .... 4+ 185
BURIED ALIVE .... 4+ 196
CHIA .... 3+ 187
CHIA DIRECT 4 188
CHIA PET 3 5.7 187
CHOCKSTONE CHIMNEY 4 188
CLAWSICLE 4/5 196
CLOAK AND DAGGER 4 183
COCAINE .... II 4+ 182
COSMONAUT 3 184
DIAMONDS AND RUST .... 4+ 183
DOUBLE BARREL .... 4+ 186
DRACULA .... 4+ 195
DRACULA RIGHT SIDE 4/5 196
DROPLINE .... II 5 194
EXTENSOR .... 4+ 199
FALLING ANGELS 3-4 188
FANG .... II 4+ 182
FIRST ASCENT GULLY .... II 4 181
GANDALF THE GREAT 4 187
HARD RANE 4 187
HOBBIT COULOIR .... 4+ 187
HOUSE OF BLUE 2-3 198
ICE ROCK CAFÉ .... 3+ 183
LAST EXIT .... II 5 194

CRAWFORD NOTCH
Frankenstein Cliff (continued)

LOST IN THE FOREST	2-3		190
MEAN MISS TREATER	4		191
PEGASUS	3-4		187
PIGLET	2-3		198
ROBOT LOGIC	3+		198
ROCK FINISH	3+ 5.6		187
RUSSIAN ROULETTE	4		184
SCRATCH AND SNIFF	4		194
SCRATCHING POST	4+		198
SCREAMING	M5		186
SHOOTING STAR	4		183
SILVER HEELS	II 4		181
SLIM PICKEN'S	5		185
SLIM PICKEN'S DIRECT	4		185
SMEAR	3-4		186
SOMETHING ABOUT YOU MAKES ME WILD	M8		198
STANDARD LEFT	3		192
STANDARD RIGHT	3+/4-		193
STANDARD ROUTE	II 3+		192
TAP TAP CRASH	3+		199
THE BLOBS	2-3		188
THE BROWN RECLUSE	5		190
THE CAVE ROUTE	3+		189
THE COFFIN	4+		195
THE COSSACK	2		184
THE HOWLING	4+ X		191
THE PENGUIN	II 4		193
THE SNUGCICLE	2-3		198
THE SPACEMAN	4+		183
THE STEPPE	1-2		184
THE SWORD AND THE STONE	4+		182
THE WIDOW'S CAVE	4+		189
THE WINDOW ROUTE	3		193
THE WRATH OF THE VALKYRIE	II 4+ M5		182
TRESTLE CUT FLOWS	2-4 M5		190
WATERFALL	3		192
WELCOME TO THE MACHINE	II 4/5		194
WHITE RUSSIAN	3		184
WIDOW'S RUN	M7		190
WIDOW'S WALK	5		189
WILD THING	4		185
WINGTIP	5.6		187
WITHIN REASON	6		197
WITHOUT REASON	5+		197
WPP	3+ M1 R		191
YOUNG FRANKENSTEIN	2-3		181

Mount Avalon

DANG'S GULLY	3-		212
MELLOW YELLOW	3		212
PEER PRESSURE	3		212
TALLY HO	II 2		212
THE BATTLE OF THE BULGE	3		212

Mount Tom

TOM'S DONUT	4+		213

Mount Webster

CENTRAL COULOIR	III 3+		201
CENTRAL COULOIR VARIATION FINISH	4+ 5.8		201
FOOLS PARADISE	III 3		202

GREEN CHASM .... III 3 5.6 201
HALF BREED .... II 3 5.2 202
HEART PALACE 4- 201
HORSESHOE GIULLY .... III 1-2 200
LANDSLIDE GULLY .... III 1-2 201
NORTH SLABS 1-2 202
SHOESTRING GULLY .... III 2 (5.5 3) 200
THE PILGRIMAGE .... II 3 202
VO2 GULLY .... 3+ R 201
VO2 MAX 3 201

Mount Willard

CANDLEPIN 4 204
CAULIFLOWER GULLY 2-3 207
CINEMA GULLY .... II 2 205
CORNIER DE LA MOUSE .... II 3+ 204
DAMSEL IN DISTRESS 4 5.8 209
EAST FACE SLAB 3 207
EAST FACE SLAB RIGHT .... 3/3+ 209
ELEPHANT HEAD GULLY .... 3+ 211
FLAT FOOT FLOOGIE .... 2+ 203
FREEZE FRAME .... II 3 5.7 A0 205
GOATBELL GULLY .... 3+ 211
GREAT MADNESS .... II 5 205
GULLY #1 1/2 .... 4+ 204
GULLY #1 .... II 4 204
GULLY #1: DIRECT START 3-4 204
GULLY #2 1/2 .... II 3 204
GULLY# 2 .... II 3+ 5.7 204
HITCHCOCK GULLY 3- 208
LEFT HAND MONKEYWRENCH 3 208
LONG DISTANCE LOVE 3 209
OLD ANXIETY .... 5+ M3 210
OUT OF TOUCH 5 209
PARALLEL UNIVERSE .... III M6 5 R/X 206
PEACE OF MIND M5 4 208
READ BETWEEN THE LINES 4 209
REAR WINDOW .... II 4 207
RIKKI-TIKKI-TAVI .... II 5- 206
SILVER CASCADE 1-3 211
STREAMLINE .... II 2 203
SURPRISE PARTY BUTTRESS .... 3+ 207
THE CLEFT 2-3 209
THE CORKSCREW 5 209
THE FLUME II-2 211
THE SNOT ROCKET 3-5 (M5) 210
THINKING OF JANET .... 4+ 209
TRESLE GULLY 3 210
UNKNOWN .... 3+ 210
WILLARD SLAB RIGHT 2 209
ZIG PIG M5 4 208

Mount Willey

WILLEY'S SLIDE .... II 2 202

E

EVANS NOTCH

East Royce Mountain

BALCONY SEAT .... II 4 235
BASHO .... III 4 5.6 237
CALIFORNIA KID 4- 234
CURTAIN CALL 4 235

EVANS NOTCH
East Royce Mountain (continued)

EXIT STAGE LEFT .... 4+ 235
EXIT STAGE RIGHT 3 236
FRACTURE POINT 3/4 238
FRENCH CANADIAN REALITY 5 236
HAGAN'S HIGHWAY 2/3 238
LOVE DIET .... 5+ 236
OPENING NIGHT JITTERS 4 235
PILGRIM'S PROGRESS .... III 4 237
PROMPTER'S BOX 2 236
RIGHTS OF SPRING .... II 4 5.6 234
THREE'S COMPANY .... II 4 236
WHEN FRIGHT MEETS MIGHT .... 4+ 234

Shell Pond
SHELL POND ROUTES 3-5 233

The Basin
BICKFORD BROOK 3 234
BLOWING BUBBLES .... II 3 233
BUBBLE GULLY .... II 3+ 233
COLLARBONE GULLY 3 234
MICA MINE 2-4 233

F
FRANCONIA NOTCH
Big Slide
SHORT STACK 4 115

Cannon Mountain
ABORIGINAL RHYTHMIC IMPLEMENT .... III 3+ 5.9 A0 98
ACROSS THE GREAT DIVIDE .... IV 5.7 A4 98
ADAM'S SLIDE .... II 2 104
CANNONADE .... II 2-3 5.4 102
CRACK UP 4- 5.7 A1 103
DARK CRYSTAL .... III 5 M4 100
DUET .... III 5.7 102
FAFNIR .... IV 5 100
FRUIT CUP WALL .... V 5.8 A4 103
HASSIG'S DIRECT 5 100
HENDERSON .... II 5.5 96
ICARUS .... IV 5.8 A4 (11B) 102
LA DEEPFREEZE .... III 2-4 96
LABYRINTH WALL .... V 5.7 A4 103
LAKEVIEW .... II 2 5.5 104
LILA DIRECT .... III 5+ M5 R 101
LILA .... IV 4+ M6 (A2) 101
LILA VARIATION FINISH .... 4+ M3 101
MAGICAL MYSTERY TOUR .... V M5 5 A0 104
MOBY GRAPE .... III 5.8 103
NORTH-SOUTH-WEST .... III 5.8-9 103
OLD CANNON .... III 5.6 104
OMEGA .... IV 5+ 96
ONE DROP OF WATER .... IV 5.9 A3 M4 102
PROZAC .... IV 6R M6 98
QUARTET ICE HOSE .... IV 5+ M6 5.10 102
SAM'S SWAN SONG .... III 5.7 102
THE BLACK DIKE .... IV 4-5 M3 99
THE GHOST .... IV 5.7 A3 102
THE HORRIFYING EAR .... II 5.9 MIXED 104
THE WHITNEY-GILMAN RIDGE .... III 5.7 98

UNION JACK .... III 5.9 103
UNNAMED .... III 3+/4+ 104
VERTIGO .... III 5.9 103
VMC DIRECT DIRECT .... IV 5.10 (5.7 A2) 103
WIESSNER'S BUTTRESS .... II 5.6 104

East Side

ACE OF SPADES 4 115
ALPINE DIDDY .... 3+ 109
ALPINE GRUNGE .... 3+ 108
AMPHITHEATER ICE .... 2-3+ 108
AZTEC WARRIOR .... II 3+ 5.6 111
BONSAI GULLY 4R 110
BURN STATION .... II 3 5.6 113
CARPET PATH .... 3+ 5.6 108
CRUCIAL EVIDENCE 4 107
DIGGING TO CHINA 3 5.6R 112
EAGLE VISION .... II 4 5.5R 114
ED'S WEED BE GONE TO SPIRIT WITHIN 4 5.6 107
EYE OPENER 5 109
FEAR OF THE UNKNOWN 4R 111
FERRETT LEGGER .... 3+ 5.6 106
FINAL CONFRONTATION .... 4+ 109
FIRE AND ICE .... M6 4+ 112
FLUSHOT .... II 4 112
GARCIA-VEGA 4 112
GOD, I LOVE THIS 4 110
GRAVITATIONAL PULL .... 4 MIXED 113
HEIGHTENED AWARENESS .... II 3+ 113
HELL BENT ON BIRCH .... 3+ 108
HOLLOW HELL 4 105
HURRY UP I'M HUNGRY 4 110
LATE NIGHT WITH YELLOW TOE .... II 3+ 113
LIP SERVICE 4 M7 107
LOST MIND .... 3 MIXED 114
MACK JAM 4 105
ONE SWING AWAY .... 3+ 106
OVERBID .... 4+ 115
PATELLA SWELLA .... 3+/4 109
PRAYER GIRTH 4R 110
PSYCHOTIC REACTION 4 5.6R 109
PSYCHOTIC SATISFACTION (DIRECT FINISH) 4 108
RESOLUTION GULLY .... II 3+ 114
ROCK A BYE BILLY BOY 3 105
SACKLESS 3 5.7 106
SCOTTISH GULLY .... 3+ 5.4 106
SHORT TRICK 3 115
SIDE STEPPING THE ISSUE .... 3+ 5.6 105
SLEEP IN THE DRY SPOT .... 3+ 5.6 108
SLICE OF MEAT IN A ROCK SANDWICH .... II 4 R MIXED 114
SOCIAL EXPERIMENT .... 4+ 107
SPANKING BILBO .... 4+ 109
SPIRIT WITHIN 4 5.7 106
SWEET SECRETS .... 3+ 5.6 111
SWING EASY, CLIMB HARD .... 3+ 5.6R 108
SYKO'S PILLARS .... 4+ 108
TARDY BUT STILL FIRST 3 5.6 106
THANK GOD FOR TURF 3 5.6 109
THE ARÊTE .... 3+ 5.8 111
THE HERMIT .... 4+ 109
THE SHIELD .... 3+ 5.7 107
THINSICLE .... 3+ R 109
THREADING THE ALPINE NEEDLE .... 2+ 5.5 106

FRANCONIA NOTCH

East Side (continued)
TOOTHLESS WONDER 4 5.7R 110
TRUMP CARD 3 115
VAPORUB 3 108
WESLEY'S ASPIRATION .... 4+ 107

Lonesome Lake
LEAP OF FAITH .... 3+ 116

Mount Garfield
BAD DOG .... II 4 116
MAD DOG .... II 5 117
POSTHOLE ALFONSO .... II 4+ 116
SICK PUP .... II 4+ 117
THE BIG ONE .... II 5 116

The Flume
ONE PICKLE SHY (OF THE WHOLE BARREL) .... M7+ R 96
SWAIN'S PILLAR .... 4+ 96

The Nubble
THE NUBBLE FLOWS 3-4 117

K

KANCAMAGUS HIGHWAY

Black Mountain
LONG WAY HOME .... III 2-3 136

Champney Falls
CHAMPIN' AT THE BIT .... M8+ 139
CHAMPNEY FALLS 3-5 M5-8 139
CRANKIN' IN COTTON .... M5+ 139

Crack in the Woods
ANGELS DON'T SHATTER 3 140
BOSSANOVA 3 140
COLUMN IN THE WOODS 4 140

Mad River Notch
AYE KARUMBA .... M5 4+ 137
BEAUTY AND THE BEAST .... 3+ 138
ON THE DROOL OF THE BEAST .... II 5- 137
THE BEAST WITHIN 4- 138

Mount Hedgehog
CHOCKSTONE CHIMLEY 3 5.6 138

Mount Huntington
SHEER ELEGANCE .... II 4+ 5.6 138

Painted Walls
LEFT OF THE WILDERNESS 4 141
STORMY MONDAY 4 5.7 141
WAY IN THE WILDERNESS .... II 5 141

Rainbow Slabs
RAINBOW SLABS .... 2-3 (3+ 5.4 A0) 140

Sundown Ledge
ICE CAPADES 3 143
ICE FALLIES 4 143
PIMPSICKLE M6 143
QUALUDE (IT'S WORTH THE TRIP) 5 143
THE COVERED BRIDGE ICE FLOWS 3-5 142
THE MONGOL M7 142
WINTERLUDE .... II 3+ 143

	IV 4 5.6	278
	IV 4+	278
	III 1-2	277
	IV 4	278
	IV 4- 5.7	278
	II 3+	268
	II 3+	277
	3+	277
	M4+	277
	III 3	279
	4+	277
	II 5	264
	II 4	264
	II 4+	265
MINI-PINN...	II 2	263
MINI-PINNACLE #3	2	263
SOUTH OF THE BORDER	II 4	265
STAIRWAY TO HEAVEN	II 4	264
STRANGE BREW	II 3	263
WALK ON THE WILD SIDE	II 5	264
WHERE DO THE CHILDREN PLAY	II 4+	264
WICKED LEFT	3	264
WICKED RIGHT	4-	265
ZORRO	II 4	263

South Basin Headwall

AMBEJEJUS BOOM HOUSE BUTTRESS	III M4 3	272
ARMADILLO	IV 3+ 5.7	271
BLACK GULLY EAST	III 3	272
BLACK GULLY WEST	III 3	272
CATHEDRAL GULLY #1	II 1	275
CHAUVIN-COLE ROUTE	III 3+	273
CHAUVIN-COLE VARIATION START	II 3+5.6	273
CILLEY-BARBER	IV 4	270
DILLO DIRECT	IV 4	271
DOUGAL'S DELIGHT	II 2+	275
GALLERY ROUTE	III 3+ 5.6	272
GULLY #3	II 2	275
HEADBANGER	III 3 5.4	272
HEATH'S FINISH	II 4 5.6	271
LITTLE CHIMNEY (FALSE CHIMNEY)	II 3	268
PIGGY-WIGGY	II 3	273
RHYTHM AND BLUES PILLAR	4+	271
RUDE LITTLE MAN	IV 4- 5.5	273
STEEL MONKEY	III 2 5.6	268
THE CHIMNEY	II 2	268
THE DIAMOND	IV 3+	272
THE FUNNEL	II 2+	275
THE PRIMITIVES	IV 4-	271
TOWER RIDGE	IV 4 5.5	269
UPPER CATHEDRAL SADDLE (CATHEDRAL GULLY #2)	II 1	275
WATERFALL BUTTRESS	III 3+ 5.5	270
WATERFALL GULLY EAST	IV 4	269
WATERFALL GULLY	IV 4	269
WATERFALL LEFT	IV 4	269
WEXLER ROUTE	IV 3 5.6	269

The Furries

PAMOLA DIRECT WEST GULLY	III 3+	267

KATAHDIN

The Furries (continued)

PAMOLA FOUR .... III 2+ 5.6 267
PAMOLA WEST RIDGE (PAMOLA III) .... IV 5.2 266
PAMOLA'S FURY LEFT .... III 3+ 265
PAMOLA'S FURY RIGHT .... III 3 266

L

LAKE WILLOUGHBY

Crystal Lake

CRYSTAL LAKE FLOWS 3-5 90

Jobs Pond

JOB'S PILLAR .... II 4 90

Mount Hor

ARCTIC CROSSING .... II 4 89
TAKE BACK VERMONT .... II 3+ 89
TAKE BACK YOUR EMPTYS .... II 3+ 89
THE BOISSONNEAULT-CATTABRIGA ROUTE 4 89
WOOBER GOOBER GULLY .... II 3+ 88

Mount Pisgah

AURORA DIRECT .... 5+ 80
AURORA .... IV 4+ 5.8 A2 80
BRINTON'S FOLLY 4 80
BULLWINKLE .... III 5+ 83
CALL OF THE WILD .... II 6 76
CALLED ON ACCOUNT OF RAINS .... IV 5+ M4 R 78
CHINA SHOP .... IV 5+ 81
CHOP SHOP .... 5+ 81
CRAZY DIAMOND .... 4+ 85
EXTENSIVE HOMOLOGY .... III 5 84
FIVE MUSKETEERS .... IV M6+ 5+ 79
FLOAT LIKE A BUTTERFLY (LAND LIKE A TOMATO) .... III 4+ 84
GLASS MENAGERIE .... III 5 84
INTENSIVE DRIPOLOGY 5 M5 85
LEDGE APPROACH .... III 4 78
MINDBENDER .... II 5+ 78
ORION .... IV 5.6 5 80
PATIENCE .... III 5 83
PLUG AND CHUG .... II 5 76
POWER TEST .... III M7+ 5+ 82
REIGN OF TERROR .... III 5 83
RENORMALIZATION 4 78
ROCKY THE SQUIRREL .... III 5 M5+ 83
SHAKER HEIGHTS .... III 4 (5, 4+ 5.7) 78
SHAKEY HEIGHTS .... III 3+ MIXED 78
STARMAN .... IV 5+ M4 80
STORMY MONDAY .... III 4+ 81
SUPER NOVA .... IV 4+ M4 A2 79
TABLET CENTER .... 3+ 88
TABLET LEFT .... II 3+/4+ 88
TABLET RIGHT 3 88
THE GANTLET .... II 5+ 79
THE LAST GENTLEMAN .... IV 5 81
THE PROMENADE .... IV 5+ 82
THE WHITE STRIP III 5 M6   84
TWENTY BELOW ZERO GULLY .... III 4+ 84
WHO'S WHO IN OUTER SPACE .... IV 5 81
ZEPHYR .... II 3 5.4 85

Mount Wheeler
BEAUTIFUL DAY .... III 3+ 5.7 90

P

PRESIDENTIAL RANGE
King Ravine
GREAT GULLY .... III 1-2 230
KING RAVINE HEADWALL .... III 1-2 229
P.F. FLYER .... II 3-4

Madison Gulf
EXCLAMATION POINT .... 3+/4 228
LINK'EM UP .... UNRATED 229
POINT DU PINCEAU 4 2 28
POINT .... II 3+ 228
POINT OF NO RETURN 4 227
POINTILLISM 2-3 227
POINTLESS .... 3+ 228

Mount Washington
CENTRAL GULLY .... II 1 224
CLOUDWALKER .... II 4 5.7 224
COUNTERPOINT .... II 4 228
DAMNATION BUTTRESS .... II 3 225
DAMNATION GULLY .... III 3 226
DIAGONAL .... II 2 224
DODGE'S DRIP .... 2+ M3 219
GLEN ELLIS FALLS .... 2+ 218
GREAT GULF HEADWALL .... III 1-2 226
HEADWALL ROUTES .... II 1-4 220
ICE-CENTRIFICLE FORCE .... 3+ 218
ICEMEN DON'T EAT QUICHE 4- 218
JACK FROST 2-3 218
LEFT OF LEFT 3 219
LEFT OF RIGHT .... 3+/4 220
LEFT WALL OF CENTRAL GULLY .... 2+/3 224
NORTH GULLY .... II 3 226
ODELL'S GULLY .... II 2-3 223
PASS THE QUICHE M7 218
PINKHAM CASCADE 2 219
PINNACLE GULLY .... III 3 224
SOUTH GULLY 1 223
THE ESCAPE HATCH 1 223
THE SHURUYEV-MIRKINA-DYNKIN ROUTE .... III 5.9 A2 3 223
WAIT UNTIL DARK GULLY .... III 3 226
YALE GULLY .... II 2-3 225

S

SACO RIVER VALLEY
Arethusa Falls
ARETHUGGISH .... 3+/4 M4/5 177
DRIPETHUSA .... 3+/4 177
MAIN FLOW 3 177
MAIN FLOW LEFT .... 3+ 177

Cardiac Crag
CARDIAC ARETE .... 3+ 173
CORONARY BYPASS 4- 172
EKG 3 173
EMERGENCEY ROOM 1-2 173
HARTLESS 3- 172
PACEMAKER 2-4 172

SACO RIVER VALLEY
Cathedral Ledge

5¢ CIGAR 5 153
ALPHA CORNER 5 153
ANGEL'S HIGHWAY .... III 5.8 A2 159
BLACK CRACK 5 M7 5.10R 155
BONGO FLAKE/PENDULUM LINK-UP .... IV 4+ A3 158
CATHEDRAL DIRECT .... III 3-4 5.7 A2 159
CHICKEN DELIGHT 5 154
DIAGONAL .... III 5 5.6 157
DIEDRE III 5 5.9 .... M4 160
DOUBLE VEE 5 154
DRESDEN 4 M6 153
FOREST OF FANGORN .... IV 5.7 A3 158
FUNHOUSE 5.7 155
GOOFER'S DIRECT .... II 3 156
GRAND FINALE .... IV 5.8 A3 157
JACK THE RIPPER A3 (5.11) 161
JUST LAUGHING .... 4+ M6 162
LAYTON'S ASCENT 5 154
MINES OF MORIA .... IV 5.7 A2 158
MORDOR WALL .... IV 5 A4 158
MORDOR/DIAGONAL LINK .... IV 5 A4 158
NOMAD CRACK .... 5+ 154
NORTH END PILLARS 3-4 163
NORTH END SLAB 2 163
NUTCRACKER 5 153
OFF THE HOOK 5 154
PENDULUM ROUTE .... IV 5.8 A2 (5.11) 5 158
PENDULUM TO CATHEDRAL DIRECT TO OPTION 9A .... IV 5.10 158
POOH 5.7 155
RECOMPENSE .... III 5.9 155
REFUSE .... II 3 5.5 154
REMISSION DIRECT START .... 5+ 160
REMISSION .... IV 5+ 5.8 159
REPENTENCE .... III 5 159
STANDARD ROUTE .... III 4 5.6 157
SUBMISSION 5 159
SUPER GOOFER .... II 5- 156
THE BIG FLUSH .... II 4+ 156
THE POSSESSED A2 (5.12) 161
THE PROW .... III 5.6 A2 (5.11+) 156
THE THRESHER SLAB .... 3/3+ 163
THE UNICORN .... 4+ 162
THIN AIR .... III 5 5.6 156
THREE BIRCHES .... II 4 5.8 155
WARLOCK .... II 5.8 A4 160
YELLOW BRICK ROAD .... III A2 156
YELLOW PERIL 5 162

Ducks Head
LUNAGLACE .... 3+ 168
OVERLOAD .... 5+ 168
THE LAMINATE 5 168
WHEN LIGHT MEETS NIGHT 4 168

Eagle Cliff
COLD COLD WORLD .... M8+ 169
EAGLE'S GIFT .... 5+ 169

Giant Stairs
ACROSS THE RIVER AND INTO THE TREES .... II 4 170

Guide's Wall
5.12 PILLAR 4 152
ONTHIN ICE 2-3 152
SEASON'S GREETINGS 3 152
SOLDIER OF FORTUNE 3 152

Hart Ledge
DUAL HEARTS .... II 4 5.8 172
HART OF THE MATTER .... II 3 171
ICE TEARS .... II 5- 172

Humphreys Ledge
BARNABUS COLUMN .... 3+ 167
BLACK PUDDING GULLY .... 4+ 166
BLACK PUDDING GULLY LEFT .... 4+ 165
BOISSONNEALUT-PHILIBERT ROUTE .... 3+ 5.7 164
BPG VARIATIONS M4-5 166
DARK SHADOWS 4 5.6 167
DOG TIRED .... 4+ 167
HAGGIS SLAB 2 165
HOLLOW FLOWS 2-4 164
HOLLOW TIERS 3-4 164
SOUL SURVIVOR .... II 5 M5 165
SUNNY SIDE OF THE STREET 3 165
THE DESCENT CHIMNEY 3 5.4 165
THE SENATOR .... II 5 164
TRIPECICLE .... II 5 166
WIESSNER ROUTE 3 5.8 165

Iron Mountain
FRIENDSHIP ROUTE .... II 3 170
MISGUIDED 3 170

Moat Range
HANCOCK FALLS 1 147
MOAT MOUNTAIN ICE FALL .... II 2 147
RED EAGLE BROOK ICE FALL .... II 1 147

Mount Bemis
DANCING AT THE RASCAL FAIR .... 3+ 176
ENTREPRENEUR 4 176
VISION THING .... 4+ 177

Mount Tremont
CASPER THE FRIENDLY GHOST .... II 2 173
OPEC ICE FALL 2 176
XANADU FALLS .... II 3 173

Texaco Slab
ANKLES AHEAD 4 175
ANKLES AWAY .... 3+ 174
DOUBTING THOMAS 4 175
EMBARGO 2-3 176
EUGENE'S WOODY 6 175
GASOLINE ALLEY 2 5.4 176
TEXACO SLAB 2-3 176
THE DUNKING 3 174
THE IMPASS .... 3+ 5.8 174
THE LOWE DOWN 6- M5 175

Whitehorse Ledge
AN ALCHEMIST'S DREAM .... III 4 150
BEGINNER'S ROUTE .... II 2-3 R 148
DREAMS OF REGURGITATING WHITE HORSES ...... III 4 5.6 R 149
ENDANGERED SPECIES .... III 4+ 5.7-8 151
MOMENTO .... III 5.4 R 3-4 149
SLABS DIRECT .... III 4 R 149
SLEEPING BEAUTY 5 M5/6 150

SACO RIVER VALLEY

Whitehorse Ledge (continued)

SLIDING BOARD .... III 4 5.7 R 149
SOUTH BUTTRESS DIRECT .... IV 5.8 A3 (5.11 AO) .. 151
STANDARD ROUTE .... III 3-4 R 148
THE ELIMINATE .... IV 5.8 A3 151
THE GIRDLE TRAVERSE OF WHITEHORSE .... IV 3-4 5.9 AO 151
THE MYTH OF SISYPHUS .... III 5 151
WEDGE .... III 4 5.6 R 149

White's Ledge

STALACTITE .... 3+ 171
WHITE'S GULLY .... II 3+ 5.5 170

SMUGGLERS NOTCH

Bear Notch

BEAR LEFT 4 71
BEAR RIGHT .... 5/5+ 71
CUB SCOUT .... 3+ 71
GRIN AND BEAR IT .... 3+ M4 71
THREE BEERS 4 71

Bristol Cliffs

BRISTOL CLIFF FLOWS 2-4 71

East Side

BLUE ROOM .... II 3+/4- 69
DAVE'S SNOTSICLE .... II 3-4 69
DOUG'S ROUTE .... II 4 70
ELEPHANT'S HEAD GULLY .... II 3 67
ELEPHANT'S HEAD, THE SOUTH FACE .... II 4 M4 67
FREEZE DRIED .... II M6/7 68
H&D GULLY .... 2+/3 66
ICE SCREAM .... MIXED (HARD) 67
INTELLIGENCE BYPASS 3 66
LEFT BASTARD .... 3+ 70
LEFT SKI TRACK .... 2+/3- 70
LOUIE'S LEAP .... BOULDERING 65
MIDDLE BASTARD 4- 70
ORIGIN OF INTELLIGENCE IN CHILDREN .... III 4-5 66
PRENUPTIAL AGREEMENT .... 5+ 70
RAGNAROCK .... II 4+ 68
RIGHT BASTARD 4 70
RIGHT SKI TRACK 3- 70
SARGENT-SEVERIN .... 3+/4+ 68
SINK 'EM AND WEEP 4 70
STERLING CLIFFS AREA 3-/4- 66
TALL TALES .... 4/5 M5 R 68
THE PLAYGROUND 3-4 66
UNNAMED .... 4+/5 66
WATERSHIP DOWN .... II 3+/4+ 67
WORKOUT WALL .... 2+/4+ 65

West Side

A'S ANGUISH (AKA GOLDEN ICE CHIMNEY) .... 4/4+ 62
BLACK SUNSHINE .... 3+/4 62
BLIND FAITH .... II 3 58
BLIND FATE .... III 4 58
BLUE ICE BULGE .... II 3- 57
CALIFORNIA DREAMING .... II 4 58
CASS'S GULLY 1-2 59
DOMINATRIX .... II M6 4+ 61
DRIVING FORCE .... 2-3+ 57
EASY GULLY 1-2 59

ENT GULLY	II 2	64
FRENCH TICKLER	M6 A0 4	61
GRAND CONFUSION	3+	60
GRAND CONTUSION	3+	60
HALFWAY GULLY	3	63
HAPPY BIRTHDAY	3+ M4	65
HIDDEN GULLY	II 3/4-	59
HIGHER RENT	3- R	64
JEFFERSON SLIDE	2-4	64
LOW RENT	M1	64
NATTY ICE	M5+	64
NATURAL LIGHT	3- MIXED	64
NORTH GULLIES	2+/3+	64
NORTON-GIBNEY	II 4	58
PICK AND CHOSS	M4	58
POSITIVELY 4TH STREET	3+	63
POSTER CHILD	4/4+ M4	60
PUB CRAWL	M4	63
QUARTZ CRACK	II 5.8R	62
RAINY DAY WOMEN	3-/3+ M4+	63
RUBBLE GULLY	3 MIXED	62
SCREAM QUEEN	M5 4+	61
TERROR-TORY	2-3	57
THE BEGINNING OF THE END	5 M7+	64
THE BUSHWAY ROUTE	M4+	63
THE END OF THE BEGINNING	5 M6	64
THE GOLDEN SHOWER	3+	65
THE GRAND ILLUSION	4+	61
THE RUSTINATOR	3+ M5	65
THE SNOTCICLE	II 4+/5-	62
THREE SHEETS	II 4	61
TRI-SCAM	3+ MIXED	62

Notes

Notes

Notes

Notes

RICK & PETER, 2002*

Rick Wilcox

Rick has been climbing since the 1960's and living in NH since 1971. He managed the Eastern Mountain Sports (EMS) store and the EMS Climbing School in North Conway, NH until 1979 when he became the president of International Mountain Equipment (IME). He has been the President of the Mountain Rescue Service since 1974 (participating in over 250 technical rescues) and an owner/officer at the International Mountain Climbing School (IMCS) since 1986. His climbing and guiding resume includes an incredible 38 expeditions to mountains over 18,000 feet around the world (he was the leader on most of them), with the high-point undoubtedly being his successful 1991 climb of Everest. He has guided high-altitude peaks in Peru, Ecuador, Argentina, Alaska, Mexico, Europe, and Asia, specializing in mountains over 18,000 feet. He has climbed in northern New England for over thirty years with highlights including being on the first step-less ascent of Pinnacle Gully with Jim McCarthy in 1970, making the first ascent of Repentence in 1973, and doing the second ascent of the Black Dike, also in 1973. In addition to running his store and climbing school, Rick is a frequent lecturer using his climbing experiences to get people excited about being alive. He lives in Eaton, NH with Celia Davis and children Jake (17), Mariah (15), Russell (13) and Reed (13).

S. Peter Lewis

Peter Lewis has lived and climbed in the White Mountains of New Hampshire for most of the last 22 years working as a mountain guide, a photojournalist, and author. The blackflies drove him to Colorado in the mid 1990's where he worked as the executive director of the American Mountain Guides Association until 1999. He came back because he missed his friends, four real seasons, and trees. He has written or co-written six books on climbing, worked as book editor for The Mountaineers Books, and published many photos and articles. In early 2002 he joined two friends to start TMC Books, the publishing arm of the wilderness medicine school SOLO, and now spends all his time writing, illustrating, and designing books. He lives in a 180 year old farmhouse in western Maine with Karen, the lady he has loved and been married to for over 20 years. He has a son, Jeremiah (18) and a daughter, Amanda (10) who are his best friends. He is writing a photography how-to book and is currently building a 200 square foot, timber frame treehouse (with electricity, a woodstove, etc., and yes, he's writing a book about that too). He still climbs as much as his knees allow and can crank 5.7 or grade 3 ice right off the couch. He's not sure what he's going to be when he grows up.

*The photo has been digitally altered to simulate aging so readers will be able tell the difference between this and the author's photos from the 1992 edition of this guide.

Techy Publishing Stuff

Text: Tahoma and Maiandra True Type font families used throughout

Art: drawings were produced using a #14420 Jet-Black, Extra-Smooth, Design Ebony, pencil

Photos: slides were scanned on a Nikon LS 2000; prints and drawings were scanned on some cheap Memorex thing

Hardware: all design, editing, photo, art, and production work was done on a PC (can you believe it!)

Software: Adobe Pagemaker 6.5, Photoshop 5.5, Illustrator 9.0, and Microsoft Word

Paper: cover: 93.5# Cornwall C2S Rcy Cv
inside" 60# Ris Value Gloss Tx

Coffee: Colombian Supremo and French Roast consumed throughout

TMC Books

TMC Books is made up of three guys, some computers, two parrots, a giant lizard, several dogs, and lots of cats—in fact there are just too many cats.

Our dream is to publish books and other things that effervesces people—that informs and instructs them, that stretches their minds, that makes them better at what they do, and more than anything, that fills them with enthusiasm and inspiration.

Our vocational backgrounds are eclectic. At some point at least one of us has been: an artist, a physician, a professional mountaineer, a sailor, businessman, a photojournalist, a church builder, a woodworker, a teacher, an author, a boat builder, a school-builder, and a graphic artist. This mix of experience and expertise has led to a title list that defies pigeonholing. While we specialize in books that support the vision of Stonehearth Open Learning Opportunities (SOLO), the country's most respected wilderness medicine school, we are much more than that. If something stirs us, brings us a smile, makes us jump and shout, we'll publish it. And whether it's the quality of the content and the writing, the beauty of the photos or the illustrations, or the effectiveness of the design, we do everything to make it the best job possible.

We're just three guys with a bunch of computer hardware and assorted animals in a converted barn in the mountains. We're turning our dreams into books, and we hope you get as much enjoyment and fulfillment by reading them as we get by making them.

If you would like to order more copies of this book just rip this page right out (it's okay; go ahead) and mail it to us with a check. You can also order this and our other titles from our website. For up-to-date information on all our projects or to request title brochures, please visit TMCbooks.com

NAME _____

ADDRESS _____

CITY _____

STATE/ZIP _____

PHONE & EMAIL _____

NO. OF ICE GUIDES _____ x $29.95 = _____ + $5 (for 1 book) or

$7 (for 2 books) for shipping equals a **GRAND TOTAL** of _____

If you visit TMC and stick your head in our mailbox you'll see this stunning view of 6,288' Mt. Washington the crown of the White Mountains and a frequent distraction for us. (No, wait, actually, you'll see the back of the mailbox. To see the splendid view you'll just have to stand in the driveway and look north.)